Cognitive Bias in Intelligence Analysis

T0373872

Series Editors: Richard J. Aldrich, Rory Cormac, Michael S. Goodman and Hugh Wilford

This series explores the full spectrum of spying and secret warfare in a globalised world.

Intelligence has changed. Secret service is no longer just about spying or passively watching a target. Espionage chiefs now command secret armies and legions of cyber warriors who can quietly shape international relations itself. Intelligence actively supports diplomacy, peacekeeping and warfare: the entire spectrum of security activities. As traditional inter-state wars become more costly, covert action, black propaganda and other forms of secret interventionism become more important. This ranges from proxy warfare to covert action; from targeted killing to disruption activity. Meanwhile, surveillance permeates communications to the point where many feel there is little privacy. Intelligence, and the accelerating technology that surrounds it, have never been more important for the citizen and the state.

Titles in the *Intelligence, Surveillance and Secret Warfare* series include:

Published:

The Arab World and Western Intelligence: Analysing the Middle East, 1956–1981
Dina Rezk

The Twilight of the British Empire: British Intelligence and Counter-Subversion in the Middle East, 1948–63
Chikara Hashimoto

Chile, the CIA and the Cold War: A Transatlantic Perspective
James Lockhart

The Clandestine Lives of Colonel David Smiley: Code Name 'Grin'
Clive Jones

The Problem of Secret Intelligence
Kjetil Anders Hatlebrekke

Outsourcing US Intelligence: Private Contractors and Government Accountability
Damien Van Puyvelde

The CIA and the Pursuit of Security: History, Documents and Contexts
Huw Dylan, David V. Gioe and Michael S. Goodman

Defector: Revelations of Renegade Intelligence Officers, 1924–1954
Kevin Riehle

Cognitive Bias in Intelligence Analysis: Testing the Analysis of Competing Hypotheses Method
Martha Whitesmith

Forthcoming:

The Snowden Era on Screen: Signals Intelligence and Digital Surveillance
James Smith

https://edinburghuniversitypress.com/series-intelligence-surveillance-and-secret-warfare.html

Cognitive Bias in Intelligence Analysis

Testing the Analysis of Competing Hypotheses Method

Martha Whitesmith

EDINBURGH
University Press

Edinburgh University Press is one of the leading
university presses in the UK. We publish academic
books and journals in our selected subject areas across
the humanities and social sciences, combining cutting-
edge scholarship with high editorial and production
values to produce academic works of lasting
importance. For more information visit our website:
edinburghuniversitypress.com

Edinburgh University Press Ltd
The Tun – Holyrood Road, 12(2f) Jackson's Entry,
Edinburgh EH8 8PJ

First published in hardback by Edinburgh University Press 2020

Typeset in 11/13 Adobe Sabon by
IDSUK (Dataconnection) Ltd, and
printed and bound by CPI Group (UK) Ltd,
Croydon, CR0 4YY

A CIP record for this book is available from the
British Library

ISBN 978 1 4744 6634 9 (hardback)
ISBN 978 1 4744 6635 6 (paperback)
ISBN 978 1 4744 6636 3 (webready PDF)
ISBN 978 1 4744 6637 0 (epub)

Contents

List of Figures and Tables

Acknowledgements

I would like to thank Simon Saintclair-Abbot and Philip Gregory of the Professional Heads of Intelligence Analysis team in the Cabinet Office. Without their support and assistance this book would not have been possible. Their passion and dedication to improving the quality of training available for intelligence analysts in the UK and their enthusiasm for supporting the academic community in this work is commendable. Thank you to Professor Mike Goodman for your advice and encouragement, and your forbearance in having to peer-review statistical analysis. Finally, a huge thank you to Nick, for your constant support, and never begrudging the time this book took away from us.

Introduction

A significant proportion of human cognition is spent on trying to anticipate danger from the world around us. Our brains have evolved to identify threatening behaviour from the multitude of signals we receive from our external environment with minimal conscious effort. The speed of our ability to react to adverse situations can mean the difference between life and death. Being able to anticipate threats in advance allows an even greater advantage: the ability to enact defensive measures. The more that we can prepare for the likely threats we face, the better the chances we have of minimising the damage they may cause. Intelligence analysis has formed a significant part of this activity throughout human history. For at its core, intelligence is concerned with defence, whether the adversary comes from the physical environment, is a natural predator or is in the form of the competition for resources and social dominance within our own species.

However, like many efforts of human understanding, intelligence analysis is by no means easy. Our cognitive faculties are fallible and prone to error. We understand knowledge as a revisionary concept: that the best theories available to academia can be enhanced and refined over time when they are shown to be false by better argument or previously unseen evidence. Intellectual error is both natural and inevitable, and absolute and incontrovertible truth is an elusive goal. However, the potential costs of failing to achieve an absolute standard of truth in intelligence are arguably much higher than in many other areas of intellectual enquiry. The consequences of failures of intelligence, though rare, stand out clearly in Western history: from the attack against Pearl Harbor in 1941, the 1950 Korean war, to the Bay of Pigs invasion in 1961. The price of intelligence failure to human life can be devastating, and the tolerance of what is at heart a natural and inevitable limitation of human knowledge and cognition is often low. But how far are the limitations of human cognition inevitable?

Cognitive biases are mistakes in reasoning or other cognitive processes, produced by information-processing rules that the brain uses to make decisions. Cognitive biases affect the way we form beliefs and choose to behave. Cognitive biases affect both of the central stages of analysis: the formation of initial beliefs, and the adjustment of beliefs during the processing of information. Dozens of cognitive biases have been identified affecting a range of analytical tasks from probability judgements (Tversky and Kahneman 1974), mathematical calculations (Hendrick and Costantini 1970b), the impressions that we form of other people's characters (Hendrick et al. 1973) and the judgement of causational empirical relationships (Chapman and Chapman 1967). Although intelligence failures are not necessarily the result of errors in analytical judgements, they are held to be factual inaccuracies that arise in the process of intelligence analysis, due largely to inaccurate, forgotten or wrongly discarded hypotheses (Johnson 2012). In this capacity, cognitive biases stand as a significant causal factor for intelligence failures.

Cognitive biases are not inherently good or bad. Some are incredibly useful and even essential to our survival (Laqueur 1985). It all depends on the context of the beliefs that you are trying to acquire. Cognitive biases enable faster decisions when timeliness is more valuable than accuracy. This could feasibly apply to intelligence analysis that is required to inform operational decisions where little time is available and there is a high risk to human life. However, beyond this limited context cognitive biases can arguably only impede the quality of analytical judgements in intelligence. Cognitive biases have been identified as contributing factors to several significant intelligence failures in the twentieth and twenty-first centuries that have been attributed at least in part to analytical error, including the invasion of Iraq by the US in 2003 (Commission on the Intelligence Capabilities of the United States Regarding Weapons of Mass Destruction 2005), the Yom Kippur war of 1973 (Bar-Joseph and Kruglanski 2003) and the al-Qaeda attacks against the US on 11 September 2001 (National Commission on Terrorist Attacks upon the United States 2004). The detrimental impact cognitive biases can have on intelligence analysis poses a significant risk to human life.

* * *

A significant proportion of research in intelligence studies has focused on intelligence failure and strategic surprise in warfare. There are three main schools of thought on the causes of intelligence failure, and each supports different solutions as to how intelligence failures should or could be prevented. The first school of thought holds that intelligence failures are the result of cognitive biases (Richards 2010). Proponents of the cognitive-failure approach have suggested different solutions to intelligence failure. Some argue for a methodological approach to intelligence analysis in the rigorous application of analytical methods and methodologies that are employed in other areas of academia (Heuer and Pherson 2010; Agrell 2012), whilst others argue that intuition (or critical rationalism) should be relied on instead (Treverton and Fishbein 2004). This division of opinion is known colloquially as the art versus science debate.

The second school of thought on intelligence failures holds that the root of the problem is faulty bureaucratic structures or practices within intelligence communities: failures within the underlying intelligence system (Betts 1979; Zegart 2009). Academia in this category has predominantly focused on identifying the current structures and bureaucratic processes through which intelligence is conducted and seeks to identify and correct faults in the system. In the system-failure school of thought, intelligence failures are the result of either inadequate collection of raw intelligence information through faulty calibration, inadequate requirements or technological hurdles, or inadequate mechanisms to communicate analytical judgements, either in collection or in warning.

Whilst the cognitive-failure school of thought places the root of intelligence failure in the hands of the analyst, and the system-failure school of thought points the finger at faults in the intelligence machine, the third school of thought holds that intelligence failures are the result of poor decision-making drawing upon raw intelligence or analytical judgements. In this action-failure school of thought, decision-makers are held to react inadequately to analytical judgements in which multiple hypotheses are equally supported by ambiguous information and fail to enact appropriate defensive measures.[1] Research into intelligence failures faces the problem of trying to disentangle the inter-relations between the three factors of cognitive-failure, system-failure and action-failure. Richard K. Betts observed that it is particularly difficult to separate intelligence failures from policy failures. This is largely because intelligence collection and analysis exists in an essentially interactive relationship with decision-making at a policy-making level (Betts 1979). Further, intelligence failures can have multiple causes, and a single intelligence failure could have causes from each of these three schools of thought. Whilst cognitive biases form the central point of intelligence failure in only one of these schools of thought (cognitive failure), analytical judgements are a key component of all three identified ways in which intelligence failure can occur. In the cognitive-failure school of thought, analytical judgements that have been formed under the influence of cognitive bias are the root cause of intelligence failure. In the systems-failure school of thought, intelligence failures are caused by inadequate collection of raw material that informs analytical judgements, inaccurately focused analytical judgements or inaccurate communication of analytical judgements. In the action-failure school of thought, intelligence failures are caused by faulty decision-making informed by analytical judgements. Given the nature and scale of the consequences that can result from intelligence failures, there is considerable interest in identifying ways in which the impact of cognitive biases can be reduced or mitigated in intelligence analysis. Reducing the impact that cognitive biases can have on analytical judgements drawing on raw intelligence can contribute to improving the quality of decisions made in the interest of both national and international security.

Normative theories of mitigating cognitive bias in intelligence analysis fall into two camps: the argument that intelligence analysis should be based on intuition and the argument that it should be based on structured analytical methods. Studies in this area have drawn on psychological studies from the late twentieth century (Heuer 1999), information theory and anthropology (Johnston 2005), with some attempts to adapt theories from the philosophy of science (Kuhns 2003). One camp argues for the reliance on intuition, arguing that our brains are physically configured to allow us to reach the best and most accurate analytical judgements (Treverton and Fishbein 2004). Some authors have suggested that to mitigate cognitive biases, intelligence analysts need to develop the capacity to be able to detect when they are subject to cognitive biases, or develop a heightened awareness of bias during the analytical process (Richards 2010; Treverton and Fishbein 2004).[2] However, cognitive biases are not learned behaviours which can be detected and unlearned through a process of conditioning: they are instinctive mental behaviours that have evolved with our species. Cognitive biases occur without our awareness, on a subconscious level. It is difficult to see how an individual could develop a conscious awareness of what is occurring in their subconscious.

The second camp of academics argue that using structured analytical methods to conduct intelligence analysis can reduce the likelihood of cognitive biases occurring or mitigate the influence of cognitive biases on analytical judgements. There are two main arguments as to why structured analytical methods may be more likely to reduce or mitigate cognitive biases in intelligence analysis over intuition alone. The first is that by following a structured process for attempting to acquire knowledge, the justification for believing a specific hypothesis to be true is made explicit and can therefore be subject to peer review (Heuer and Pherson 2010). If having no justification for our beliefs means we have no rational basis to accept them as true, then providing no justification for our beliefs gives others no obvious rational basis for taking our beliefs to be true. The second argument is that by using and recording the use of structured methods to develop and test hypotheses, the methods for testing the hypothesis in question can be repeated, thereby allowing hypotheses to be refuted or strengthened (Heuer and Pherson 2010). Following a set methodology allows accurate replication, and therefore offers opportunities for validation or refutation. Overall, supporters of the argument for the use of structured analytical methods in intelligence analysis claim that, whilst the application of a structured methodology may not be enough to counteract instinctive mental behaviours that may lead us into error, by making the basis of justification for our judgements explicit, an analyst has better chances of being able to spot cognitive biases and errors in judgement.

Those that adhere to the school of thought that it is best to rely on our innate cognitive abilities to acquire knowledge have argued that using structured analytical methods is a time-intensive process that is unnecessary when our innate cognitive abilities have evolved to enable speedy decision-making (Treverton and Fishbein 2004). However, the most important argument for using structured analytical methods rather than relying on intuition in intelligence analysis is that our intuitive cognitive faculties are fallible. Whilst in some cases cognitive biases allow a greater efficiency in our cognitive judgements, they can also lead to illogical interpretations of information, inaccurate judgements and distorted perceptions of the world around us.

*   *   *

A significant body of psychological research into human judgement has been accumulated over the past sixty years. A large proportion of this research has focused on the limitations of human cognitive abilities. It is widely agreed that human judgement is consistently affected by cognitive biases. Whilst a notable portion of this research has focused on making mathematical judgements of probability, there is a considerable body of research into the process of making general analytical judgements. The research on this topic can be usefully split into research into how people generate hypotheses and how people evaluate hypotheses.

There has been relatively little research that has examined the process of hypothesis generation. However, the research that has been conducted has provided several interesting results. Fisher et al. (1983) and Mehle et al. (1981) found that participants only generate a fraction of the total number of plausible hypotheses for consideration. Mehle (1982) conducted a study where mechanics were asked to generate plausible hypotheses about why a car would not start. The study found that the mechanics were deficient at generating a wide range of plausible hypotheses, only generating between four and six options. Moreover, the participants were overconfident that the sets of hypotheses they generated were more complete than they were. Other research has shown that participants tend to generate hypotheses that they believe are highly likely and ignore hypotheses that they believe are unlikely or implausible (Dougherty et al. 1997; Weber et al. 1993). Research has also shown that the judged probability of the preferred hypothesis (the focal hypothesis) decreases as the number of alternative hypotheses generated increases (Dougherty et al. 1997). This indicates that the more alternatives that are considered, the less chance there will be of overconfidence in analysis. Barrows et al. (1982) showed that individuals are unlikely to consider hypotheses that are not generated at the beginning of an analytical task. A study by Gettys and Fisher (1979) was conducted into how individuals develop new hypotheses to an already established analytical task. The results indicated that new hypotheses were introduced to analysis only if they were considered plausible enough to make them strong competitors for the focal hypothesis. A study by Fisher et al. (1983) found that some hypotheses are generated based on a few pieces of available information rather than all the available information, and that sometimes hypotheses are generated based on anomalies amongst available evidence that focus an individual's attention. There are no studies that have published analysis regarding the generation of hypotheses in intelligence analysis. As such, there is no evidential basis from which to compare the results of psychological studies into hypothesis generation. However, there is no obvious theoretical reason why intelligence analysis would provide a different environment in which hypotheses are generated compared with other forms of analysis.

Whilst the body of research into hypothesis generation is small, it has several implications for the debate over intuition versus structured analytical methods as the most effective approach to mitigating the impact of cognitive biases in belief acquisition. The first is that an intuitive approach to conducting analysis is likely to involve the consideration of only a small proportion of plausible hypotheses. In addition, if an individual conducts analysis using an intuitive process with only a small number of hypotheses, available research implies that the hypotheses most likely to be considered are those judged to be highly probable by the analyst. As such, an intuitive approach to analysis may reduce the ability to predict rare events of high impact to defence and national security, such as the al-Qaeda attacks against the World Trade Center in September 2001. Further, research implies that were only one hypothesis to be considered for analysis, individuals may be over-confident in their assessment of the likelihood that this hypothesis is true. It therefore follows that intelligence analysis would be better served by the consistent consideration of multiple hypotheses. However, the second implication from available research into hypothesis generation is that, where individuals consider more than one hypothesis using an intuitive approach, they are unlikely to be able to generate a complete set of plausible hypotheses. In this capacity, structured analytical methods that stipulate the consideration of multiple hypotheses may offer an advantage over intuition.

There has been considerable research investigating hypothesis evaluation in both cognitive and social sciences. Research has shown that the process whereby individuals check the consistency of information against generated hypotheses happens at high speed (Fisher et al. 1983). Research has also shown that people have different approaches to how they evaluate hypotheses. A study by Wason (1960) showed that some people evaluate a hypothesis based on a small number of supportive or confirming pieces of evidence (induction by simple enumeration), but do not seek disconfirming evidence (induction by eliminative enumeration). This runs the risk of incorrect assessment, as confirming evidence does not necessarily prove a hypothesis, whereas any instance of disconfirming evidence will necessarily disprove it. Studies by Dougherty et al. (1997), Gettys and Fisher (1979) and Koehler (1994) have indicated that when an individual judges the likelihood that a hypothesis is true, he or she does so by comparing the likelihood against rival hypotheses. However, the rival hypotheses must be retrieved or generated from memory. Tversky and Koehler (1994) argue that the probability of a focal hypothesis is assessed by comparing the strength of evidence against the focal hypothesis and alternative hypotheses. Others have argued that the probability of a focal hypothesis is judged by comparing the strength of evidence with the focal hypothesis and the alternative that is considered the next strongest in terms of likelihood (Windschitl and Young 2001). These studies are consistent in their agreement that hypothesis evaluation conducted by intuition is accomplished by taking one hypothesis at a time and comparing it against others. Research has also indicated that working memory capacity plays a significant role in hypothesis evaluation and generation, as it constrains the number of alternative hypotheses that an individual can retain for comparative analysis. As such, the probability of the focal hypothesis is likely to be judged by comparing it to a small number of alternative hypotheses, rather than an exhaustive set (Dougherty and Hunter 2003). Working memory affects analysis in other ways. Research has shown that the number of pieces of relevant information that an individual can maintain focus on is very small and that the number varies between different individuals (Engle, Tuholsk et al. 1999). Other research has also shown that people are unable to prevent non-relevant information from entering their focus of attention (Hasher and Zacks 1988).

This research has multiple implications. It indicates that when hypothesis evaluation is conducted by intuition, it is done at speed, and will involve only a small number of hypotheses for consideration due to constraints on working memory. Whilst some people will verify hypotheses in an efficient way – by seeking to falsify and eliminate hypotheses (eliminative induction) – others will only seek a few pieces of confirming evidence before making a conclusion (enumerative induction). Working memory constrains the amount of information an individual can focus on, and not all the information that is retained in focus will be relevant to the task at hand, leading beliefs to be influenced by irrelevant information. On an initial examination, the research looking at how people generate and evaluate hypotheses offers very little support to the argument of relying on intuition to mitigate cognitive biases in intelligence analysis. It also provides some support for the argument that structured analytical methods may have an advantage over an intuitive approach in mitigating cognitive limitations. For example, using a structured approach may slow down the process of hypothesis generation and reduce the cognitive strain of having to retain key items of information in focus by using a ranking and voting system to process a larger volume of information and compare each piece of information one by one against a set of hypotheses. In addition, using a structured analytical method designed for the approach of seeking to disconfirm hypotheses rather than only seeking confirmation may improve the efficiency of hypothesis validation. Further, whilst the application of a structured methodology to reach judgements may not be enough to counteract cognitive biases, by making the basis of justification for judgements explicit, an analyst may have a better chance of being able to identify biases and errors in judgement.

* * *

Although most works that look at the prevention of intelligence failure are dedicated to the mitigation of cognitive biases in intelligence analysis, only a small proportion follow the methodologist school of thought and focus on the application of structured analytical methods to achieve this. Those that do tend to focus on applying systems analysis programmes to threat prediction. Since the 1990s, the structured analytical methods approach to reducing the risk of cognitive bias has been recommended by the US intelligence community and has since been widely adopted in the West, forming both the guidance and professional training provided to intelligence analysts. There is a wide range of structured analytical methods (also referred to as structured analytical techniques) for intelligence analysis that have been borrowed or developed by Western intelligence communities since Pearl Harbor.[3] These range from brainstorming to Bayesian probability statistics. However, few of these methods were designed as a comprehensive methodological approach to intelligence analysis, encompassing both the formation of hypotheses and the processing of information. Rather, most provide specific methods for encouraging greater creative thinking at different stages of the analytical process. Only one structured method recommended by Western intelligence communities provides a comprehensive methodology for all stages of intelligence analysis.[4] The Analysis of Competing Hypotheses (ACH) was developed by the Central Intelligence Agency (CIA) specifically to mitigate against the cognitive bias of confirmation bias, the tendency to interpret new evidence as confirmation of one's existing beliefs. ACH is the principal method currently recommended by both the US and UK intelligence communities for mitigating cognitive biases in intelligence analysis (Jones 2017). Since its creation, the ACH method has been widely adapted in the private sector and multiple variations of the technique have been developed. But can it deliver what it promises?

A substantial body of research in the social sciences indicates that intuition cannot be relied upon to mitigate bias. However, the comparative ability of structured analytical methods to mitigate cognitive biases in analysis has not yet been put to substantive empirical validation (Jones 2017). The current body of empirical research into the ability of structured analytical methods to mitigate cognitive biases comprises one published study, by Cheikes et al. (2004). This study focused on the efficacy of the ACH method using a consistency of information scoring system against confirmation bias in an intelligence analysis scenario. It found that ACH did not mitigate against cognitive biases impacting belief acquisition in intelligence analysis. However, only one variation of ACH information scoring systems was tested against two cognitive biases. There are four central scoring systems that have been used in versions of ACH to date and numerous cognitive biases that can affect human behaviour. As such, whilst there is currently no evidence that structured analytical methods can provide higher mitigation for cognitive biases over intuition, the research is by no means conclusive. The utility of structured analytical methods in mitigating bias is currently unknown.

A significant proportion of empirical research in the social sciences has focused on the existence and extent of cognitive biases. However, limited empirical research has been published on the extent to which cognitive biases negatively affect intelligence analysis, ways to effectively combat the negative effects of cognitive biases in intelligence analysis or the efficacy of structured analytical methods to combat cognitive biases in intelligence analysis. It is likely that the lack of research into the impact of cognitive bias specifically in an intelligence analysis context is the result of this research having been almost exclusively conducted within the social sciences, as opposed to intelligence or defence studies. It is possible that the limited research into the efficacy of structured analytical methods for intelligence analysis is due to the limited knowledge or application of these methods beyond the intelligence world. However, it is more likely that this dearth of research is due to the very limited focus on experimental research that has been seen to date within the field of intelligence studies.[5] Whilst limited effort has been spent in identifying the relevant implications of available social science research into cognitive biases for intelligence communities, it is possible that this wide body of research has direct implications that can be utilised for enhancing analytical training.

* * *

The 'art versus science' debate regarding how best to reduce the risk of intelligence failures resulting from intelligence analysis has stagnated in recent years. Whilst the two opposing theoretical positions have been clearly outlined, the debate lacks empirical validation: the art has so far outweighed the science. This book aims to redress this imbalance. To do so, it will apply two approaches. The first is to add to the empirical validation of the efficacy of structured analytical methods in mitigating the risk of cognitive bias: to use current knowledge from social science to validate the art side of the debate. The second is to identify whether alternative approaches to structured analytical methods can be identified from existing social science research: to pit a homage to science developed by Western intelligence communities against science itself. However, these approaches cannot be achieved by an empirical approach alone. The ability to apply the research from social sciences into cognitive bias to an intelligence context depends on whether intelligence analysis differs in either nature or degree from non-intelligence analysis: whether intelligence analysis involves a uniquely different process for forming beliefs, or whether some factors that have a causal impact on belief formation affect intelligence analysis to a substantially different degree compared with non-intelligence analysis. Further, the results of empirical validation of structured analytical methods need to be addressed in a theoretical context. If structured analytical methods fail to mitigate against cognitive bias, why is this the case, and is there any way in which the methods can be improved to achieve mitigation? Likewise, if some structured analytical methods are found to provide mitigation against cognitive bias, how have they achieved this, and can they be enhanced to have higher efficacy or efficiency? These are questions of both science and philosophy, and any attempt to answer them requires a multidisciplinary approach, drawing from both philosophical theory and empirical research. This book attempts to provide this multidisciplined approach.

Testing the efficacy of ACH in mitigating the risk of all cognitive biases currently identified in social science is beyond the scope of this book. Instead, I will focus on two cognitive biases that have been identified as having previously contributed to intelligence failures that derived from analytical error and have a sufficient volume of empirical research dedicated to them in social sciences. These cognitive biases are confirmation bias and serial position effects.

A significant body of research in the social and psychological sciences has shown that both recall of information and judgements based on a cumulated body of information are significantly influenced by the sequence in which the information is presented or processed. This phenomenon is known as serial position effects (also referred to as information order bias, serial order effects and order effects). Serial position effects were first observed by Solomon Asch in 1946, as part of his research into how people form impressions of other people's personalities. Asch conducted ten studies in which participants were read a list of descriptions about a fictitious individual, after which they were tested as to the impression they had formed of the individual's character. In one of the studies, Asch observed that information provided early in the experiment had a directional impact on how subsequent pieces of information were processed. Asch claimed that subsequent information was interpreted using the first piece of information as a reference point, or anchor. Asch referred to this phenomenon as a primacy effect (alternatively referred to as the anchoring effect, anchoring bias and focalism). Primacy, within the context of the impact of serial position effects on belief acquisition, is understood as the phenomenon whereby information processed at the beginning of a series of information has a disproportionately high impact on an individual's belief formation or adjustment process. A second serial position effect, recency, has since been recognised in addition to primacy. Recency is the phenomenon whereby information processed at the end of a series of information has a disproportionately high impact on the belief adjustment process. A separate and larger field of research has examined the way in which serial position effects impact working memory. Primacy, in this application, is understood as pieces of information processed at the beginning or the end of a series of information being more vividly or easily recalled compared with information in the middle of a series of information.[6] Research into serial position effects on recall has traditionally associated primacy with the functioning of long-term memory, whereas recency has been associated with the functioning of short-term memory (Capitani et al. 1992), although the association between recency and short-term memory has been challenged (Henson 1998). It has also been argued that primacy and recency occur in recall because information at the beginning and end of a series of information are more distinct (Henson 1998) or are more contextually distinct (Glenberg and Swanson 1986). However, the way in which serial position effects affect memory and the way in which they affect belief acquisition have been treated as separate areas of research in the social sciences. Serial position effects have the potential to pose significant implications for belief adjustment. If the order in which information is processed has the potential to drastically influence assessments, then the accuracy of analytical judgements has the potential to be reliant on chance, rather than on analytical skill or rigour.

In comparison, confirmation biases are a group of biases that affect the way in which people interpret information, and what information people seek when evaluating hypotheses (Fischoff and Beyth-Marom 1983). The concept of confirmation bias has changed since the term was first used in social science research in the 1960s. The term 'confirmation bias' is originally attributed to Wason (1960). Wason conducted a study into the hypothesis testing strategies employed by young adults, to see whether there was a preference towards seeking to confirm hypotheses (enumerative induction) or disconfirm hypotheses (eliminative induction). Wason developed a conceptual task in which seeking to confirm evidence would almost always lead to erroneous conclusions (the 2-4-6 card selection task). Using this task, Wason found that some of the participants were unable or unwilling to change from enumerative induction to eliminative induction as a hypothesis testing strategy, despite enumerative induction leading to multiple erroneous conclusions. Wason termed this phenomenon confirmation bias (or verification bias (Wason 1968)).[7]

Both serial position-effects and confirmation bias are highly likely to have an impact on intelligence analysis. Confirmation bias has been specifically attributed to at least two cases of significant intelligence failures: the invasion of Iraq by the US in 2003 and the Yom Kippur War. However, there is equal likelihood that serial position effects could have been at play in both of these cases.[8] ACH has been described as a method specifically designed for reducing the risk of confirmation bias in intelligence analysis, as well as offering a way of reducing the risk of other biases. However, it remains to be seen if ACH can deliver a reduced risk of either confirmation bias or serial position effects.

* * *

This book comprises two parts. Part 1 will provide the theoretical and philosophical elements of the research. It will attempt to answer the following questions: (1) Is belief acquisition in intelligence a unique epistemological act? and (2) Does ACH provide a theoretically valid framework for establishing epistemic justification? Part 1 draws on the leading theories from the philosophical school of epistemology, the study of knowledge and belief to provide a foundation for the testing of ACH against empirical research. Part 2 will provide the empirical elements of the research. It will look to answer the following questions: (1) Does ACH have a mitigating impact against confirmation bias or serial position effects in intelligence analysis?; (2) What analytical conditions are associated with an increased or reduced risk of confirmation bias and serial position effects?; and (3) Do serial position effects or confirmation bias affect intelligence analysis differently compared with non-intelligence analysis? Part 2 of the book will present the results of a study looking at the efficacy of ACH in mitigating the cognitive biases of serial position effects and confirmation bias. The study was facilitated by the Professional Heads of Intelligence Analysis team at the Cabinet Office. Part 2 will also explore the efficacy of an alternative approach to mitigating cognitive bias: using experimental research to identify whether any of the conditions under which analytical tasks are conducted are associated with a reduced or increased risk of cognitive biases. Based on these findings, I propose alternative models for predicting serial position effects and confirmation bias. These models argue that whilst the risk of occurrence of serial position effects and confirmation bias are impacted by different analytical conditions, they share an underlying cognitive process: a force towards forming a focal hypothesis early on in belief acquisition.

Notes

1. Most research in this area is derived from historical case studies and lessons-learned exercises that bear relevance to contemporary contexts.
2. Other academics have argued that biases can be overcome by intensifying the level of knowledge you have of your adversary (Handel 1984).
3. This can be seen from the analysis of several internal training manuals from the UK and US intelligence and defence communities that are now available in open source: *Quick Wins for Busy Analysis* (Cabinet Office 2015), *Criminal Intelligence Manual for Analysts* (United Nations Office on Drugs and Crime 2011), *Handbook of Warning Intelligence: Assessing the Threat to National Security* (Grabo 2010), *A Tradecraft Primer: Structured Analytical Techniques for Improving Intelligence Analysis* (United States Government 2009), *Strategic Early Warning for Criminal Intelligence: Theoretical Framework and Sentinel Methodology* (Criminal Intelligence Service Canada 2007), *Intelligence Essentials for Everyone* (Krizan 1999), *Creating Strategic Visions* (Taylor 1990) and *Strategic Intelligence for American World Policy* (Kent 1949).

4. It could be argued that Subjective Bayesianism falls into this category, if it includes the specific instruction to generate a range of hypotheses for consideration. However, not all applications of Subjective Bayesianism contain this instruction, whereas it is a fundamental element of the ACH method.

5. It is also possible that more empirical research has been conducted internally within intelligence communities on these areas that has not been made available to the public.

6. Key research in this field includes: Bjork and Whitten (1974), Bower (1971), Capitani et al. (1992), Conrad (1960, 1965), Corballis (1967), Crowder (1979), Fuchs (1969), Glenberg (1990), Glenberg and Swanson (1986), Greene (1986), Healy (1982), Healy et al. (1987), Henson (1998), Hintzman et al. (1973), Houghton (1990), Jahnke (1963), Jahnke et al. (1989), Jordan (1986), Kahneman (1973), Kidd and Greenwald (1988), Lashley (1951), Lee and Estes (1977), Lewandosky (1994), Lewandosky and Murdock (1989), Madigan (1971, 1980), McElree and Dosher (1989), McNichol and Heathcote (1986), Murdock (1968, 1983, 1993, 1995), Neath and Crowder (1990), Robinson and Brown (1926), Seamon and Chumbley (1977), Shiffrin and Cook (1978), and Smyth and Scholey (1996).

7. Following Wason's introduction of the term, multiple studies have been conducted examining the application of enumerative induction, seeking to replicate Wason's 'confirmation bias' (Klayman and Ha 1987; Klahr and Dunbar 1988; Mynatt et al. 1977). However, there has been controversy regarding the use of the term 'confirmation bias' to refer to the examination of enumerative induction (Whetherick 1962; Koslowski and Maqueda 1993; Evans 2016). This is because enumerative induction is not equivalent to confirmation bias as it is currently defined: an individual may use enumerative induction to compare information against a hypothesis without interpreting the information in a biased way.

8. Identifying the presence of cognitive bias in an analytical process is highly problematic if applied retrospectively, as in both the Iraq war and the Yom Kippur war. Further, the serial position effect of primacy is very difficult to distinguish from confirmation bias, as both occur in the first stages of information processing and result in information processed early on in an analytical task having a disproportionate impact on belief adjustment and formation.

PART I

Intelligence, Bias and Belief Acquisition: A Theoretical Perspective

I   Intelligence and Belief Acquisition

To identify if intelligence analysis is subject to cognitive bias in a different way from non-intelligence analysis we need to examine whether intelligence analysis is different from non-intelligence analysis: if it is a unique form of belief acquisition. To do this, two things must be established. The first is whether intelligence analysis is different in nature (or kind) from non-intelligence analysis. The second is whether intelligence analysis differs in degree from non-intelligence analysis. Both these are questions of a philosophical nature. The nature of a concept or entity concerns its essential properties: the necessary characteristics that define the identity of a thing. If two things differ in nature, then they differ in their fundamental properties. In comparison, if two things differ in degree, it means that they share the same fundamental properties but either behave differently or are affected differently by external factors. If intelligence analysis differs in nature from non-intelligence analysis, then it is rational to assume that it could be affected in different ways by cognitive bias. Likewise, if intelligence analysis and non-intelligence analysis do not differ in nature but differ in the degree to which they affect or are affected by external factors, this also could have ramifications for the relative impacts of cognitive bias. To establish whether intelligence analysis is unique in nature from non-intelligence analysis, and therefore may be affected in a unique way by cognitive bias, the nature of intelligence must be established.

Academics have yet to formulate an agreed theory of the essential nature of intelligence (Laqueur 1985). This is for two reasons. The first is that many previous definitions of intelligence have attempted to incorporate all objects, concepts and activities that

21

are or can be associated with the term 'intelligence' into a single taxonomic class that provides an account of the essential nature of intelligence. This practice falsely assumes that the essential nature of a single entity must include all relationships of association between that entity and other entities or concepts. The second is that academics have formulated definitions of intelligence on the assumption that the individual conditions that are necessary to intelligence must also each be unique to intelligence, rejecting conditions that can be found outside the intelligence world. However, it is the total sum of necessary characteristics that are required to pick out a unique entity. Overcoming these two errors should allow the development of an agreed theory of intelligence. The essential nature of intelligence will be defined by the characteristics necessarily associated with the term. In this chapter, I will put forward a case for identifying the necessary characteristics of intelligence and suggest a single overarching taxonomic class for intelligence: that the essential nature of intelligence is the covert pursuit of justified beliefs.

* * *

For decades, academics have struggled to agree on a suitable definition of intelligence.[1] Some academics have defined intelligence by the goals that it is used to achieve. Laqueur (1985) defined the purpose of intelligence as 'to obtain information and to assess it correctly'. Lowenthal (2002) defined intelligence as 'collected and refined information that meets the needs of policy makers'.[2] Warner (2002) defined intelligence as 'secret, state activity to understand or influence foreign entities'.[3] Warner argued that (1) intelligence is dependent on confidential methods and sources to be fully effective: that secrecy is a key component; (2) intelligence is performed by officers of the state, directed by the state, for state purposes, and that the focus of intelligence is on other states: that it has a foreign focus; (3) intelligence is linked to the production of information and is a method of influencing other states by unattributable means; and (4) secrecy is the primary variable distinguishing intelligence from other intellectual activities, as the behaviour of the participant under study changes if the participant is aware of being observed. In contrast, Turner (2005) argued that the inclusion of secrecy as a necessary component for defining intelligence was insufficient, as any act conducted in secret by a government would fall under the definition of intelligence. This, argued Turner, is too simplistic. Turner instead defined intelligence as the collection and analysis of policy-relevant information for the purposes of informing or assisting state decision-makers in national security or foreign policy.

Other academics have attempted to define intelligence by both the activities it encompasses and its overall aims. Johnston (2003) defined intelligence as a secret activity aimed at understanding or influencing other entities: 'secret state or group activity to understand or influence foreign or domestic entities'. Although Johnston described his definition as a slightly modified version of the definition provided by Warner (2002), the expansion to include domestic intelligence focusing on non-state actors is a significant divergence.[4] Warner later provided a contrasting understanding of intelligence to his proposed definition in 2002. He argued that most people interpret intelligence as being two things: information for decision makers, and secret state activity designed to influence foreign entities (Warner 2006).

Although these definitions share multiple areas of overlap, none has been deemed sufficient to adopt as a standard taxonomic definition of intelligence. There are two reasons why an agreement has yet to be reached between these previous attempts. The first is due to a misunderstanding of definitions. A definition is a formal statement of the meaning of a word. However, there are different types of definitions. Extensional definitions list the objects or activities that a term describes. Enumerative definitions (a type of extensional definition) provide an exhaustive list of all entities that fall under the term in question. Intensional definitions try to express the essential nature of a term.[5] In seeking to provide an adequate definition of intelligence, academics are trying to establish the essential nature of intelligence, and therefore an intensional definition of intelligence. However, most definitions that have been suggested for intelligence take the form of extensional or enumerative definitions: they attempt to express the essential nature of intelligence by providing a single statement that incorporates all objects, concepts and activities that are or can be associated with the term.

Seeking to provide a definition of the essential nature of intelligence by listing all activities associated with the term falsely assumes that the essential nature of a single entity must include all relationships of association between that entity and other entities or concepts into a single taxonomic class. However, extensional definitions are arguably only appropriate to use for terms that have a small, fixed set of objects or concepts which fall under the term in question. This is arguably not appropriate for intelligence, as not only is the term associated with a wide variety of objects, activities and concepts, including but not limited to covert operations; foreign policy; domestic policing; national and international law; the collection of information; the analysis of information; and military operations, but the range of activities conducted under the auspices of intelligence may vary between different cultures. At heart, the debate about the requirement of an agreed definition of intelligence is one of taxonomy. Taxonomy seeks to classify objects and concepts based on shared characteristics: to identify what it is about an entity that separates it from others.

A Taxonomy of Intelligence

Taxonomies attempt to identify the essential nature of an object or concept, or a class of objects or concepts: they seek to provide intensional definitions. The traditional, and most authoritative, way to identify the essential nature or essential characteristics of significant terms and the concepts or objects they refer to is to identify their necessary conditions.[6] 'Necessity' as a philosophical term is what must be the case and cannot be otherwise: a necessary condition is what must be true and cannot be false (Vaidya 2011). In contrast, 'sufficiency' is what could be the case, but what also may not be the case: a sufficient condition is one that may or may not be true (Nolan 2011).[7] A necessary condition guarantees the truth of an entity or concept. In comparison, a sufficient condition acts as a truth condition for an entity or concept in some conditions, but not in others. Take for example, the following statement:

'If Matthew is human, then Matthew is a mammal'. Given the fact that all humans are mammals, the truth of the proposition 'Matthew is human' necessarily guarantees the truth of the proposition 'Matthew is a mammal'. However, whilst it is necessarily the case that 'all humans are mammals', it is not necessarily the case that 'all mammals are humans'. As such, the truth of the proposition 'Matthew is a mammal' is sufficient to guarantee the truth of the proposition 'Matthew is a human'. To provide a taxonomy of 'intelligence' (or an intensional definition), the necessary conditions of intelligence must be identified.

The second reason that previous definitions of intelligence have failed to provide a sufficient taxonomy is the false requirement that the conditions that are necessary to intelligence also be unique to intelligence. Random (1958) argued that to provide a definition of intelligence by identifying necessary conditions, you must identify the unique operations of intelligence.[8] Characteristics of intelligence that are arguably necessary have been dismissed by academics because they are not unique properties of intelligence. For example, Turner (2005) dismissed the notion that intelligence being a secret activity was a necessary characteristic of intelligence by arguing that most work conducted by a government is secret, but not all this work is intelligence. Therefore, secrecy is not a unique property of intelligence. However, neither logic nor linguistics works in this manner. The characteristics of one concept or entity do not have to be unique only to that entity or concept. Many intensional definitions contain necessary characteristics that are shared with the intensional definitions of other terms. For example, consider the definitions 'war' and 'violence'. Violence is behaviour involving physical force intended to hurt, damage or kill someone or something. War is a state of armed conflict between different countries or different groups within a country. Violence is arguably a necessary condition of war, but violence is not unique to war. For example, violence is also a necessary characteristic of the definition of 'assault'. The necessary characteristics of intelligence must identify the term as a unique entity or concept. However, it is the total sum of the necessary characteristics that must form a collectively unique entity or concept, not the individual characteristics.

The variety of definitions for intelligence provide multiple suggestions of what its characteristics are: intelligence as a secret activity; intelligence as conducted by states; intelligence as targeting foreign entities; intelligence as intended to influence foreign entities; intelligence as derived from special sources; intelligence as action-guiding analytical product; and intelligence as competitive advantage. These components can be grouped into three categories of characteristics: the characteristics of intelligence as a form of behaviour or activity; the characteristics of the sources from which intelligence derives and the characteristics regarding the aims or purposes of intelligence. But how many of these are necessary conditions of intelligence?

Intelligence as Action

Definitions of intelligence provided by Kent (1949) and Herman (2001) explicitly include the characteristic of action. Intelligence can be defined as an act or set of actions undertaken by humans: that it involves a human or group of humans doing something. The argument that intelligence necessarily requires human action is an obvious truth. It is difficult to see how intelligence could exist without anything being done, or as an activity that necessarily cannot be undertaken by humans.[9] It is both uncontroversial and intuitive to argue that intelligence necessarily refers to activity conducted by humans. However, it is also uncontroversial to argue that there are multiple human actions that can vary in their essential nature. For example, compare the act of charity to the act of murder. Charity is the voluntary act of helping those in need, whereas murder is the unlawful or premeditated killing of one human being by another. The essential nature of charity includes the attempt to prolong the life of another being, whereas the essential nature of murder includes the destruction of the life of another being. These concepts share the necessary condition of being or involving human action, but it does not follow that the essential nature of charity and murder are equivalent to each other. We need to consider what additional characteristics render intelligence a distinct human activity, or a distinct class of human activities.

Almost all definitions of intelligence include the characteristic of the pursuit of information (Random 1958; Kent 1949;

Laqueur 1985; Herman 2001; Lowenthal 2002; Warner 2002; Turner 2005; Johnston 2003; Warner 2006; Simms 2010). The first part of Kent's (1949) definition explicitly equates intelligence with knowledge. Each of us understands the various meanings of the word 'knowledge'. We understand that knowledge is a theoretical or practical understanding of a subject, or an awareness or familiarity gained by experience. If knowledge is a necessary condition of intelligence, then it logically follows that anything that is not knowledge is not intelligence. This would mean that neither belief nor justified belief can be conditions of intelligence. The concept of knowledge is closely related to the concepts of belief and justification. Every traditional account of knowledge includes belief as a necessary component. Furthermore, where knowledge is difficult to obtain, then justified belief is widely accepted as the alternative goal. When knowledge cannot be obtained, justified beliefs are looked to in order to guide behaviour and decision-making. Some philosophers have argued that the requirement for attaining knowledge is so high as to be virtually impossible to reach, and therefore justified beliefs are more important than knowledge (Russell 1912).[10] It could be interpreted that, according to the first part of Kent's (1949) condition, to believe (and be justified in believing) that Islamist terrorism poses a future threat to the national security of the United Kingdom, but to fall short of knowing this to be true, cannot occur under 'intelligence'. This claim is obviously false. It is logically impossible to know the future.[11] Intelligence assessments made about future scenarios necessarily fall short of knowledge. However, it is uncontroversial to assume that intelligence assessments are produced about future events. It is also uncontroversial to assume that intelligence assessments made about the present and the past may also fall short of knowledge. It is unlikely that all intelligence assessments will be made from a complete and reliable basis of information. Given the likelihood of falling short of knowledge in intelligence predictions, the exclusive equation of intelligence with knowledge is unsatisfactory. However, although intelligence can fall short of the epistemological status of knowledge, it is not controversial to suggest that the pursuit of justified beliefs is a necessary condition of intelligence.

A second characteristic in current definitions of intelligence is that intelligence is conducted by an organisation or a group of people (Kent 1949; Johnston 2003). If it were true that intelligence is necessarily conducted by more than one person, it would follow that intelligence cannot be conducted by an individual. But is it impossible for a single individual to conduct an act of intelligence in isolation? This is not obviously true. Whilst we tend to associate intelligence activity as being conducted by a group, it does not follow that a single individual cannot collect intelligence, process intelligence and be influenced by this intelligence. Consider the following thought experiment:

> Jeff's son has been kidnapped by a neighbouring tribe. Jeff wants to rescue his son, but Jeff's own tribe is not willing to help him do so, due to the neighbouring tribe's superior military strength. Jeff decides that he will rescue his son on his own. To plan his mission, Jeff sneaks to the edge of the neighbouring tribe's encampment and conducts reconnaissance. He identifies which structure his son is being held in, and the guard movements around the camp. He uses this information to plan a rescue mission.

It is not controversial to suggest that in this scenario, Jeff is engaged in an act of intelligence. There is no obvious reason why activities related to intelligence would only ever be conducted by a group of people. As such, being conducted by an organisation or group arguably does not stand as a necessary characteristic of intelligence as an activity.

This argument is related to a second characteristic in multiple definitions of intelligence that describe intelligence as a behaviour: intelligence as conducted by a state (Random 1958; Warner 2002; Johnston 2003). The term 'intelligence' is predominantly associated with activities conducted by state intelligence agencies or communities. However, whilst intelligence activity may predominantly be conducted by a state, it does not follow that intelligence is exclusively conducted by a state. Warner (2006) argued that intelligence pre-dates nation states, and that intelligence dates to the earliest days of humanity where groups decided to war with other groups for control of territory. There are no obvious reasons why non-state actors cannot engage in intelligence activity. For example, guerilla or insurgency groups could collect and analyse information on a nation state that they seek to target in an armed conflict. As such, intelligence should not be restricted to applying only to state activity, even if states are the predominant practitioners of intelligence. There is no reasonable case why being conducted by a state is a necessary characteristic of intelligence as an activity.

A third key characteristic of intelligence as an action cited in definitions by Random (1958), Warner (2002), Johnston (2003) and Warner (2006) is the argument that intelligence is conducted in secret. For secrecy to be a necessary component of intelligence as an action, it must be impossible for intelligence to be conducted without secrecy. It is widely held that secrecy is essential for intelligence to be effective: that intelligence often involves collecting information on an enemy or adversary and that conducting such an act in public would lead the target of information to become aware of this activity and make efforts to hide his or her activities, thereby increasing the difficulty of collecting information on them (Warner 2006). Further, some intelligence practices may conceivably involve collecting information on an ally. To do so in public risks the ally being made aware of the act of information gathering and may place alliances at risk. It seems obviously true that the activity of intelligence being conducted in secret (being intentionally kept hidden from the object of intelligence collection) would probably increase the effectiveness (or efficacy) of intelligence, and therefore would stand as an ideal condition for intelligence. Further, if intelligence is an act of collecting information, and being conducted in secrecy is not a necessary condition of its nature, then what distinguishes intelligence from research? It seems obviously true that something about intelligence as an act distinguishes it from the open collection of information. However, it is not obviously true that it is impossible for intelligence to occur without secrecy. For example, an intelligence agency may be obtaining accurate information on the activities of a terrorist group from a human source who is a member of the terrorist group in question. However, this human source is also providing accurate information about the actions and locations of the intelligence agency to the terrorist group. Both the intelligence agency and the terrorist group believe that their activities are hidden from the other; however, this is not actually the case. As such, their intelligence activities are not conducted in secrecy. In this capacity, it can be argued that being an act or activity that is intended to be hidden from an individual or group of individuals who are the subject of the intelligence act is a necessary condition for intelligence, but that the guarantee of secrecy is not. In this sense, intelligence can be understood as an intentionally covert activity that is not openly acknowledged or displayed.

The Aims of Intelligence

From an examination of the characteristics that are associated with intelligence as an activity, it can be argued that the essential nature of intelligence as an act is the covert pursuit of information. But what is the purpose of this behaviour? One of the defining characteristics suggested by current definitions of intelligence is the purpose of influencing an individual's or group of individuals' behaviour or beliefs. The question of whether intelligence can exist without the ability to influence an individual's behaviour or beliefs depends on the target of influence. On one hand, the aim of intelligence can be understood as to influence the belief acquisition process of the individual or individuals who are conducting the intelligence act (covertly collecting and processing information): to enable them to form and adjust beliefs based on the information that they have collected. It is obviously true that intelligence is necessarily intended to influence this first type of target: the intelligencer (or intelligencers). The argument that intelligence is fundamentally driven by the intent to influence behaviour has some merit, if you take the target of influence as being broad in scope. Intelligence is arguably intended to enable individuals to make informed decisions. Further, newly acquired information can influence beliefs that were based on a previously acquired body of information. In this sense, intelligence can be validly taken to have a necessary purpose of informing beliefs. However, it is not obviously true that collected information will necessarily influence an intelligencer. For example, information may be received that is of sufficiently poor quality or insufficient relevance that it has no impact on the behaviour, beliefs or decision-making process of the intelligencer. In this capacity, the activity of covertly collecting information can be understood as necessarily having the purpose of influencing the intelligencer or intelligencers, even if this does not consistently occur. There is arguably little merit in collecting information that is not intended to have some impact on the beliefs of the individual or group attempting to collect it.

Further, it is not controversial to argue that the aim of intelligence is to enable decision-making. This is a key characteristic of intelligence identified in multiple definitions (Lowenthal 2002; Warner 2006; Simms 2010). This is a core concept of our pursuit of knowledge, and it is therefore not controversial that this should also be a core component of intelligence. The aim of influencing the behaviour of an individual or group engaging in intelligence activity would logically be included within the aim of influencing beliefs of individuals engaging in intelligence activity. It is intuitive to assume that the decisions consciously made by an individual will be necessarily based on what that individual believes to be true or false. In this capacity, a necessary component of intelligence as an activity is the purpose of influencing beliefs. But in what capacity do we mean that a belief will be influenced? This could feasibly take the form of a previously held belief being reinforced or altered on the receipt of new information through an act of intelligence collection. However, it could also take the form of acquiring entirely new beliefs. The different ways in which beliefs may be influenced by an act of intelligence can be combined under the pursuit of justification for beliefs. It has already been established that knowledge is not always obtainable. As such, where knowledge is not an option, justification for beliefs is sought instead. Further, it is widely held that justification of beliefs is a necessary requirement for knowledge. In the context of intelligence, justification can be sought to influence already held beliefs or to warrant the formation of new beliefs. As such, a necessary condition for the aims of intelligence would be more appropriately identified as the pursuit of justified beliefs.

On the other hand, intelligence can also be understood to be collected and processed information used by the individuals who collected and processed it in order to influence a separate individual or group: to have the capacity to enable an individual or group to influence the behaviour of another individual or group. For example, Random (1958) and Warner (2002) include the influencing of foreign entities as a defining characteristic of intelligence. But does the influencing of foreign entities stand as a necessary condition of intelligence? The notion that intelligence is necessarily defined as influencing foreign entities is not obviously true. This notion has been countered by Warner (2006) who argued that understanding intelligence as specifically targeting foreign entities fails to consider domestic intelligence focusing on citizens of the state. Even if domestic intelligence includes foreign states or citizens as a target for intelligence analysis, it would not exclude intelligence gathering on its own citizens or exclude the existence or investigation of internal threats to national security from foreign nationals.[12] The accepted concept of intelligence-led policing is enough to discount intelligence as targeting foreign entities as a necessary characteristic of intelligence. The fact that intelligence is used for domestic purposes, and can focus on domestic citizens, invalidates the notion that the purpose of intelligence is exclusively to influence foreign entities. As such, the purpose of influencing foreign entities cannot stand as a necessary condition of the essential nature of intelligence.

It is not obviously true that the capacity to influence the behaviour or decision-making of a second party is a necessary purpose of intelligence. For this argument to be true it would follow that intelligence necessarily serves a dual purpose of influence: to influence the decisions and behaviour of the intelligencer, and to enable the intelligencer to influence a second party. However, there are plausible cases where intelligence is only intended to influence the behaviour or decisions of the intelligencer alone. Consider the previous thought experiment of Jeff and his kidnapped son. Jeff's pursuit of intelligence would not influence the beliefs of any individual other than Jeff, as it would not be shared with other individuals. Further, Jeff was not intending to use the intelligence gained to influence the behaviour of members of the neighbouring tribe, but to conduct a successful rescue mission. As such, the ability to influence a second party is not a necessary purpose of intelligence.

Some academics have argued that the purpose of intelligence is to enable policy-makers (Lowenthal 2002). This argument assumes that intelligence is only meant to influence the behaviour and decisions of individuals in senior governing positions within a state. However, this argument is not obviously true. This would prevent intelligence from being conducted by non-state groups, or by individuals. Further, it would necessarily follow that intelligence could not have the capacity to influence the decisions or behaviour of intelligence practitioners who are not responsible for making policy decisions. However, there are plenty of actions undertaken by intelligence agencies that do not necessarily require the authority of policy-makers: for example, domestic policing and counterterrorism operations. It would be unfeasible to expect all policing decisions that have been influenced by intelligence to be made by policy-makers. As such, it is invalid to restrict the ability or purpose of intelligence to influence decision-making and actions to a single hierarchical level within a group of individuals.

* * *

A second characteristic that has been put forward as a necessary purpose of intelligence is that of gaining competitive advantage. Simms (2010) argued that to achieve competitive advantage, either the information gathered must be better than that of the opponent, or the opponent's ability to collect and produce intelligence must be degraded. Following this, Simms argues that intelligence has three main functions: (1) to collect information that allows the anticipation of a competitor's actions; (2) to collect information that allows timely communication to enable decision-making; and (3) blocking or manipulating information received by a competitor to disrupt or degrade his or her decision-making (Simms 2010). A method of gaining a competitive advantage is arguably an important component of intelligence. It is plausible to argue that the overall purpose of acquiring knowledge or justified beliefs through intelligence is to be able to gain a competitive advantage over an adversary, whether the adversary poses a threat to national security or is a competitor in terms of economic status or resources coveted by an individual, group or state. An adversary is defined as an opponent in competition, conflict or dispute. An adversary for intelligence in this sense could be an ally, enemy or neutral party. Further, if you take secrecy to be a necessary component of intelligence as an activity it could be argued that this is to ensure or protect the ability to gain a competitive advantage over an adversary: one is necessitated by the other. If you had no requirement to gain a competitive edge, it is arguable that secrecy would not be a necessary requirement of intelligence activity. It is intuitive that intelligence would be sought to gain an advantage over an adversary. However, it is less obvious that it is a necessary component. It does not follow that gaining an advantage over an opponent is always realistic. It is possible for there to be situations where gaining an advantage is neither practical nor likely. However, you could look to lessen the disadvantage you have: to lessen the advantage that an adversary or an opponent has over you. Further, it is plausible that intelligence can be sought to gain an equal status with an opponent, rather than a position of advantage. Whilst doing so would convey an advantage to one individual or group, it would not provide the individual or group with an advantage over their opponent. Intelligence will not always result in one person or group being in a position of advantage over another person or group. Further, it is arguable that information can be sought in an act of intelligence to fulfil knowledge gaps, without necessarily being required to fulfil the goal of providing a competitive advantage. As such, it does not follow that gaining an advantage over an opponent is a necessary characteristic of intelligence.

The Basis of Intelligence

A third category of characteristics of intelligence provided by previous definitions refers to the sources from which intelligence is based. Bruce (2008) argued that what separates intelligence is that it is derived from special sources of information. But is this necessarily the case? When the term 'source' is used as a noun, it means a place, person or thing from which something originates or can be obtained, or a person who provides information. When we use the phrase 'the sources of intelligence' we use the term 'source' as a noun to cover all objects, people or places from which individual pieces of information obtained in intelligence collection originated. To describe a source as 'special' implies that it either produces information of higher quality than other sources of information, or that it is in some way different from most other sources of information: that it is an exception. Intelligence is necessarily concerned with seeking justification for beliefs. As such, when we talk about sources of intelligence, we refer to the sources from or by which we seek to gain justification for beliefs. A source of knowledge or justification is something that at least partially supports that a proposition is true.[13] Our beliefs may arise from a multitude of sources, such as desires, biases, perceptions and rational thought. If our beliefs are to be taken as justified, then they need to have come from sources that we have sufficient reason to consider reliable. In epistemology, the sub-field of philosophy that focuses on belief and knowledge, sources of knowledge and justification are taken to be testimony, introspection, perception, memory and reason (Steup 2014). Further, we can distinguish between primary knowledge and justification, and secondary knowledge and justification. Primary knowledge and justification do not depend on evidence provided by the justification or knowledge of someone else, whereas secondary knowledge and justification do. For example, if Simon's justification that a proposition P is true is dependent on the evidence provided by the testimony of Brian, Simon's justification for believing P to be true is secondary. However, If Simon's justification that a proposition P is true is dependent on his personal perceptions, his justification would be primary (Audi 2002).

Perception is a basic source of both justification and knowledge (Audi 2002). When we talk about perception as a source of knowledge, we refer to the capacity to perceive. Our perception is traditionally taken to consist of the five classical senses: sight, sound, touch, smell and taste.[14] However, the definition of senses is not actually restricted to five, or to any number for that matter. The natural sciences have discovered a significant number of perceptual senses that humans possess and continue to identify more. Perceptions can be split into two types of experiences: necessary and contingent (or sufficient). A necessary perceptual experience is where a perception entails that a proposition P is necessarily true, whereas a contingent experience entails that a proposition P could be true but could also be false. This distinction shows that perceptions can be fallible.[15] Perception is a basic source of both justification and knowledge. Perception includes information that is used to acquire a posteriori knowledge. The term 'a posteriori' refers to knowledge that is derived from sense experience, observation and empirical data or processes: a posteriori knowledge is dependent on empirical evidence or experience.

Introspection is a basic source of both justification and knowledge. Introspection is the capacity to analyse one's own mind. This can include abstract objects and concepts, sensations, emotions, thoughts, and other mental entities and states. Introspection is considered to have a special status in comparison to perception. Perceptions can be false or misleading, whereas introspection is considered less prone to error (Steup 2014).[16]

Memory can be defined as our capability of retaining past knowledge. Like perception, memory is also fallible. Memories can be wholly false or partially inaccurate.[17] Memory is a basic source of justification. However, it is not a basic source of knowledge. Memory is an essential source in that without it we could not sustain the possession of an individual piece of knowledge once it has been established, nor of a body of knowledge. However, we cannot know anything through memory without that knowledge being dependent on another source. Memories are obtained through reason, perception, testimony and introspection, but memories cannot come into creation through memory alone. Memory is memory of something. Therefore, whereas memory stands as a basic source of justification, it is not a basic source of knowledge. It is also important to note that what can be known or justified based on memory can also be acquired by other means. For example, what memory can provide as a source of justification and knowledge could also be provided by the testimony of another individual that derives from a basic source of justification and knowledge (say perception or reason). This shows us that a basic source of justification or knowledge need not be unique (Audi 2002).

Reason is taken both in philosophy and in general to be a reliable method of epistemic justification, and therefore a reliable route to knowledge. There are some beliefs that can be justified solely by a process of reason. This kind of knowledge and justification is referred to as 'a priori'. An example of a belief that is a priori justified is the belief that 2 + 2 = 4. Mathematics is based on a conceptual framework of internally consistent laws. The rules of mathematics therefore provide a form of a priori justification for believing the truth of the results of mathematical calculations. Another example of a priori justification is formal logic. As the rules of a priori justification are internally consistent and conceptual, a priori knowledge is commonly accepted to be necessarily true. Reason is a basic source of both justification and knowledge. However, the term 'reason' is arguably ill-suited for our purpose as it can mean different things. For example, 'reason' covers both reasoning and reflection. However, although reflection does not have to rely on independent premises, reason necessarily relies on these. To use the term 'reason' as a basic source for justification and knowledge we must tighten our definition. For reason to stand as a basic source of justification and knowledge of a proposition it must be derived from an exercise of reasoning about the proposition. Reason as a basic source of knowledge and justification is predicated on a process of reasoning about the propositional content of the knowledge or justification in question. However, reason is not necessarily a fallible source of knowledge. Logic is a process of reasoning that establishes validity but not truth: a proposition can be logically valid and still be false in the real world. However, knowledge is necessarily true (Audi 2002).

Testimony is distinguished by having its own cognitive faculty. To gain knowledge that a proposition is true through testimony, you must know that the proposition is true based on someone else saying that the proposition is true. There has been controversy over whether to include testimony as a basic source of knowledge and justification. One criticism against the notion that testimony is a source of knowledge is that it is not always possible to know if an individual's testimony that a proposition is true was derived from a reliable method or from sufficient evidence. In addition, some philosophers argue that a witness's reliability and credibility should be considered in judging if their testimony is a reliable source of justification for knowledge. Testimony is considered to be non-basic as it is dependent on other sources. It is obvious that testimony cannot stand as a basic source of justification. However, it has been argued that testimony can stand as a basic source of knowledge. For example, you do not have to believe in Brian's testimony to know that Brian has testified, or to know what Brian's testimony contains. In this capacity, you can have knowledge derived from a testimony, and this knowledge does not have to depend on additional sources. Therefore, testimony can, in specific circumstances, stand as a basic source of knowledge. However, this example concerns knowledge by acquaintance, rather than propositional knowledge. You cannot claim to have knowledge that a proposition that Brian provided through testimony is true merely because you perceived Brian providing the testimony. As concerns propositional knowledge, testimony cannot stand as a basic source of knowledge or justification: it will always be dependent on another source.

It is important to distinguish between the sources of knowledge and justification, and the basis for knowledge and justification. A source supplies an accessible basis for knowledge. In this capacity, sources are causes of knowledge and justification. In contrast, a basis is an underlying support or foundation for knowledge or justification. In this sense, a basis can have more than one source. An individual source can be a basis for knowledge or justification on its own, but this is not always the case. Further, a source of knowledge and justification is not in itself a basis for knowledge and justification. If Simon claims to know that there is an oak tree in front of him because he visually perceives an oak tree in front of him, the source for his knowledge claim is perception, but his basis for knowledge is empirical evidence. However, his visual perception does not stand as empirical evidence without independent confirmation. Sources indicate the kind of basis to expect an individual to have when he or she claims to have knowledge through that source (Audi 2002).

For sources of knowledge and justification in intelligence to be classed as special and to stand as a unique characteristic of intelligence, it follows that there must exist a set of sources of knowledge or justification that either are unique to intelligence (that is, that only provide information for intelligence activity) or provide information of higher value to intelligence activity than to non-intelligence activity. The current categorisations for intelligence sources are human intelligence (HUMINT); signals intelligence (SIGINT); geographic intelligence (GEOINT); measurements and signals intelligence (MASINT); and open source intelligence (OSINT).

Human intelligence (HUMINT) is a category of intelligence source that is collected and provided by humans.[18] Human intelligence sources include agents, informants and observers (Krizan 1999).[19] The most appropriate term to use in describing what exactly is provided by HUMINT is 'claims'. When a human source makes a claim, he or she states or asserts that something is the case, without necessarily providing evidence or proof. A claim is an assertion that something is true. A claim does not have to be from first-hand access or experience; it could be based on a claim made by a separate individual. A human source provides a claim that something is the case, irrespective of whether he or she believes in its truth or its reliability. HUMINT is therefore best understood as a category of intelligence derived from claims collected and provided by humans. An important distinction of HUMINT as a source of intelligence is that it is consciously reported by a human to a group, organisation or individual seeking information. In this capacity, HUMINT, as a definition, describes the manner of delivery or collection of a claim, rather than the source of the information on which the claim is based. It is not obviously true that HUMINT is a unique source or basis of knowledge or justification, or one that is of higher quality than others. HUMINT can arguably provide all the five sources of knowledge and justification: testimony, introspection, perception, memory and reason. Human sources may provide intelligencers with the testimony of a second individual, insight that they gained from a process of introspection or reason, an account of something which they directly perceived, or something which they recalled in memory. HUMINT is therefore not a distinct category of information, but a method of collection that covers all types of sources and basis of knowledge and justification. Further, there is no obvious reason to believe that HUMINT necessarily provides a higher-quality basis of justification and knowledge than others. As it can encompass all types of sources and bases of knowledge and justification, it cannot be validly claimed that HUMINT is necessarily of higher quality.

Signals intelligence (SIGINT) refers to information derived from communications intelligence, electronic intelligence and instrumentation signals intelligence (United States Department of Defense (hereafter US DoD) 2014).[20] SIGINT, in this categorisation, would apply to detectable phenomena given off by electromagnetic energy and human-made electronic devices. SIGINT has been subject to more attention than HUMINT in intelligence studies, but rarely in terms of what it provides as a source of intelligence. Rudner (2004) argues that SIGINT provides valuable information for intelligence analysis in the form of clear language interceptions, direction finding and electronic traffic analysis in addition to the provision of enciphered communications and electronic emissions. SIGINT is an overarching taxonomic class with multiple sub-categories (or taxa). These sub-categories include communications intelligence (COMINT); electronic intelligence (ELINT); and telemetry intelligence (FISINT). COMINT is defined as technical information derived from foreign communications (US DoD 2014). ELINT is defined as technical and geolocation intelligence derived from foreign non-communication, and electromagnetic radiations (not including nuclear detonations or radioactive sources) (Krizan 1999). Telemetry intelligence (FISINT) is technical information derived from missiles or other remotely monitored devices such as warheads. Telemetry collects data regarding location, speed and engine status (Watson 2008).[21]

Like HUMINT, SIGINT is a method of collection or delivery for claims, information and data derived from intelligence sources. Like HUMINT, SIGINT is also an umbrella term that can plausibly provide information from all five types of sources of knowledge and justification. SIGINT can provide all the same information as HUMINT. The only difference is that HUMINT is consciously provided by humans, whereas SIGINT is unconsciously provided by either humans or objects. SIGINT is likewise not a distinct source of justification or knowledge. It is also not obviously true that SIGINT provides a higher-quality source or basis of justification or knowledge. SIGINT can collect empirical (a posteriori) information that is not gained from humans, but from inanimate objects. However, whilst this type of information may be of higher quality than human testimony or introspection, as SIGINT does not exclusively provide empirical information, it cannot be validly held to necessarily provide a higher-quality source or basis of justification and belief.

Geospatial Intelligence (GEOINT) is defined as imagery and geospatial information relating to physical features of objects and activities that have a geographical reference (US DoD 2014). GEOINT is acquired by associating data with a geographic location, for example the assignment of latitude and longitude coordinates or postal addresses. The category of GEOINT can overlap into SIGINT, specifically with COMINT and ELINT. GEOINT is any type of information that can be given a geolocation. This can plausibly apply to any information that was sourced from signals intelligence, communications intelligence or electronic intelligence. Rather than being a source of information, GEOINT is a method of coding information after it has been received. In this capacity, GEOINT is arguably not a source of intelligence, but a method of classification of information collected from other types of intelligence sources.

Measurement and Signatures Intelligence (MASINT) is defined as technical measurements relating to the physical attributes of objects and events (US DoD 2014). MASINT includes the subsets of Imagery Intelligence (IMINT), and Scientific and Technical Intelligence (S&TL). IMINT is defined as information providing imagery of an object or event (US DoD 2014).[22] S&TL is defined as information relating to scientific and technological capabilities and activities of an adversary (US DoD 2014). Krizan (1999) describes MASINT as including acoustic intelligence (ACINT) and radiation intelligence (RADINT). MASINT is the analysis of technical and scientific data. The sources of MASINT are emanations from both sentient and non-sentient objects. As such, MASINT is not in itself a specific source of intelligence analysis but derives from specific types of sources. MASINT is an umbrella term that includes several sub-categories or taxa. Sources of MASINT include, but are not exclusive to, RADINT, ELINT and ACINT. MASINT falls under the category of perception as a source of knowledge and justification. It is not obviously true that MASINT is a special source of information. Whilst MASINT arguably provides a higher-quality basis of information than other sources as it exclusively concerns the collection of empirical information, it is not obviously true that MASINT is a unique source. Any individual who has a perceptual faculty can gain information through MASINT. In addition, MASINT is arguably used for other activities whose aim is gaining knowledge or justification for beliefs that fall outside of intelligence, such as scientific research. As such, MASINT is not a unique or uncommon source of information.

Open Source Intelligence (OSINT) is defined as information derived from openly available information (US DoD 2014). Krizan (1999) describes OSINT as including: public documents, books and journals, newspapers, television and radio.[23] Steele (2007) describes OSINT as including information from the internet, subject-matter expertise and commercial geospatial information.[24] OSINT is distinguished by the fact that it is publicly available. However, it is not a distinct type of source for intelligence analysis, as it can feasibly comprise HUMINT, ELINT, GEOINT, MASINT, ACINT, RADINT, COMINT and SIGINT, provided the information is in the public domain. OSINT is distinguished by the type of access a collector can have to sources of knowledge or justification for beliefs. As such, OSINT does not stand as an uncommon, unique or higher-quality source of information.

The current categories of intelligence sources are determined exclusively according to the method through which information is obtained: the physical method of collection or delivery of the information. HUMINT is delivered by human agents; SIGINT, MASINT, IMINT and GEOINT are collected via technology; and OSINT is obtained from publicly accessible information. None of these are distinct categories in terms of the provision of knowledge or justification of beliefs. Further, none of these categories, or the sources and basis of knowledge and justification of beliefs that they encompass, are uncommon or unique to intelligence, or provide a body of information that is necessarily of higher quality than sources and basis of knowledge and justification that is available outside of intelligence activities. As such, the sources of information from which intelligence derives are not special. All that distinguishes intelligence in terms of its sources is that the information is intended to be collected in a covert manner. As intelligence is necessarily a covert pursuit of information, it is intuitive to assume that the ideal sources of information for intelligence would be those that are hidden from the target of information collection, or sources that the target of information collection does not know are providing information about them.

*   *   *

From an examination of multiple definitions of intelligence that have been offered in academia, we can identify the following as necessary conditions of intelligence: (1) that intelligence is a covert human behaviour; and (2) that intelligence seeks to gain knowledge or justification for the beliefs of the individual engaged in intelligence. By combining these necessary conditions, we can form an intensional definition, or taxonomy of intelligence. The essential nature of intelligence is the covert pursuit of justified beliefs. By this definition, it will be obvious that belief acquisition in intelligence differs in nature from belief acquisition that occurs in a non-intelligence capacity. Both are directly concerned with belief acquisition, and with acquiring beliefs that are epistemically justified. However, intelligence differs from belief acquisition in a non-intelligence context by one necessary characteristic: it is a covert activity. For belief acquisition in intelligence to share the same nature as belief acquisition in a non-intelligence context, both would have to share this necessary characteristic. However, whilst there may be circumstances in which belief acquisition in a non-intelligence context is intended to be hidden from the subject of belief acquisition, this is arguably not a necessary characteristic. If we accept that the covert element is a necessary characteristic unique to intelligence, and not to the pursuit of justified beliefs in a non-intelligence context, then it follows that intelligence analysis and non-intelligence analysis differ in nature. This difference in nature could have significant ramifications concerning how one is impacted by cognitive biases compared with the other. Having identified the root of this difference, we can narrow down the potential ways in which such a difference may occur. To establish whether there are any theoretical grounds for arguing that cognitive bias has a different impact on belief acquisition in an intelligence context compared with a non-intelligence context, we need to examine whether the covert characteristic of intelligence would result in belief acquisition being impacted differently by cognitive bias. To do this we need to start by getting a greater understanding of the act of belief acquisition itself.

Intelligence as an Epistemological Act

If the essential nature of intelligence is the covert pursuit of justified beliefs, it follows that intelligence is by nature epistemological. Epistemology is the field in philosophy that studies the nature of and requirements for knowledge and for justification for our beliefs. In a broad sense, epistemology looks at issues about the acquisition of knowledge in any subject area where knowledge is sought. In a narrow sense, epistemology is defined as the study of justified belief and knowledge (Steup 2014).[25] Given that all arguments are intended to be true, we first need to have an agreed understanding of how we can distinguish a true argument from a false one. For this, we must understand how to distinguish what is true from what is false, and how we can be certain that what we believe to be true is in fact true: by what method can we know when an argument is true? Epistemology, as the philosophical field that attempts to provide a theory of the fundamental nature of knowledge, works to provide this. The methods identified by epistemology for establishing knowledge and justification for our beliefs will apply not only to all areas of philosophy but to all areas of intellectual enquiry where an individual seeks to acquire knowledge. This includes intelligence. The answers to the central questions that epistemology has sought to answer, and which theories have current primacy, will therefore have a key bearing on intelligence as an act of belief acquisition.

Epistemologists have attempted to define the different types of knowledge that exist. One traditional distinction of knowledge types is between a posteriori knowledge and a priori knowledge.[26] In a posteriori reasoning, empirical evidence or experience is used to deduce probable causes. In contrast, knowledge or justification that is derived by internal thought processes alone is known as a priori reasoning. A priori reasoning can be used to identity valid inferences by conceptually constructed connections, such as mathematical proofs or logical inferences. Other traditional distinctions are between knowledge by acquaintance, propositional knowledge and capacity knowledge. Knowledge by acquaintance covers all cases in which we know a thing that exists in space and time by personal acquaintance. This includes knowing a person, knowing a place and knowing an object. Propositional knowledge concerns knowing that a proposition (a declarative statement) is true. Capacity knowledge covers all cases in which a conscious being knows how to do something. There are complex interconnections between these three different kinds of knowledge. For example, it may be the case that knowledge by acquaintance is reducible to propositional knowledge (Everitt and Fisher 1995). However, the central focus of epistemology is on propositional knowledge: when we can justifiably claim that a statement or proposition is true.

How Can Knowledge Be Acquired?

The most obvious truism we can say about the nature of knowledge is that knowledge must be true. But this truism doesn't get us very far in identifying the nature of knowledge. Defining the fundamental nature of knowledge as truth does not allow us any insight into how we can acquire knowledge. What are the standards by which we can legitimately say we know something to be true? It is by no means an easy task to identify what the standard for knowledge is, although it may be easy to see when we fail to achieve this standard. In contemporary epistemology, attempts at tackling the question 'what is knowledge?' have concentrated on giving a definition of the term 'know'. The verb 'to know' has multiple uses: knowing how to do something, knowing a place or a person and knowing that something is the case. Epistemology has traditionally focused on this third type of knowledge: propositional knowledge. Propositional knowledge follows the form 'S knows that P', where 'S' stands for a subject or individual, and 'P' stands for the proposition that the subject or individual knows. A proposition is essentially a statement or an assertion: a declarative sentence. A second widely accepted truism about knowledge is that we must believe that something is true to claim to know that it is true. Knowledge is therefore also defined by human agency. This is obviously true, for example, how can I claim to know that I exist if I also claim that I do not believe that I exist? However, it is also logically possible that an individual can believe something to be true when it is actually false: I can believe that I do not exist when I actually do exist. Belief on its own is therefore not a necessary condition for knowledge. One widely held argument that has been put forward in philosophy is that the concept of justification is essential to knowledge: that you can claim to have knowledge if you have the right to be sure that your belief is true. An individual must have an adequate basis for his or her belief to be justified in believing it to be true: that he or she has followed an accredited route to knowledge.

Epistemological efforts into answering the question of what knowledge is have concentrated on identifying the necessary conditions for propositional knowledge. Given the commonsense argument that knowledge requires that you believe something to be true, that it is actually true and that you must have some justification for taking your belief to be true, we could respond with the answer: knowledge is a justified true belief. This response would entail the following criteria for knowledge:

1. P is true
2. S believes that P is true
3. S is justified in believing that P is true

This is known in philosophy as the tripartite analysis of knowledge, or the 'justified true belief' (JTB) criteria of knowledge. The first and second criteria of the tripartite analysis of knowledge are intuitive: to know that P is the case it must be true that P is the case. Further, for an individual to know that something is true it follows that an individual believes P to be true as well. It would be a contradiction to say that an individual knows P to be true but believes that P is false. The third criterion of the theory of knowledge is that for any proposition to be true there must be an objective fact of the matter that makes it true. It is this third criteria that is the least obviously true of the three criteria for knowledge in the tripartite analysis of knowledge theory.

The philosopher Edmund Gettier successfully refuted the tripartite analysis of knowledge theory by demonstrating that some formulations of this tripartite criterion of knowledge failed to provide a necessary and sufficient condition for knowledge (Gettier 1963). Gettier presented two hypothetical cases in which an individual acquires a false belief through a method of justification.[27] Gettier's cases demonstrated that the criteria that an individual's being justified in believing a proposition is a necessary condition for knowing a proposition is false, as there are cases where an individual can be justified in believing a proposition that is actually false. What Gettier's cases showed was that the relationship between justification and knowledge needs to be strengthened to be taken as a sufficient or necessary condition for knowledge. The relationship needs to be refined to avoid acquiring knowledge through false belief or by luck. The relationship needs to be one of a reliable or, if possible, an infallible cognitive method. A large part of contemporary epistemology has focused on trying to find the additional requirements for the tripartite analysis of knowledge to avoid being 'Gettiered'. If having 'good enough' justification is too weak to stand as a criterion of knowledge, then what is required for complete justification? This presents two issues. The first is: what is meant by complete justification? The second is: how do we avoid the concept of complete justification being so exacting that we can rarely claim to know anything at all? (Everitt and Fisher 1995)

Epistemologists' attempts to provide a Gettier-proof theory of knowledge have taken different approaches. The theories that are taken in epistemology to be the strongest contenders for providing a criterion of knowledge or justification are evidentialism, reliabilism and indefeasibilism.[28] Evidentialism argues that justification is satisfied if it is reasonable or rational from the subject's point of view. Furthermore, the subject needs to be in possession of sufficient evidence that supports the truth of their belief. In essence, evidentialism is the theory that the degree to which a belief is justified is the degree to which it fits the evidence available to the subject. Reliabilism sees the role of justification as ensuring that a belief has a high objective probability of being true: a belief is justified if the odds are in its favour.[29] Reliabilism argues that a belief is justified if, and only if, it originates from a reliable cognitive method (Steup 2014). Indefeasibilism argues that justification must be 'indefeasible': that it cannot be defeated by counterargument or contrary evidence. What all responses to the Gettier problem have in common is the argument that there is a law-like, necessary connection between a true belief and knowledge. The requirement of a relationship between a truth and what makes it true is one of necessity and relevance. It follows that to accord an individual the right to be sure, his or her justification for a true belief should also be a connection of necessity and relevance. Reliabilism, evidentialism and indefeasibilism all differentiate between sufficient justification and necessary justification for beliefs. This suggests that where necessary justification cannot be established, sufficient justification may stand as a practical substitution. However, each of these approaches has implications in circumstances where belief acquisition is pursued covertly, as in the case of intelligence.

* * *

The reliabilist theory of knowledge was put forward by Goldman (1976). It follows the form that for an individual to have knowledge of P, the following criteria need to be fulfilled:

1. P is true
2. The subject S believes that P is true
3. The subject S is justified in believing that P is true
4. The subject S is justified in believing that P is true if and only if the belief was acquired by a reliable method

This theory faces a serious objection. There is no guidance on how reliable 'reliable' must be. For example, does a method need to be totally reliable or can it be partially reliable to count? This may seem like a ridiculous objection: clearly a method must be totally reliable to be considered reliable. However, there are methods that are theoretically reliable in general, but in specific instances fail to provide the right answer. This can be demonstrated by adapting the classic example put forward by Bertrand Russell:

The Clock Case: Tim walks past a town hall clock every morning on the way to work. Tim leaves the house at the same time over a period of two weeks. During these two weeks, each time he looked at the clock on this way to work it showed the accurate time of 08:00. However, what Tim doesn't know is that the town hall clock is broken and stuck at showing the time 08:00. (Russell 1948)

The clock has coincidentally, but generally, provided the right answer over a time period of two weeks, but this is clearly not a sustainable method of telling the time. The notion of 'reliable' is therefore too vague to be used to provide a criterion of knowledge without additional precision. This criticism essentially comes down to what exactly is meant by 'method', and how far reliability can be considered an intrinsic quality of the term (Everitt and Fisher 1995). It could be argued that a reliable method would be fit for purpose for a narrow range of applications in which it would necessarily be consistently reliable. This solution would require an agreement of what would be required for a method to yield necessarily reliable results, and the identification of the shared quality between all reliable methods in guaranteeing this necessary connection.[30]

The reliabilist approach to justification has specific implications for intelligence. Reliabilism directly concerns the methods by which information is collected. The central purpose of reliabilism is to establish whether information collection methods are sufficiently reliable for the information they produce to automatically qualify as being epistemically justified. However, the covert nature of intelligence places restrictions on what mechanisms can be used to collect information. Some intelligence is derived from empirical or a priori information. These sources of knowledge can be taken as being reliable, where empirical knowledge is collected by a scientifically rigorous process, and whereby a priori information is collected from a rationally rigorous process. However, other intelligence information is derived from testimony, memory and authority. These sources of knowledge are less likely to be qualified as sufficiently reliable in general terms to provide sufficient epistemic justification without additional judgement criteria applied. Further, the information from which intelligence analysis derives faces one variable that is arguably more predominantly encountered in intelligence analysis than most other areas of formal intellectual activity: intentional deception and misinformation. This variable has been distinguished as a key difference between belief acquisition in intelligence analysis and belief acquisition in other intellectual activities (Garst 1989).[31] This argument was supported by Warner (2002), Johnston (2005) and Hulnick (2010). Intentional deception is obviously not limited to intelligence analysis and can occur in other domains. However, it has been argued that for intelligence analysis, it must be assumed that all pieces of information collected could be the product of intentional deception (Johnston 2005). Therefore, the quality of the information from which intelligence analysis derives must be initially doubted. The factor of intentional deception is arguably intrinsically linked to the nature of intelligence as a covert action. It must be assumed that the subject of intelligence collection is making an active effort to provide false information. Further, the high premium placed on information of national or international security interest, and the difficulties in acquiring it, heighten the incentive for intelligence fabricators to provide false information to intelligence collectors. A high subjective bar would have to be applied to determine whether individual human sources were reliable mechanisms for gaining knowledge, and there would inevitably be great variation in the reliability of human sources. Reliabilism therefore cannot stand alone as a way of establishing epistemic justification for intelligence that derives from mixed information sources, or from memory, testimony or authority.

* * *

The evidentialist theory of knowledge follows the form that for an individual to have knowledge of P, the following criteria need to be fulfilled:

1. P is true
2. The subject S believes that P is true
3. The subject S is justified in believing that P is true
4. The subject S is justified in believing that P is true if and only if S possesses sufficient evidence to support the belief that P is true

The most significant criticism against evidentialism is that it is not clear what is meant by being in a position of possessing sufficient evidence to support the belief that P is true. Some evidentialists argue that you need to be in a mental state that 'represents P as being true' (Steup 2014). This can include the registering of sensory evidence, memory, intuition and introspection. You are justified in believing P to be true if you have an experience that represents P to be true. This criticism comes down to which sources of knowledge are accepted as providing evidence. However, this criticism is not directed at the argument that a sufficient degree of evidential support that P is true can be taken as sufficient justification for believing P to be true.

Evidentialism also has specific issues for intelligence. The first issue concerns determining what sources of knowledge are taken to count as providing sufficient evidence. It would be reasonable to argue that information gained through scientifically rigorous empirical processes would constitute a high-quality source of evidence. However, information gained through the empirical senses of a human which are then recounted through memory (which could be collected as HUMINT or SIGINT) are arguably a lower-quality source of evidence. Further, some epistemologists have argued that memory and intuition can constitute sources of knowledge that provide sufficient evidence for epistemic justification. However, this faces similar issues to the reliabilist approach. The issue of intentional deception renders information gained through introspection and memory as potentially less reliable in intelligence, meaning that these sources of information would be of potentially lower quality than they would be in some non-intelligence contexts. The second issue concerns how much evidence would be required to constitute epistemic justification. It is reasonable to argue that evidence would have to provide a comprehensive case of support for a particular belief to be taken as a sufficient basis for epistemic justification. An evidential case that contains key gaps would not meet this standard. However, as intelligence is necessarily a covert activity, this places inevitable limitations on the ability to collect comprehensive evidence on any given subject. Intelligence collection is highly likely to contain gaps in information, even if derived from sources of information that are accepted to provide a high quality of evidence. As such, the implications for intelligence are that if evidentialism is accepted as the best way of establishing justification for beliefs, only a portion, and probably only a small portion, of beliefs acquired through intelligence would constitute as being epistemically justified.

* * *

The indefeasibilist response to the Gettier argument is that, to be justified, a subject's belief should not be susceptible to valid counterarguments: that it is undefeatable, or indefeasible.

1. P is true
2. The subject S believes that P is true
3. The subject S is justified in believing that P is true if their justification for believing that P is true is indefeasible (Lehrer and Paxson 1969)

Indefeasibilism faces similar difficulties to reliabilism: counterarguments can both partially and totally defeat justification for a belief. Total counterarguments would show that the original justification was necessarily false, whereas a partial counterargument would prove that the original argument was only conditionally true, and therefore merely a sufficient, but not a necessary, justification for the original belief. Theoretically, according to the indefeasibilist argument, an individual can be justified in believing something to be true even if he or she only has a conditionally true justification for taking the belief to be true (Everitt and Fisher 1995).[32]

Indefeasibilism also has specific implications for intelligence. The likelihood of incomplete information or gaps in information collection means that there may be insufficient intelligence information available to provide counterarguments for beliefs acquired in intelligence. Total counterarguments only apply to arguments that are necessarily true or false: arguments that are logically deductive, where truth or falsity is necessarily entailed. Total counterarguments cannot apply to conditionally true arguments: to logically inductive arguments, where truth or falsity has some support, but is not necessarily entailed. Only partial counterarguments can be applied to inductive arguments, and each premise of an inductive argument requires a counterargument. As such, multiple pieces of evidence would be required to provide counterarguments to conditionally true (inductive) beliefs. However, the covert nature of intelligence inevitably leads to restrictions on the comprehensiveness of the information available for collection. Adversaries could be actively trying to hide information or be in geographical areas where you have no or limited access for intelligence collection. It is likely that the evidence required to provide the multiple counterarguments needed to provide a total counterargument for a conditionally true argument may not be available for collection. If only partial counterargument can be provided for a conditionally true belief, then according to indefeasibilism, an individual would be epistemically justified in accepting that belief to be true. However, it is possible that the evidence required to provide a total counterargument exists, but just cannot be collected. If indefeasibilism is accepted as the best mechanism for establishing justification, then it follows that many actually false beliefs could be acquired and accepted through intelligence as having epistemic justification in the absence of comprehensive evidence.

To establish the strength of justification for a propositional belief, you need to differentiate between the qualities of different types of conditional justification. It follows that to adapt the theories of evidentialism, reliabilism and indefeasibilism as ways of establishing epistemic justification in intelligence, standards must be agreed as to when each of these approaches can provide both necessary and sufficient epistemological standards for knowing or being justified in believing whether a proposition is true or false. These approaches are not without flaws and require substantive development to establish their granular application in an intelligence context. Whilst it is not within the scope of this book to provide this, I argue that these approaches stand as the strongest philosophical basis for the development of further theory concerning epistemological approaches for intelligence.

Epistemological Implications for Intelligence

Intelligence is essentially an act of belief acquisition. However, intelligence is necessarily concerned with acquiring beliefs that are epistemically justified: beliefs that have a rational basis for being accepted as true. Whilst belief acquisition in intelligence derives from the same sources of knowledge and justification, belief acquisition in intelligence differs in its nature from belief acquisition in non-intelligence contexts. The covert nature of intelligence means that intelligence faces a greater challenge of dealing with epistemic complexity than belief acquisition in non-intelligence context. This has potentially significant implications for acquiring beliefs that can be taken to have epistemic justification in intelligence.

Despite the different arguments between what form or requirement justification takes, very few philosophers in contemporary epistemology reject the inclusion of justification in the criterion of what knowledge is. Those that do reject the justification requirement instead suggest a method of connecting a belief with truth that is some way infallible. This can be taken as a non-conscious form of justification for distinguishing knowledge from true belief. The relationship between justification and knowledge needs to be one of a reliable or, if possible, an infallible cognitive method. However, it is questionable that belief acquisition in intelligence can be based on a reliable or infallible cognitive method. Given the variety of collection methods for potential information, and the predominant reliance on claims made by humans, intelligence faces the likelihood that some of the information from which it is derived will comprise unintentionally imparted falsehoods, and falsehoods knowingly imparted in the guise of truth. Further, the information from which intelligence derives faces the likelihood of containing gaps of information, some of which may prove to be significant, or lead to false conclusions even via reliable methods. The existence of deceptive measures taken by one adversary to deceive another implies that information available for intelligence analysis is not guaranteed to be comprehensive, or representative of the subject being analysed. This arguably renders establishing the quality or degree of epistemic justification provided by the information from which intelligence derives as a greater challenge in comparison to other types of belief acquisition. In this capacity, it is reasonable to argue that the acquisition of justified beliefs in intelligence can, in specific cases, face greater epistemic complexity compared with belief acquisition in a non-intelligence context. This epistemic complexity takes three forms: establishing the epistemic quality of available information; establishing epistemic justification where available information is not comprehensive; and drawing in part or in total from information collected by an epistemically unreliable method.

It is plausible that the greater challenges faced in intelligence in establishing epistemic justification for beliefs means that cognitive biases impact belief acquisition in intelligence differently from how they impact belief acquisition in non-intelligence contexts. Cognitive biases have a variety of causes, which include limitations in the brain's ability to process information (Hilbert 2012).[33] The forms of epistemic complexity that intelligence faces could feasibly place greater strain on the brain's information-processing capability. A greater strain on cognitive ability to process information would arguably result in a greater susceptibility to cognitive bias. It is therefore theoretically valid to argue that belief acquisition in intelligence could be more vulnerable to cognitive bias.

Notes

1. This debate has taken place solely within a Western-centric view of intelligence.
2. This focus is on intelligence as a process of analysis rather than on intelligence as an organisation. This definition does not include the specific goals of intelligence: just that it is goal-oriented in an action-guiding capacity.
3. Warner's definition is based on the definition provided by Random (1958).
4. Johnston described his definition as synthesising Warner's definition with data collected from interviews with US law enforcement and intelligence agencies (Warner 2002).
5. Yet another type of definition, ostensive definitions provide the meaning of a term by using examples (Lyons 1977).
6. In analytical philosophy, the essential nature of terms has traditionally been identified by looking for truth conditions which are both necessary and sufficient. In the standard theory of truth functions in logic (Hintikka and Bachman 1991), necessary and sufficient conditions derive from the logical formula of 'if p, therefore q'. The relationship between p and q is one of material implication: if p is true,

then q is also true, and, conversely, if q is false then p is also false (Brennan 2011). According to the standard theory of truth function, it is necessary that q be true for p to also be true. As such, the truth of q is a necessary condition for the truth of p. The propositions p and q each stand as converse truth conditions for the other. If the truth of p is a necessary condition for the truth of q, then q is a necessary condition for p. However, the notion of necessity and sufficiency has yet to be defined in an unproblematic way. See Brennan (2011) for further reading.

7. Sufficient conditions are also known as either contingent or possible conditions.
8. This practice was also followed by Bruce (2008).
9. It could feasibly be argued that intelligence is an activity that can be conducted by non-humans.
10. In intelligence analysis the debate as to whether knowledge is possible or impossible is framed in the debate regarding the distinction of 'secrets' and 'mysteries', where secrets are held to be knowledge that is possible but difficult to obtain, and mysteries are held to be knowledge that is impossible to obtain. For further reading on this debate see Marrin (2012b).
11. In his *Treatise of Human Nature*, the Scottish empiricist philosopher David Hume showed irrefutably that all inferences made about future events that are based on the premise of a similarity to past events are logically invalid (Hume 1738–40).
12. See Treverton et al. (2006) for further discussion on this topic.
13. Most sources of knowledge are widely held to also be sources of justification.
14. These are known as the empirical senses. In classical empiricism, reasoning is considered to be both an individual sense and the primary sense.
15. It could be argued that perception is not a basic source of knowledge and justification as it is dependent on introspection (or consciousness). However, this could be resolved by adopting the Audi (2002) definitions of perception as 'perceptual consciousness' and introspection as 'internal consciousness' (Audi 2002). Internal consciousness is strictly understood as including conscious possession of abstract images, interpretations or concepts about physical phenomena; purely abstract concepts that are not about physical phenomena; beliefs; emotional states; and desires. Perceptual consciousness, on the other hand, is strictly understood as conscious activity that is causally linked via perceptual senses to physical phenomena that is outside the brain.

16. One argument to account for this view is the special authority we attribute to first-person accounts, and the ability to provide a first-person account of one's own mental states. Introspection provides a first-hand account of how we process our perceptions: of how the world appears to us through our perceptive faculties. However, introspection is not infallible (Steup 2014).

17. A key issue about memory as a source of knowledge is the difficulty in distinguishing between accurate memories and false memories that people believe are true. This is arguably difficult to achieve through the process of introspection, and the natural and cognitive sciences have not yet reached a stage of advancement where memory can be externally validated. This creates an issue for memory's place as a method of justification: is memory only a legitimate form of justification when it is reliable? Or is it only a legitimate form of justification if the memory is coherent with a subset or total corpus of an individual's beliefs?

18. The US Department of Defense defines human intelligence as information collected and provided by humans (US DoD 2014).

19. Source attributes for HUMINT encompass subject matter experts, professional researchers, first-hand observers or participants, information specialists and professional researchers. Krizan cites Clauser and Wier's categorisation of intelligence sources by their analytic use. Clauser and Wier group intelligence sources as falling into four categories: people, objects, emanations and records (Clauser and Weir 1975). In this categorisation, HUMINT comprises the category of people.

20. In Clauser and Weir's categories of intelligence sources, SIGINT falls under emanations and records (Clauser and Weir 1975). Emanations are classified as detectable phenomena given off by natural or human-made objects; electromagnetic energy; heat, sound, footprints, fingerprints, and chemical and material residues.

21. See Brandwein (1995) for further reading on telemetry analysis.

22. Krizan (1999) describes IMINT as including photographs/digital, electro-optical, multispectral, infrared and radar imagery. In Clauser and Weir's categories of intelligence sources, IMINT falls under objects and records (Clauser and Weir 1975). Objects are classified as physical characteristics of equipment, materials or products, such as texture, shape, size and distinctive markings (Clauser and Weir 1975).

23. OSINT does not feature as a category in Clauser and Wier's (1975) categorisation of intelligence sources.

24. To this can be added the sub-category of information drawn from social media (SOCMINT).
25. The word 'epistemology' comes from the Greek terms *episteme* (knowledge) and *logos* (logic). The contemporary term 'epistemology' has therefore taken on the meaning 'theory of knowledge'.
26. This distinction is alternately referred to as the analytic-synthetic distinction.
27. The first case presented by Gettier is as follows: Smith and Jones have applied for a job. Smith has strong evidence to believe that Jones will get the job, as the director of the company told him that this was the case. Smith knows that Jones has ten coins in his pocket. Smith knows this because he counted the coins in Jones's pocket himself. Based on this, Jones entails proposition (a): Jones is the man who will get the job, and Jones has ten coins in his pocket. This entails proposition (b): the man who will get the job has ten coins in his pocket. Suppose that unknown to Smith, it is Smith who has actually got the job, and that, also unknown to Smith, Smith has ten coins in his pocket. Proposition (a) is false, but proposition (b) is true. According to the traditional criterion of knowledge, Smith knew that (b) was true, believed that (b) was true, and is justified in believing (b) to be true. But at the same time, in this case Smith does not know that (b) is true. Smith based his belief and justification for inferring (b) on a false premise, that Jones would get the job and that Jones had ten coins in his pocket. The second case presented by Gettier is as follows: suppose that as long as Smith has known Jones, Jones has owned a Ford. Jones has just offered Smith a ride whilst driving a Ford. Smith has another friend named Brown, of whose whereabouts Smith is ignorant. Smith formulates the following three hypotheses: (a) either Jones owns a Ford or Brown is in Boston; (b) either Jones owns a Ford or Brown is in Barcelona; and (c) either Jones owns a Ford or Brown is in Brest-Litovsk. Smith decides to believe all three of these hypotheses. As it so happens, Brown is in Barcelona, and Jones does not at present own a Ford, and is in fact driving a rented car. Smith has based the propositions (a), (b) and (c) on the basis that Jones has always owned a Ford. In this case, Smith does not know where Brown is, but he believes that (b) is true, and is justified in believing (b) is true based on evidence.
28. A fourth approach argues that justification is not a requirement for knowledge and can be replaced with appropriate causal connections between belief and truth. This is known as the appropriately caused true belief theory. A fifth approach similarly denies the requirement

of justification for knowledge and argues that instead that their needs be a connection between objective reality and what an individual believes to be true to claim knowledge. This is known as the true belief that tracks reality theory. However, both face incontrovertible flaws. The appropriately caused true belief theory argues that if a true belief is the result of an appropriate causal connection, then it is knowledge. The principal argument against the appropriately caused true belief theory is that it does not allow for purely conceptual knowledge such as mathematics. Mathematics is based on a purely conceptual framework that is metaphysically neutral: it has no material existence, and therefore has no causational ability. A second argument against the theory is that it fails to account for true beliefs that are acquired by deviant causal chains (Everitt and Fisher 1995). A deviant, or inconvenient, causal chain is where an actor causes an event that he or she intended to cause, but not in the way that he or she intended to cause the event to happen. A classic example of a deviant causal chain was provided by Chisholm (1966), in the case of the accidental inheritance. A final argument against the causational argument is that false beliefs can be also causally connected to events. This was demonstrated by the Barn County Case counter-example provided by Goldman (1976). The true belief that tracks reality theory (or the 'tracking account' of knowledge) was put forward by Nozick (1981). The tracking account has been criticised for failing to account for the Goldman (1976) Barn County Case.

29. This can falsely be interpreted along the lines of Pascal's wager. Pascal's wager refers to a philosophical argument developed in the seventeenth century by the French philosopher Blaise Pascal. Pascal posited that rational people should believe in God. This would entail that they suffered a finite loss, but stand to receive infinite gains, represented in the eternal afterlife. As such, believing in God increased the odds that an individual would receive gains over the odds that they would suffer loss. However, the odds expressed in Pascal's wager relate to the odds of benefit to the subject being higher if the belief were hypothetically true rather than the odds being higher if the belief was in fact objectively true.

30. Some 'reliabilists' have argued that you can abandon the justification criteria. Their argument is that if we take knowledge to be a reliably formed true belief then it does not require justification. There are therefore two forms of reliabilism: a reliabilist theory of knowledge and a reliabilist theory of justification.

31. It could be argued that intelligence faces more time pressure or time sensitivity in the acquisition of justified beliefs than other areas of intellectual enquiry. However, this is not obviously true. There are many professions which require the timely acquisition of justified beliefs to enable swift decision-making, for example the emergency services (Garst 1989). The time pressures for intelligence analysis and any other attempt to acquire justified beliefs would depend on the timeframe for which decision-making may be required. This would vary on a case-by-case basis.

32. A similar argument, known as infallibilism, was put forward by Dretske (1971) and supported by Armstrong (1973). Infallibilism argues that S knows that P is true if there is a law-like connection between P and S's belief that P is true. This criterion of a law-like connection can be interpreted as a necessary justification.

33. Other causes include limitations in memory retrieval (Simon 1955); social influences; and evolved information-processing shortcuts that enable efficiency over accuracy (Kahneman et al. 1982).

2 The Efficacy of ACH in Establishing Epistemic Justification and Mitigating Cognitive Bias

It is theoretically valid that belief acquisition in intelligence can face greater challenges in establishing epistemic justification than in non-intelligence contexts, due to the nature of intelligence as a covert activity and the subsequent limitations that the nature of intelligence places on both the quality and comprehensiveness of available sources of knowledge and justification. The increased likelihood of greater epistemic complexity in belief acquisition may also lead to greater strain being placed on cognitive faculties, thereby rendering belief acquisition in intelligence more vulnerable to cognitive bias. This has significant implications for approaches to mitigating cognitive bias in intelligence. Mitigating cognitive bias in intelligence contexts needs to directly address the higher degree of epistemic complexity that is likely to be involved in intelligence analysis. Mitigation of cognitive bias in intelligence should be primarily concerned with reducing the cognitive strain in determining epistemic justification for beliefs, thereby reducing the reliance on cognitive shortcuts. A body of social science research has demonstrated that belief acquisition that relies on intuition is prone to a variety of cognitive biases. But can structured analytical methods fare any better?

This chapter examines the theoretical basis for whether the predominant structured analytical method recommended for belief acquisition in Western intelligence, the Analysis of Competing Hypotheses (ACH), can provide mitigation for cognitive biases. ACH will be examined in three ways: (1) by evaluating whether it provides any mechanisms to reduce epistemic complexity and cognitive strain, thereby reducing the risk of cognitive bias; (2) by evaluating whether it provides any mechanisms for preventing or reducing cognitive bias from impacting belief acquisition when using the ACH process; and (3) by evaluating whether it provides any mechanisms for making cognitive biases visible to external peer review.

The ACH Method

Structural analytical methods are formal methods or processes used to conduct analysis. Most structured analytical methods that have been recommended or specifically designed for use in intelligence analysis are inspired by, and attempt to use, a methodological process that was designed for formal logic, mathematics or the natural sciences. Others have been borrowed from the field of economics, or from methods devised by private corporations. Few of these techniques were designed to stand as a comprehensive methodological approach to analysis, covering all stages of the analytical process from hypothesis generation to hypothesis evaluation; rather, they provide specific techniques for application at different stages of analysis. Structured analytical methods that are recommended in training manuals produced since the late 1990s by military and intelligence communities in the United States, the United Kingdom and Canada can be split into two categories: structured analytical methods for generating hypotheses, and structured analytical methods for evaluating hypotheses. Whilst the generation of hypotheses for analysis inevitably dictates and restricts the breadth of possible beliefs that can be acquired by an analyst, it is with structured analytical methods that are designed for the evaluation of hypotheses, of processing information, with which belief acquisition is principally concerned.

The only structured analytical method that has been developed for the evaluation of hypotheses in intelligence is ACH.[1] [2] ACH is widely credited as having been developed by ex-CIA analyst Richards Heuer Jr. ACH requires the analyst to develop multiple hypotheses to explain a phenomenon, and then match all available relevant information against each hypothesis, looking to refute hypotheses, rather than to confirm them. The hypothesis that is most likely to be deemed true by ACH is the hypothesis that has the least evidence that counters it (Heuer and Pherson 2010). ACH was inspired by the scientific methods of eliminative induction, such as those developed by Francis Bacon and Karl Popper. The earliest forms of a systematic rational approach to developing scientific theories began with the ancient Greeks in the pre-Socratic school in the Archaic Period (650–480 BC).[3] The Greek philosopher Thales was the first to reject religious and mystical interpretations of the natural world and argued instead that every event in nature had a natural cause. Although this period saw contributions from the likes of Democritus, Lucretius and Plato, it was Aristotle who provided the most significant contribution to the development of the modern and contemporary sciences: he was the first philosopher to propose what can be described as a scientific method. Every attempt at developing a scientific theory since Aristotle, including that of eliminative induction, has been founded on an acceptance or rejection of Aristotle's nomic-deductive method.

Aristotle argued that general laws about the natural world can be known inductively from knowledge of particular observations; however, this process alone was insufficient for establishing scientific knowledge. He argued that the identification of general laws is a key preliminary step in scientific discovery, as it allows the development of hypotheses to be tested by a process of deductive, syllogistic reasoning.[4] Aristotle saw formal logical processes as a tool through which humans could seek explanations about the physical world. He believed that demonstration by experimentation revealed the deductive causal structures underlying natural phenomena but acknowledged that not all knowledge was demonstrable in this way (Shields 2014). Aristotle's system was an entirely closed logical process that allowed general laws (universal truths) to be logically inferred from particular observations of the natural world, and particular truths about the natural world to be inferred from these identified general laws. Aristotle's system was exclusively dedicated to discovering causational relationships in natural phenomena. As such, his method was a dual system of inference: from particular observations to general laws, and from general laws to particular laws.[5] Although Aristotle's scientific method is not strictly empirical, he was the first to apply an empirical approach to the discovery of scientific knowledge.

Francis Bacon rejected the traditional approaches based on the logical principles outlined by Aristotle to develop laws about the natural world. Bacon rejected what he referred to as the anticipation of nature by logic, and instead argued that knowledge about the natural world should be acquired by the interpretation of nature. Bacon argued that logical induction, and not logical deduction, should be used in the sciences. Bacon's inductive process starts with sense experience or observations, from which inductive truths, or laws, are identified. These laws, once accepted as knowledge, can be used as a basis for further scientific discovery, and act as foundations for further inductive inferences that lead to the discovery of more laws. Bacon assumed that fundamental laws of nature could be induced from the general laws identified by his inductive process. He envisaged sense experience in his inductive process as observed and confirmed facts about the physical world. These facts would be methodically compiled in tables from which presence, absence and comparisons of degree could be analysed and causational relations between collected observed facts could be identified (Bacon 1620). Bacon believed that only by employing a rigorous method of analysis could the imperfection of our senses be corrected.

Bacon's eliminative induction relies on experimentation to eliminate competing alternative theories. Experiment played two roles in Bacon's method: in collecting facts to form tables and in eliminating uncertainties. Hypotheses emerged through experimentation. The biggest contribution that Bacon's method provided to the development of scientific method was the process of analysis by exclusion (Sessions 1990; Von Wright 1951c). When tables of facts have been set up for comparison, the causal relationship between the two tables is established by excluding irrelevant facts by a process of induction. Bacon was the first scholar to introduce a method of falsification into scientific discovery (Klein 2012).

In 1934 Karl Popper similarly refuted the argument that logical induction should be used in the scientific method to confirm or falsify hypotheses. However, unlike Bacon, Popper posited that logical deduction should be the primary focus of scientific enquiry (Popper [1934] 2002). Popper referred to the application of deduction in science as critical rationalism. Like Bacon, Popper also advocated empirical disproof as the preferred method to select between competing hypotheses, and that the scientific method should provide predictive hypotheses that can be empirically tested and rejected if falsified. Popper embraced the primacy of explanatory force (abduction)[6] but rejected the notion that the hypothesis that has the most explanatory force will necessarily be the most likely to be true (Thornton 2017).[7]

ACH incorporates the central element of eliminative induction from Popper and Bacon's scientific methods: it seeks to falsify rather than prove hypotheses. The basic steps of the original ACH method developed by Heuer are as follows:

1. Develop at least three (and up to seven) mutually exclusive competing hypotheses (only one can be true) (Heuer and Pherson 2010). Aim to cover all reasonable possibilities in the hypotheses.
2. Make a list of relevant evidence. This can include information gaps and assumptions made by the analyst.
3. Score each piece of evidence (or information) for how diagnostic it is against each of the hypotheses. Different information ranking systems can be used instead of diagnostic value.
4. Refine the table by adding new hypotheses, or combining hypotheses together, if required/appropriate.
5. Make probabilistic judgements about the likelihood of each hypothesis being the true hypothesis. The hypothesis that is consistent with the largest volume of information is the most likely to be true, and the hypothesis that is inconsistent with the largest volume of information is the least likely to be true.
6. Review judgements as to the diagnostic strength of the information and readjust the scoring if required.
7. Report the conclusions of the ACH.
8. Identify indicators for future observation. This requires a set of two indicators, one on future events that would support the hypothesis assessed to be most likely to be true, and a list of indicators that would reduce the likelihood that this hypothesis is true. (Heuer 1999; Heuer and Pherson 2010)

ACH was originally developed by Heuer between 1979 and 1999 as a way of identifying deception in counterintelligence (Heuer 2009). Heuer claims that it was designed as a method of identifying the 'relative likelihood' of multiple competing hypotheses (Heuer 1999). The likelihood of a hypothesis is measured by the degree of support that information and assumptions give for each competing hypothesis. In early versions of ACH the degree of support was identified by consistency of available information to the competing hypotheses. The more consistent the information is with a hypothesis, the more likely the hypothesis is to be true (and vice versa). The hypotheses that are least consistent with the information in the matrix are eliminated from the analytical process (Heuer 1999; Heuer and Pherson 2010). The 'correct' or 'most likely' hypothesis will have the least inconsistent information (or none) ranked against it (Pherson 2017; Heuer and Pherson 2010). In this sense, 'likelihood' refers to a measure of likelihood that each hypothesis is the true hypothesis (as only one can be true). However, Heuer also describes ACH as requiring analysts to select the hypothesis that 'best fits the evidence' (Heuer and Pherson 2010), an approach more in line with the notion of abduction. Attempting to identify a likelihood or probability that a given hypothesis is true or false is problematic in philosophical terms. This is because truth is in no way probable. For something to be assigned a probability value, it has to be capable of being more than two different states. For example, to assign the probability of a horse winning a race it has to be capable of both winning and losing. To assign probability to a truth value, a hypothesis would have to be capable of being both true and false. However, this is impossible; a truth categorically cannot be false and a falsehood cannot be true. Describing truth in probabilistic terms such as 'likely' or 'probable' is inaccurate. Instead, what ACH is attempting to do is identify the truth value of multiple hypotheses: to identify which hypothesis one would be most epistemically justified in believing to be true.

The Ability of ACH to Reduce Epistemic Complexity

Reducing epistemic complexity in belief acquisition in intelligence centres on the ability to identify the epistemic justification that information of variable quality provides to beliefs. This essentially rests on the ability to determine sufficient epistemic justification of information collected in intelligence. The process by which information is ranked within ACH determines the results of the method regarding which hypothesis is deemed most likely to be true. As such, it is these scoring systems that ACH employs to judge epistemic justification for a competing set of possible beliefs. The ability of ACH to reduce epistemic complexity rests on the ability of these scoring systems to determine whether the underlying information provides either necessary or sufficient justification for believing a particular hypothesis to be true. The process of ranking information in most versions of ACH involves either one or a combination of the following scoring systems: consistency of information; diagnostic value of information; credibility of information; and the application of base rate probability values to each item of information (subjective Bayesianism).[8] But can any of these scoring systems provide a theoretically valid basis for establishing, and comparing the degree of epistemic justification for believing that a hypothesis is true?

A system to rank information in ACH needs to do several things to provide a method of establishing epistemic justification. As was outlined in Chapter 1, the requirement of a relationship between a truth and what makes it true is one of necessity and relevance. As such, information ranking systems in ACH need to provide a method of establishing epistemic justification that provides the required relationships of relevance and necessity (or where this is unattainable, sufficiency) between a belief and truth. The leading theories within epistemology for how to provide this are: that the degree to which a belief is justified is the degree to which it fits the evidence available to the subject (evidentialism); that a belief is justified if it originates from a reliable cognitive method (reliabilism); and that a belief is justified if it cannot be defeated by counterargument or contrary evidence (indefeasibilism). Information ranking systems in ACH should incorporate at least one of these approaches to stand as a theoretically rigorous method of establishing epistemic justification. Further, ACH should provide guidance on how these methods can be used to identify the epistemic justification provided by information that could have been the product of intentional deception or unintentionally imparted falsehoods.

Second, information ranking systems in ACH need to take into account the fact that epistemic justification can take both total and partial forms. Hypotheses are arguments. Arguments contain at least two premises that are logically connected to form a conclusion. Epistemic justification can be relevant to one premise of a hypothesis but not others, providing only partial epistemic justification. ACH needs to be able to distinguish between partial epistemic justification and total epistemic justification for multiple hypotheses, as well as provide a way to identify the relative, and cumulative, degree of epistemic justification that each hypothesis has for being accepted as a justified belief. Thirdly, ACH needs to provide two levels of epistemic justification. As was outlined in Chapter 1, the covert nature of intelligence probably leads to a greater epistemic complexity in acquiring justified beliefs. This is because it must be assumed that information collected within an act of intelligence may be the product of intentional deception, or unintentionally imparted falsehoods. An information ranking system in ACH therefore needs to establish the degree of epistemic justification for accepting each piece of intelligence information as a justified belief and to establish the degree of epistemic justification that each piece of intelligence information provides to the individual premises contained within a hypothesis (the relationship of relevance and necessity or sufficiency between a belief and truth). Providing only one of these levels of epistemic justification will be insufficient to determine the degree to which each hypothesis examined under ACH can be accepted as a justified belief. It is therefore an essential requirement that ACH provide this dual-epistemic information ranking system.

Consistency of Information as an Indicator of Truth

Versions of ACH that apply a consistency of information ranking system do not provide specific accounts of what is meant by consistency of information (Chang et al. 2017). Further, some versions of ACH, including versions promoted by Heuer and the CIA, use the terms 'diagnosticity' and 'consistency' interchangeably when providing guidance on how to rank information (Heuer 2005b, 1999). Consistency is understood as an action being done in the same way over time, or a set of propositions not containing any logical contradictions. Consistency of information can be interpreted as a measurement of consistency between the intelligence information and each hypothesis under consideration. In this context, consistency of information would be a measurement of epistemic relevance. However, consistency of information could also be interpreted as attempting to match competing hypotheses against an objective reality: to examine whether each hypothesis is consistent with reality.[9] The first interpretation of consistency of information is aligned with the epistemological position in philosophy of the correspondence of truth theory, whereas the second interpretation is aligned with the coherence of truth theory. However, both these interpretations are problematic when applied as theories of epistemic justification.

Truth is widely understood as our ideas agreeing with reality, except for where the truth of a proposition explicitly references another proposition. The correspondence theory of truth in philosophy is the theory that truth corresponds to reality.[10] Modern philosophers distinguish two versions of the correspondence theory of truth: a fact-based version and an object-based version. The object-based version argues that true propositions have a subject-predicate structure. A predicate is a part of a sentence that makes a claim regarding the overall topic (or subject) of a sentence. The object-based account of correspondence of truth theory argues that a proposition is true if the predicate corresponds to the object referred to by the subject of the proposition. This argument involves a reference relation and a correspondence relation, the reference relation holding between the subject of the proposition and the object that the subject is about, and the correspondence relation holding between the predicate of the proposition and the object that the subject is about (David 2013). Fact-based versions of the correspondence theory of truth argue that true propositions do not need to have a subject-predicate structure. The classic fact-based version of the correspondence theory of truth supported by Hume (1739), Mill (1843) and Russell (1912) argues that a belief is true when it has a corresponding fact.[11] The simplest iteration of the correspondence theory of truth is:

P is true if and only if P corresponds to some fact or state of affairs

Correspondence theorists also hold that if a proposition refers exclusively to another proposition and not to the external world, then its truth condition will lie in the truth of the propositions to which it refers. Supporters of the correspondence theory of truth argue that the strongest support for the theory is that it is obviously true. It is widely accepted that truth is understood as our ideas agreeing with reality. However, opponents of the theory argue that it is too broad to be useful to all academic domains. For example, it fails to distinguish conceptual truths such as logical truths as these are not technically empirical facts. A counterargument to this would be to distinguish differences of truth in different domains, such as distinguishing logical truth from empirical or social-behavioural truths (David 2013).

Consistency of information, applied on the interpretation of the correspondence of truth theory, provides a theoretically valid method of establishing epistemic justification. It is on a par with the evidentialist approach to justification: it establishes epistemic justification by determining the degree to which a hypothesis fits the evidence available to the individual. In addition, it could theoretically act as a dual-ranking system of information in ACH, applied to both establishing the epistemic justification for believing individual pieces of intelligence to be true, and establishing the epistemic justification that individual pieces of intelligence provide to a specific hypothesis. Further, it could easily be adapted to establish the relevance that information bears to a hypothesis. Finally, if ACH is adapted to split a hypothesis into its composite premises, and its information ranking systems are applied to individual premises, as opposed to a composite hypothesis, the consistency of truth interpretation of consistency of information could also distinguish between partial and total epistemic justification. As such, this approach theoretically fulfils all the major requirements of an information ranking system to stand as a valid mechanism of establishing justification. However, this approach is problematic in dealing with the nature of intelligence and the epistemic complexity that is entailed. The correspondence of truth theory depends on a correspondence with an objective reality, or a priori facts. It can therefore only be used to determine epistemic justification for information derived from reason or perception (including empirical information) as sources of knowledge and justification. However, information derived in intelligence will rarely exclusively derive from either empirical facts or a priori information. Information that is derived from testimony, memory or authority (which in many cases will arguably form the bulk of available intelligence information) would have to be subject to a different method of ranking information. In the context of ACH, consistency between pieces of information of these types and a specific hypothesis would be determined by whether a piece of information logically contradicted a hypothesis. This application of consistency assumes that the truth of a proposition is confirmed by the degree of consistency between a set of propositions, and not objective facts. However, this is not what the consistency of truth theory argues. It is this limitation in the quality of sources of knowledge from which intelligence derives that leads the consistency of information scoring system in ACH to also draw from the coherence of truth argument.

The coherence theory of truth argues that the truth of a true proposition lies in its coherence with a specific set of propositions: the truth of a proposition lies in the truth of other propositions, rather than in an objective reality.[12] There are several versions of the coherence theory of truth, all of which differ on two issues: the coherence relation and the set of propositions to which true propositions cohere. Early versions of the coherence theory of truth argued that coherence is understood as consistency. However, this argument was refuted by the fact that this would entail accepting a set of inconsistent propositions as both being true. If the consistency argument is accepted, then the truth of a proposition is reliant on the consistency of a set of propositions. A set of propositions S and T may be consistent with the additional propositions Q and R, which are not members of the set that S and T belong to. However, if Q and R are both consistent with the set of S and T, but are not consistent with each other, the coherentist would have to accept that both Q and R are true. This leads to the acceptance of logical contradictions. It could be argued that this is a risk that could be managed in the application of ACH: the occurrence of logical contradictions within a body of information that is ranked against a hypothesis may be easily spotted if ACH is conducted by one analyst using a small volume of information. However, the risks of logical inconsistencies not being spotted increase when: (1) only sections of an individual piece of intelligence information are extracted for input into ACH, and the total set of claims within an individual piece of intelligence information are not taken into account for internal consistency or logical coherence; (2) more than one analyst is involved in processing the information, and there is not complete cross-checking of the information for internal consistency between different analysts; (3) the ACH runs over an extended period of time and details of individual reports are forgotten; and (4) when the ACH includes a large volume of information, or a moderate volume of highly complex or detailed information, and the spotting of logical inconsistency becomes difficult. However, even if logical contradictions were spotted, there is no clear argument as to how to deal with this eventuality. If both pieces of logically contradicting information are consistent with a hypothesis, then both are equally valid to be included and to be given equal scoring according to the consistency of information ranking method. To remove one of the two contradicting reports would be highly subjective.

Other coherentists have instead argued that coherence is a relation of entailment: that the truth of a proposition coheres with a set of propositions if it is entailed by the set of propositions, or that the propositions mutually support one another (Bradley 1914). However, the concept of entailment is also problematic as a method of establishing truth. The theory that entailment is the essential component of truth was put forward by Fox (1987) and Bigelow (1988). The entailment theory of truth-making is that there exists a thing that, by its very existence, entails that something is true: X makes P true if and only if X exists and X entails the representation of P (MacBride 2014). This notion of entailment is a common and widely used concept outside of philosophy, which makes it seem attractive to be used as an understanding of what makes something true. To entail is understood as a necessary connection or consequence. However, it is this notion of a necessary connection to truth that makes entailment a problematic explanation for what makes something true. Entailment theoretically allows the existence of any object to entail that something is necessarily true (Restall 1996). This is akin to arguing that the truth of the proposition 'Simon is a human' is necessarily entailed by the existence of a banana peel. The theory of entailment clearly needs an additional theoretical requirement.[13] However, coherentists do not argue that any arbitrarily chosen sets of propositions will provide the truth of any proposition. Coherentists argue that the truth of a proposition lies in its coherence with a set of propositions that are held to be true (Young 2013).[14] In this capacity, the coherence theory of truth is distinct from the coherence theory of justification. If truth is correspondence to objective facts, coherence with a set of unverified propositions does not count as a justification or proof of truth. It does not follow that a coherent set of unverified propositions must correspond to objective reality. Therefore, coherence cannot stand as an infallible method of justification and, by extension, knowledge.

The very nature of intelligence as a covert attempt at belief acquisition, and the subsequent limitations on the quality of sources of information from which intelligence derives, means that using consistency of information as a way of ranking information for epistemic justification is highly problematic. Truth is widely taken as correspondence to objective facts; however correspondence with an objective reality is unlikely to be provided by intelligence information. Individual pieces of intelligence information are more likely to take the form of unverified propositions, which require corroboration. However, coherence with a set of unverified propositions cannot stand as justification of truth and therefore knowledge, as it does not follow that a coherent set of unverified propositions must correspond to an objective reality. Even if consistency across a set of propositions is taken to be an acceptable method of distinguishing truth from falsity, it cannot be taken as a method of establishing epistemic justification.

Diagnostic Value of Information as an Indicator of Truth

Diagnostic value is used as a scoring system in versions of ACH promoted by Heuer and the CIA (Heuer 1999; Heuer and Pherson 2010).[15] The term 'diagnostic' originated in the medical sciences and biology. To be diagnostic is to provide a precise indication: a characteristic or symptom that has value in diagnosis, in allowing the classification of what an unknown object or entity is. In the context of ACH, if a piece of information has diagnostic value, it must provide an indication of which of the competing hypotheses is correct (if any). The purpose of diagnostic value is to determine whether a piece of information supports the truth or the falsity of a particular hypothesis. However, few versions of ACH provide detailed advice on what is meant by diagnostic value, and how or by what measurement it should be determined. Some instructions on how to apply ACH conflate diagnostic value with the consistency of information with specific hypotheses (Heuer 1999). However, these are not equivalent ranking systems. Information can be consistent with two propositions but provide no diagnostic value between the two propositions. For example, an ACH could be developed about whether the Islamist terrorist group the Islamic State in Iraq and the Levant (ISIL) is undertaking attack planning targeting the United Kingdom. The ACH could contain two hypotheses: (1) ISIL's senior leadership in Syria are planning an attack against the United Kingdom; (2) ISIL's senior leadership in Syria are not planning an attack against the United Kingdom. A piece of information could claim that ISIL's senior leadership is based in Syria. This piece of information is logically consistent with both hypotheses. However, it does not provide any diagnostic indicator between them.

Diagnostic value is a process of determining taxonomy or classification. It is concerned with identifying unique characteristics of a concept or entity. A piece of information has diagnostic value if it relates to a unique characteristic of one entity but has no relation to unique characteristics of alternative entities. For example, if you were trying to identify if a mystery lifeform is a mammal or an amphibian, the information that the lifeform in question is warm-blooded and has fur pertains to unique characteristics of the classification mammal, but not the unique characteristics that necessarily determine the classification of amphibian. Therefore, this piece of information indicates that the mystery lifeform is necessarily a mammal, and not an amphibian. In this capacity, diagnostic value is a necessary relationship of entailment between an object and truth: that there exists a thing that, by its very existence, entails that something is necessarily true.

Diagnostic value fails to satisfy two of the three main criteria required of an information ranking system in ACH to stand as an acceptable mechanism of establishing epistemic justification.

Diagnostic value can be used to identify both partial epistemic justification and total epistemic justification. It centres on distinguishing epistemic support for unique characteristics of one concept or entity that are not shared by a competing concept or identity. In this capacity, it can identify diagnostic support for a unique premise of one hypothesis that is not shared by a competing hypothesis within ACH. However, diagnostic value does not provide a dual-ranking system. It does not measure the degree of epistemic justification there is for believing individual pieces of information to be true or false; it only establishes the degree of justification they provide for believing that a hypothesis is true or false. Finally, it is questionable whether diagnostic value fulfils the criteria of providing a theoretically valid mechanism of establishing epistemic justification. Diagnostic value arguably satisfies all three of the strongest theoretical approaches for establishing epistemic justification. It satisfies the requirements of evidentialism, as it measures the degree to which a hypothesis fits the available evidence. It satisfies the requirements of reliabilism, in that it utilises sources of knowledge and justification that would be widely considered as having been produced by a reliable cognitive method: a priori true information and empirical facts. Further, by seeking to identify the epistemic justification for unique characteristics of one concept or entity that are not shared by others, it satisfies the indefeasibilism approach, as the epistemic justification for one hypothesis will inevitably provide contrary evidence or counterargument for a competing hypothesis. However, the focus of diagnostic value is in identifying necessary connections between information and a hypothesis. It is questionable whether diagnostic value can be used to identify sufficient epistemic justification.

Diagnostic value, as a distinction of entailment, requires an objective fact of the matter to necessarily entail the truth of a hypothesis. This is a logically deductive relationship between a hypothesis and an evidential basis. Logic is divided into two types: deductive and inductive (abduction, typically cited as a third type, is not a system of logic). Deductive logic is a complete conceptual system where premises are necessarily linked to the conclusions of an argument. In deductive logic, valid argument forms that have true premises will necessarily have true conclusions.[16]

Unlike deduction, induction does not reveal necessary connections between true premises and true conclusions. Induction offers only conditional (or sufficient) connections between true premises and true conclusions. Induction fails to preserve truth conditions between premises and conclusions and allows for true premises to lead to false conclusions (Vickers 2014). Inductive inferences are contingently true, whereas deductive inferences are necessarily true.[17]

Diagnostic value in its original context overestimates the importance of deduction over that of induction. Outside of logic, mathematics and scientific methodology, which are fundamentally based on deductive logic, all major inferences are inductive (Russell 1948). Diagnostic value faces difficulty in the cross-application from the medical sciences and biology, essentially empirical processes of establishing knowledge, to the non-empirical process of establishing knowledge that is the typical mainstay of intelligence analysis. As intelligence is unlikely to solely establish knowledge based on processes of logic, mathematics or scientific methodology, it follows that intelligence will be concerned with at least some hypotheses that comprise inductive inferences. However, information or evidence that pertains to inductive inferences does not qualify as diagnostic, as it does not necessarily entail a unique quality of a hypothesis; it can only contingently entail it. If diagnostic value is to be adapted as a reliable method of establishing epistemic justification in intelligence it needs to account for inductive inferences and inductive evidence. However, the concept of diagnostic value would have to be fundamentally altered to be able to account for sufficient epistemic justification as well as necessary epistemic justification. This is a considerable challenge. The question of how to identify good inductive inferences from bad ones, and therefore determine the relative sufficient diagnostic quality of information that is relevant to inductive hypotheses, is the biggest philosophical problem that faces the subject of induction. In epistemological terms, the central problem of induction is the question of how we can use inductive inferences to justify our propositional beliefs. No current version of ACH provides such guidance. However, it is not implausible that such guidance could be developed that derives from philosophical theory. Philosophers have provided guidance on what premises can be added to inductive arguments in order to make the truth or falsity of the argument easier to identify, provided that the truth or falsity of the individual premises can be established (Skyrms 2000).

Subjective Bayesianism as an Indicator of Truth

Subjective Bayesianism (also known as Bayesian subjectivism, personalism and subjectivism) assigns a measure of probabilistic support that a piece of evidence provides to a hypothesis based on an individual's belief. A measurement of probability is assigned based on the level of confidence an individual has in whether it is true. Subjective Bayesianism is used as a single scoring system for ACH. Using subjective Bayesianism as a scoring system for ACH requires the following steps: (1) assess the base rate for each item of evidence (using frequentist probability for items that are solely determined by available empirical evidence and subjective inferences for items that are not); (2) judge each item of information as to how likely it is that each hypothesis would be true or false if the information was true; (3) judge the likelihood that each piece of information is true or false; and (4) use these measurements as prior probabilities in automated subjective Bayesianism calculus (Pope and Jøsang 2005). In subjective Bayesianism, probability is used to express the degree of support that an analyst believes a piece of evidence gives a hypothesis: the probability of an event is the ratio between the analysts' expectation of an event occurring and the impact of an event's occurrence on the probability of additional events. Probability is altered in the light of evidence, providing a standardised mechanism. In this sense, subjective Bayesianism, although centred on subjective assessment, attempts to incorporate objective information into analysis.

Subjective Bayesianism applies a theory of probability developed by British philosopher Thomas Bayes. Bayes' central theory is that a hypothesis is confirmed by a body of information that its truth renders probable (Joyce [2008] 2016). Bayes' theorem can be deployed objectively or subjectively. Objective Bayesianism is based on empirical evidence, whereas subjective Bayesianism is based on subjective beliefs. Subjective Bayesianism is essentially the theory that a hypothesis is confirmed or refuted by the degree of belief that an individual has that the hypothesis predicts a body of information. Bayes' theorem is particularly useful when applied objectively using empirical information for inferring causes from their effects. This is because it is relatively simple to identify the probability of an effect given the presence or absence of an assumed cause (Joyce [2008] 2016). However, applying Bayes' theorem subjectively faces the problem of identifying prior probabilities (referred to as 'the problem of the priors' in philosophy). Prior probabilities are probability distributions that are used to express subjective beliefs about variables before any evidence is taken into account. The key issue that divides objective Bayesianism and subjective Bayesianism is that subjective inferences of prior probabilities face relatively weak rational constraints. The only constraint is that prior probabilities applied are probabilistically coherent. However, many inferences can be reconstructed as probabilistically coherent prior probabilities. This does not mean that these inferences are rational (Talbott 2016). There is no agreed solution on the problem of prior probabilities within philosophy. As such, it is questionable whether Bayes' theorem provides a framework for inductive inferences, or if it only translates a framework of deductive inferences into a corresponding framework of degrees of belief (Talbott 2016).

There are three key issues with subjective probability that limit its utility at establishing epistemic justification. The first is that the utility of subjective Bayesianism is dependent on the objectivity, or rationality, of the analyst and the quality of information on which prior probabilities are based. If poor-quality information or weak rationality underpins the process, then poor-quality assessment is inevitably the result. A second key issue regards its application of frequentist probability.[18] Frequentism in its basic form, finite frequentism (Venn 1876), is the theory that the probability of an attribute A in a finite set of a reference class B is the relative frequency of the actual occurrences of A within B. Using a dice example, this means that the probability of rolling the number three on a six-sided dice is the relative frequency of the actual occurrences of rolling a three on a six-sided dice. The frequency is the number of times a three was rolled, divided by the total number of rolls of the dice.[19] Finite frequentism is the predominant choice of probability interpretation in statistical analysis and in the sciences. However, finite frequentism is not without issues. Frequency interpretations of probability can give misleading or false results. For example, if an unloaded dice was rolled ten times, and eight of the ten rolls displayed a five, the probability would be 80 per cent for a five on the next roll of the dice. However, if the dice was rolled 120 times, and a five was displayed only twenty times, the probability of rolling a five on the next throw would be 20 per cent. The probability measurement provided by finite frequentism will change over time and by the size of the reference class. Further, the instruments by which we measure probability may be faulty or unfair, such as a loaded dice or faulty mechanical equipment. Probability interpreted by frequency is neither necessarily consistent nor necessarily reliable. Further, frequency interpretations of probability can only be provided for the prediction of the repetition of repeated events that have already occurred. They cannot provide a probability measurement for events that have never occurred but may occur in the future. In addition, there is the problem of single cases. Single cases are unrepeatable events. Many events are conventionally considered as unrepeatable – the assassination of US President Abraham Lincoln and the first moon landing, for example. Single-case events are not repeatable, and therefore can have no probability measurement assigned to them by frequency. Many questions that intelligence seeks to answer will concern future events that have never occurred before, or single-case events. The main problem with finite frequentism is that it associates probability and frequency too closely. The two concepts are related but not reducible to one another. Finite frequency interpretations of probability cannot therefore stand as conclusive evidence for a hypothesis (Hájek 2012).

The third issue with subjective Bayesianism is that the basis for determining the epistemic justification that a set of information gives to a hypothesis is decided by an individual's belief, and not on a relationship of necessity (or sufficiency) and relevance between the underlying information that informs a belief and the belief itself. Belief or inference on its own is not an accepted method of determining necessary or sufficient conditions for knowledge, as it fails to provide justification for beliefs. Individuals must have an adequate basis for their belief to be justified in believing it to be true: that they have followed an accredited route to knowledge.

Various philosophers have attempted to prove that probability is reducible to logic. The first concerted effort to do this was undertaken by Boole (1894), followed by Venn (1876) and later by the logicians Frege (1879, 1892), Russell and Whitehead (1910, 1912, 1913) in their landmark three-volume publication *Principea Mathematica*. Between them, Frege, Russell and Whitehead developed what we now know as predicate logic and quantificational logic. These systems were powerful enough to be applied to all deductive arguments in mathematics and the sciences, whereby the validity of deductive arguments depends solely on the logical structure found in the sentences involved in the argument in question. Some philosophers attempted to use this system to extend to inductive reasoning by extending the deductive entailment relation to include probabilistic entailment for conditional inferences. They argued that if we cannot identify a necessary deductive truth, then we can apply a probability measurement to the likelihood that a conditional inference is true: an inference will be assigned a conditional probability. Philosophers tried to extend the rules of deductive logic to an inductive probability system in various ways. Carnap (1950) attempted to assign different premise sentences a degree of probabilistic support for the conclusions they entailed by analysing the syntactical structures of arguments. Carnap's attempt drew heavily on the work of Bayes' logic.[20] It is now commonly held in philosophy that Bayes' logicism is irredeemably flawed. In addition to truth being in no way probable, it is widely agreed that a logical structure based on analysis of natural language cannot be used to determine the degree to which a premise inductively supports a conclusion. This is because all systems that try to apply probability to inductive inferences fail in that they cannot provide satisfactory prior probabilities. The prior probability of any proposition in a system of inductive logic does not depend on observational or empirical evidence: it depends on the logical-syntactical structure of the language being used. No philosopher or mathematician has yet to identify a satisfactory method for deriving prior probabilities from the logical-syntactical structure of language. Furthermore, it is not clear why the probability of an inductive proposition about the physical world being true would rely on a logical-syntactical basis, even if a way could be found to apply probability to truth values. It is therefore highly questionable that subjective probability calculations can stand as an accredited route to knowledge.

Subjective Bayesianism provides none of the three key criteria for providing a method of establishing epistemic justification in ACH. If subjective Bayesianism can be adapted to provide an accepted method of establishing epistemic justification, then it could easily be adapted to provide a dual-use epistemic justification ranking system for ACH. However, it is less clear how it could be adapted to provide a system that identifies both partial epistemic justification and total epistemic justification. The probability calculation for each hypothesis is based on all the evidence that is ranked diagnostic against it. As such, the calculations do not differentiate between partial epistemic justification and total epistemic justification; they only account for total epistemic justification. A theoretical basis for the validity of subjective Bayesianism in establishing epistemic justification may not necessarily be impossible to establish. However, as no philosopher has yet been able to achieve this despite the concerted efforts of some of the greatest minds in human history, it seems unlikely that this method will be able to stand as a reliable method for determining epistemic justification in intelligence in the near future.

Credibility of Information as an Indicator of Truth

Credibility of information is included in some versions of ACH. However, it is not used in isolation. Rather, it is combined with a second scoring system. The inclusion of credibility of information as a ranking system in ACH is to ensure that low-quality information is not given equal scoring as high-quality information if both reports have equal value on a separate scoring system, such as diagnostic value or consistency of information. Credibility of information is rarely incorporated in versions of ACH, and on most occasions where it is included, the credibility of information scores has no impact on the overall ACH scores.

Credibility is essentially a measure of epistemic justification for a belief. However, the credibility of information specifically refers to the degree of epistemic justification for believing that the claims made in a specific piece of information are true. Credibility does not measure the epistemic justification that a specific piece of information provides for a whole hypothesis. In this sense, credibility is an essential scoring system for ACH to stand as a way of establishing epistemic justification for beliefs or knowledge but requires an additional scoring system to establish the total or cumulative degree of epistemic justification that pieces of information give to a hypothesis.

A key issue with the use of credibility of information as a scoring system in ACH is that there is a lack of appropriate guidance provided in ACH manuals or instructions as to what methods or standards should be used to assess the credibility (epistemic justification) of information. This is not an issue with the concept of using credibility of information as a scoring system for processing information in an analytical task, but whether the guidance on how to identify epistemic justification for information is theoretically appropriate. If this guidance is not provided in training on ACH, then it has to be sought, or taught separately. Guidance on making assessments of the credibility of information (sometimes also referred to as the validity of information) can be found in training guides that have been produced internally by Western intelligence communities and released as open source documents. However, these face significant theoretical flaws from an epistemological viewpoint.

Only two publicly available Western intelligence training manuals currently provide instructions on how to determine the credibility of information: Krizan (1999) and the United Nations Office on Drugs and Crime (UNODC) (2011). Krizan (1999) identifies three ways to evaluate the reporter of the claim where it is derived from humans: reliability, proximity and appropriateness. Krizan argues that to establish the reliability of an individual making a claim, you need to compare the performance of that individual in providing reliable reporting over time. If a source has proved accurate in the past, then it is reasonable to infer from this a level of likely accuracy in the future. If the source has not been tested, either through being a new source or through the inability to test the accuracy of previous reporting the source has provided, then evaluation of the information must be done on its own merits: to be evaluated independently of any consideration of its origin (Krizan 1999). Proximity refers to the access that the source must have to the claim he or she has made. A direct observer or participant can present direct evidence. However, the more degrees of separation there are between the source and the claim he or she has made, the greater the chance of distortion or error. Appropriateness refers to whether the source speaks from a position of authority on the subject being reported on. An individual's capabilities and shortcomings will affect the level of validity and reliability of the claims provided and must be considered. In evaluating a claim itself, Krizan argues for the use of three criteria: plausibility, expectability and support. Plausibility refers to whether the information is necessarily true, or contingently true. Expectability is the measurement of whether the analyst evaluating the claim or piece of information would expect to see it in the context at hand. Support refers to whether the claim is corroborated or not. Corroboration can include different information reported by the same individual, or different information reported by different individuals (Krizan 1999).

The most comprehensive information available in primary and secondary sources in intelligence analysis for guiding principles or methods to evaluate sources of information is to be found in the *Criminal Intelligence Manual for Analysts*, produced by the UNODC (2011). The UNODC describes two standardised systems used in law enforcement for evaluating sources of information based on the reliability of the source and the validity of the information or claim. The first is called the '4x4' system, and the second is the '6x6' system.

In the 4x4 system, the process of evaluation begins with identifying the characteristics of the source of an individual claim. The next step is to evaluate the reliability of the source of the claim. The third step is to identify the relationship between the source of information or claim and the claim itself. The fourth and final step of the evaluation process is to evaluate the validity of the claim itself (UNODC 2011). The 4x4 system provides two ranking systems with four available scores apiece. The first is for the evaluation of the source of a claim. The second ranking system is used to evaluate the claim itself. The second ranking system described by the UNODC is known as the 6x6 system. Like the 4x4 system, the 6x6 system involves two scoring systems, the first to evaluate the reliability of the source that is reporting the claim, and the second to evaluate the validity of the data.

The ranking systems outlined by Krizan (1999) and the UNODC (2011) are designed exclusively to evaluate information derived from human sources. This implicitly indicates that information derived from mechanised sources does not require evaluation for epistemic justification. However, as intentional deception and misinformation are factors that may affect all information for intelligence analysis, it is inappropriate to assume that any piece of information does not need to be evaluated for its epistemic value: deception methods apply equally to mechanical collection devices as well as human sources. Further, some pieces of information will need to be evaluated in context. More significantly, from an epistemological standpoint, the system proposed by Krizan (1999), and both the 4x4 and the 6x6 systems proposed by the UNODC (2011) are severely problematic for application in establishing the epistemological status of information derived from human sources.

Evaluating the Credibility of Human Source Intelligence

The Krizan (1999) system of evaluating the source of a claim is to assess the source's reliability. Reliability is assessed by prior performance, the proximity of the source to the original claim and the source's appropriateness, or subject matter expertise regarding the claim that he or she is reporting. However, it is not clear whether these three measurements are considered of equal value, how they should be separated into individual, equal units against which to rank sources, and whether a source needs to demonstrate all three of these qualities to be considered reliable. Further, it is not clear why proximity and appropriateness are measurements of reliability. An individual's proximity to the original claim is not necessarily related to his or her ability to report the claim accurately. This argument is predicated on the notion that an individual who acquires a claim by perception is more reliable than a source that does not. This can be successfully countered by demonstrating that both sources in this argument are equally reliant on perception and memory in their reporting and are therefore of equal episte-mological status. Consider the following examples.

Example 1: Bill is walking home late at night when a man wearing a grey hooded jumper runs past him. Bill thinks nothing of it until a week later when an appeal from the local police is issued for any information regarding a rape that occurred in the area around Bill's home the same night he was walking home late. The suspect is described as a man wearing a grey hooded jumper. Bill provides a witness statement to the police. In recalling the event that occurred a week before, Bill remembers an image of a man in a grey hooded sweatshirt with brown hair and a beard. However, the man that ran past Bill had black hair and no facial hair. Bill believes his memory to be true.

Example 2: One evening at the local pub, George overhears the following claim being made by a man at the table next to him:

Premise 1: All dogs are birds
Premise 2: Pluto is a dog
Conclusion: Therefore, Pluto is a bird

A week later, George visits the same pub with his friend Simon. George provides an account of the conversation he overheard a week before to Simon. George passes the following information onto Simon:

Premise 1: All mice are birds
Premise 2: Mickey is a mouse
Conclusion: Therefore, Mickey is a bird

The claim that George has reported to Simon is not the claim that George overheard at the pub the week before. However, George believes that he has recalled the information correctly.

In both examples, the source acquired a claim through perception. In example 1, the claim was acquired directly by sight, and in example 2 the claim was acquired by hearing a testimony provided by a separate individual. However, in both examples the information is incorrectly reported to a second party through distorted or inaccurate memories of the individual's perceptive recollection of the claim he reported. Both perception and memory can be fallible.

Memories can be false or partially inaccurate. It is incredibly difficult, if not impossible, to distinguish between accurate memories and false memories that people believe to be true. The proximity of a source to the original claim he or she reports is arguably theoretically irrelevant, as any reporting chain, whether it is direct or indirect, is equally reliant on perception and memory. The accuracy of a claim from a source who reports what he or she observes directly is arguably as susceptible to being affected to an equal degree by distorted memory as a claim that is passed through several individuals in a reporting chain. Therefore, the proximity to information cannot be used to measure the reliability of a human source.

Krizan's third criterion of measuring the reliability of a human source is appropriateness. This is measured by whether a source stands in a position of authority on the subject being reported on (Krizan 1999). This argument is based on the premise that a subject matter expert will be a more reliable source for making claims on a topic than someone who is not a subject matter expert. However, this premise is predicated on the sub-premise that an individual who is a subject matter in X has better perceptive and memory faculties for claims related to X. Let us reconsider the example of Bill's witness testimony of the rape suspect. According to this argument, if Bill were a barber he would have been able to correctly remember that the rape suspect did not have a beard, and if Bill were a hairdresser he would have been able to correctly remember the colour of the suspect's hair. This is clearly facetious. To use appropriateness as a measurement of reliability for a source, you would have to show that there is a necessary inverse connection between the possession of subject matter knowledge, and the fallibility of perception and memory regarding an individual's claims from direct perception that have some relevance to his or her subject matter knowledge.

The 6x6 system contains several inconsistencies in its units and criteria of measurement concerning the reliability of a human source. The ranking system for source reliability contains 'integrity' as a criterion of measurement in some scoring options but not in others. This means that a source can attain the highest source of reliability score whilst lacking integrity. This is counterintuitive. The scoring system has the criterion of a 'history of unreliability', and a 'history of occasional reliability'. However, these options are arguably not theoretically distinct from another. Having a history of the occurrence of unreliability says nothing about the frequency of the occurrence of unreliability. Further, the 6x6 system for ranking source reliability includes scepticism as a criterion of measurement, using the scoring of 'doubt', 'some doubt' and 'definite doubt' (UNODC 2011). However, it is unclear what would make the scepticism of the analyst or collector a reliable method of evaluation for the reliability of a source. Scepticism is not necessarily based on a reliable method. An individual may be justified in his or her scepticism that a claim is true, but it does not follow that this will necessarily be the case. An individual may be equally likely to be unjustified in his or her scepticism of the truth of a claim.

The biggest problem with both Krizan's (1999) and the UNODC's (2011) use of reliability as a measurement applied to the credibility of human source reporting is that it is not consistent with the reliabilist interpretation of epistemic justification. Reliabilism is the argument that beliefs can be considered as justified if they were produced by a reliable cognitive method. However, the measure of reliability applied by Krizan (1999) and the UNODC (2011) is judged by the accuracy of a human source's reporting history. It makes no mention of the cognitive method by which the human source produced his or her claims. This method of quality assurance is arguably an example of veritable justification. Veritable justification is where a subject is justified in believing that a proposition is true because it actually turns out to be true. However, it does not follow that just because an individual's belief actually turned out to be true means that he or she formed that original belief based on an adequate justification. It is theoretically possible to be justified in believing that a proposition is true even if the belief turns out not to be true.

Personal Knowledge versus Impersonal Knowledge

The UNODC (2011) claims that personal knowledge is afforded a higher rating of quality than information that has been acquired by rumour or hearsay. In epistemic terms, this refers to the distinction between justification for beliefs that is derived from direct access (perception, introspection and memory), and justification for beliefs that is derived from the testimony of one or more other individuals. This is the distinction between primary knowledge claims and secondary knowledge claims. The epistemological significance of this distinction comes down to whether testimony (or authority) is inherently more open to challenge (defeasibility) as a source of justification than reason, perception, memory and introspection. This argument corresponds with the epistemological distinction between basic and non-basic sources of justification. However, it does not follow that non-basic sources of justification are more open to defeasibility than basic sources of justification. The ability to challenge a proposition by counterargument will depend on each individual proposition, not the source or basis from where the proposition was obtained.

* * *

Both the Krizan (1999) system and the UNODC (2011) 4x4 system use proximity of the human source to the original claim as a method of either assessing the reliability of the source or assessing the quality of the claim itself. Krizan uses proximity as a measurement of whether a human source is reliable. The 4x4 system uses proximity as a measurement in assessing the claim itself but does not specify what is being measured. The biggest problem with using proximity to the source of the claim is that it conflates the truth of the claim with the number of degrees in the reporting chain rather than the origin or content of the claim itself. There is no reason to assume that the degree of distance between the individual (or object) that reports a claim and the original claim is directly proportional to the truth of the original claim. On a rational level, this is patently absurd. While the chance of the original claim becoming distorted could be increased by any and every layer in the reporting chain, this has no effect on the truth of the original claim made, or the truth of the claim that is eventually delivered to the collector. The problem with reporting chains having more than one level is the challenge of establishing the relationship of resemblance between the original claim made and the claim that is received by the collector. Regarding the identity between the original claim and the final claim that is reported at the end of the chain, consider the following scenario. Brian tells George the following argument:

Premise 1: Either London is in England or it is in France.
Premise 2: London is in England.
Conclusion: London is in France.

George reports this claim to Simon, who is seeking information as to the location of London. George successfully relays to Simon the identical argument that originated from Brian, but what George has reported is a logically invalid argument form. As a logically invalid argument form, the claim is necessarily false. Just because a claim received by a collector is identical to the original claim made, it does not necessarily bear any relationship to the validity or truth of the original argument.

Consider another scenario. Brian tells George the following claim:

Premise 1: All dogs are birds
Premise 2: Pluto is a dog
Conclusion: Therefore, Pluto is a bird

However, Brian communicated this to George over a bad phone line. Believing that he has accurately recounted the claim made to him by Brian, George passes the following information on to Simon, who has asked George to tell him anything he hears from Brian about animals:

Premise 1: All mice are birds
Premise 2: Mickey is a mouse
Conclusion: Therefore, Mickey is a bird

The claim that George has reported to Simon is not identical to the claim reported to him by Brian, but it bears a relationship of resemblance to Brian's original claim, in that it follows the same logical form. However, both versions of Brian's original claim are logically valid. Just because the claim reported to the collector bears a resemblance to the original claim, it does not necessarily follow that the claim reported to the collector will be true.

Furthermore, the claim received by Simon is as relevant to his request as Brian's original claim. If the claims can be established as identical then there can be no doubt as to whether the claim was distorted along the reporting chain. However, if the claims are not identical, then the resemblance between the two will have to be established. However, neither identity nor resemblance has a necessary relation to the validity or truth of the claim itself.

The accuracy of reporting across a multiple-level reporting chain bears no necessary relationship to the epistemological status of the original claim and the final version of it. Whilst having as few levels as possible in a reporting chain is required to get accurately recounted information, this concerns processes around guaranteeing the clarity of the original information, rather than the truth of the content. Personal knowledge is not a simple notion, nor an appropriate standard by which to evaluate the truth or validity of a proposition. It is not clear why a proposition that has been reported via more than one individual in a reporting chain would be inherently less likely to be true than a proposition that has been reported through primary sources.

Evaluating the Validity of a Claim

Both the 4x4 and 6x6 systems apply validity as scoring systems of intelligence claims. Identifying the validity of claims allows a collector to identify claims that are inherently false. The validity of the claim itself can be measured by testing the claim to see if it can be represented in a logically valid argument form. The 4x4 system's ranking for the claim itself places logical validity on a par with coherence against a previous body of knowledge, and with the failure of the claim to match with the body of knowledge held by the official who is passing on the claim to the collector. However, as has previously been outlined, neither logical validity nor coherence can be used to establish the truth of information. Further, logical validity is not equivalent to coherence (consistency) against a previous body of knowledge. Logic only measures whether an argument is valid; it is not used to establish the truth of an argument. This must be determined in a separate process. An argument can be logically valid, but actually false. One of the key problems with the 4x4 ranking system for determining validity is that it is not clear what is being measured. Each score level conflates the validity of the claim with its actual truth. However, truth and validity are categorically different concepts.

The 6x6 system for ranking the validity of data is also problematic. Like the 4x4 system, it falsely equates truth with validity. Unlike the 4x4 system, the 6x6 system identifies what it seeks to measure about the claim itself: whether it is logically valid or not. However, to test if a claim has a valid logical argument form, it must be, or contain, an argument: at least two premises and a conclusion that leads from the premises. However, there is no guarantee that all claims will contain an argument. Further, there can only be two scores for this measurement: either a claim is logically valid or it is logically invalid, and therefore automatically false. The 6x6 system includes 'not illogical' as a separate criterion from 'logically valid' and 'logically invalid'. However, 'not illogical' is semantically equivalent to 'logically valid'. In addition, the 6x6 system uses probabilistic terms as a scale of validity. Probability is inappropriate for measuring logical validity, as there is no connection between the two. If something is illogical then it can neither be true nor valid, as being logically invalid renders an argument necessarily false. This makes it false, not 'improbable', as improbability allows the possibility of something being true. In addition to using probability as a measurement of validity, the 6x6 ranking system for data validity also includes whether a claim is believed to be true as a criterion of validity. However, it should be obvious that believing something to be true does not make it logically valid.

In addition to the conflation of measurements of logical validity with measurements of truth, the 6x6 ranking system for establishing validity contains several inaccuracies in its use of correspondence and confirmation as measurements of the validity of a claim. Correspondence is defined by a close similarity, connection or equivalence. Equivalence is defined as two entities having the same quantity, size, degree or value. Confirmation, on the other hand, is defined as confirming that a proposition is true. The 6x6 ranking system for establishing validity uses both correspondence and confirmation as measurements of validity. However, neither of these concepts bears any relation to validity. Correspondence and confirmation are concepts that relate to establishing the truth of a proposition or claim, not its logical validity. The 6x6 data validity ranking system uses the following units as measurements of correspondence: 'Agrees with other information on the subject', 'agrees somewhat with other information on the subject' and 'is contradicted by other information on the subject'. However, correspondence arguably does not manifest in degrees: either two things correspond or they do not.

*   *   *

If these examples of internal guidance on establishing epistemic justification for believing intelligence information to be true are representative of the current training provided to intelligence analysts, then there are considerable grounds for concern. Neither the Krizan (1999) nor the UNODC (2011) guidance provides theoretically valid ways of establishing epistemic justification for beliefs. The theoretical flaws and clear inconsistencies provide no recourse for dealing with the epistemic complexity involved in judging epistemic justification of information in intelligence. Instead, they offer false reassurance of theoretical validity. In the specific context of ACH, credibility of information is arguably the most problematic scoring system that has been used in existing versions of the ACH method. Establishing the credibility of information, or epistemic justification, is the only information ranking method that needs to be applied within ACH and is a key component of ACH for tackling epistemic complexity. However, if theoretically valid guidance is not provided to intelligence analysts in how credibility is to be determined, and what standards can be specifically tailored for dealing with the limitations of information collected in a covert manner, then the ACH process becomes self-defeating. The purpose of ACH is to establish epistemic justification that intelligence provides to competing hypotheses, and in doing so reduce epistemic complexity. If no theoretically valid method of doing so is provided, then ACH categorically fails to attain its intended outcomes.

Although ACH faces multiple issues in relation to aiding the justification of beliefs or the identification of truth and falsity, the method does have several theoretical benefits over the use of intuition. First, research indicates that intelligence analysis would be better served by the consistent consideration of multiple hypotheses, which is a stipulation of ACH. Even if research has shown that participants are unlikely to be able to generate a complete set of plausible hypotheses, considering multiple hypotheses increases the chances of a true hypothesis being considered in an analytical task. Second, using a structured approach may reduce the cognitive strain of having to retain key items of information in working memory by using a ranking system to process a larger volume of information and compare each piece of information one by one against a set of hypotheses. Third, seeking to disconfirm hypotheses (eliminative induction) rather than only seeking confirmation may improve an analyst's approach to hypothesis validation, and improves analytical efficiency compared with trying to confirm hypotheses (enumerative induction). Enumerative induction is a less optimal method of hypothesis testing than eliminative induction. This is due to the greater efficiency and epistemological certainty of proving a hypothesis to be false compared with confirming a hypothesis to be true (Von Wright 1951c). However, to be a more effective alternative for analytical judgements made by intuition, ACH needs to be able to employ a theoretically valid mechanism to establish the epistemic justification for hypotheses. All four of the scoring systems that have been proposed for use in ACH are problematic, but to different degrees. Consistency of information applied using a coherentist theory of truth interpretation, and subjective Bayesianism are not epistemologically viable methods of establishing truth or justification for beliefs. Credibility of information is necessary for establishing the epistemic justification for individual pieces of information, but it is not a mandatory score for ACH, it is used infrequently and available guidance on how to establish credibility (epistemic justification) may not be theoretically inappropriate. Diagnostic value is a viable way of establishing the degree of epistemic justification the information provides. However, it remains questionable whether the concept of diagnostic value can be adapted to account for sufficient epistemic justification in addition to necessary epistemic justification.

ACH and the Mitigation of Cognitive Bias

ACH has been described as being able to mitigate the impact of cognitive bias in two ways: by preventing cognitive bias from affecting the scoring system(s) used to process information and calculate the final scores for hypotheses, and by making the occurrence of cognitive bias explicit for external peer review (Heuer and Pherson 2010). However, it is unclear from a theoretical consideration why ACH would have an inherent capability to prevent cognitive bias from impacting the scoring systems employed by ACH to process information or reduce this impact. There is no obvious mechanism within ACH, or the scoring systems currently used as part of ACH that could theoretically prevent the scores inputted into the ACH process from being impacted by subconscious bias. Further, it is unclear why the use of eliminative induction in ACH would be any less vulnerable to cognitive bias than enumerative induction. The difference between these two approaches is one of efficiency in establishing epistemic justification: that falsification (eliminative induction) is a more efficient way to establish truth or falsity than the search for supporting evidence (enumerative induction). However, it does not follow that being theoretically more efficient in establishing truth or justification renders eliminative induction free from vulnerability, or any less vulnerable to the possible influence of cognitive bias. Eliminative induction has no inherent mechanism for impacting subconscious processes.

A separate, related benefit attributed to ACH is that it can make the occurrence of cognitive biases visible to an external observer. However, there is no obvious reason why ACH would be able to do so. To be able to identify when cognitive bias is occurring or has occurred, ACH requires a mechanism to record how the degree of belief that an analyst has in the truth of respective hypotheses changes over time, specifically in correlation with each piece of information processed. I have found no publicly available version of ACH that records the degree of belief and the degree of epistemic justification for information processing. Even if ACH was adapted to do this, its application would be restricted. It would have to be applied for the entirety of information processing during an analytical task. It cannot be applied mid-task, or retrospectively, or it will not provide an accurate capture of the impact of cognitive bias on belief acquisition. This is problematic for intelligence analysis, as it is difficult to identify when information processing for analytical judgements begins. If analysts look at a single topic over time (months or years) and conduct multiple (or repeated) analytical tasks on the same topic, information processed at the beginning of their posting or deployment could influence belief acquisition or adjustment for later analytical tasks. If ACH is used for an individual analytical judgement, it will not reliably capture information that subconsciously influenced a belief which was processed months before. Serial position effects are likely to affect subsequent tasks that are thematically linked. ACH therefore can have no efficacy in being able to identify the occurrence of cognitive biases for tasks where analysts have prior knowledge or have previously processed relevant information.

Another benefit attributed to ACH is that by employing eliminative induction rather than enumerative induction, it has the capacity to reduce the occurrence of cognitive bias in intelligence analysis. This attribute specifically refers to the ability to reduce the occurrence of confirmation bias. Confirmation biases are the tendency to search for, interpret, recall and place disproportionate weight on information that provides support for a belief, and to give disproportionately less consideration to information that contradicts the belief, or provides support for alternative possibilities. Heuer argues that by focusing on disproving hypotheses, confirmation bias is less likely to occur. This relies on the implicit assumption that the sub-conscious processes that underpin a conscious attempt to disprove a hypothesis are inherently less likely to be subject to confirmation bias than in the conscious attempt to prove a hypothesis. However, there is no theoretical reason why this would be the case. Confirmation bias could lead to searching for information which disproves alternative, non-favoured hypotheses, or less consideration given to information that contradicts a favoured hypothesis compared with information that contradicts non-favoured hypotheses.

*　*　*

ACH was arguably developed for two purposes. Its first function was to provide a way of establishing true hypotheses in intelligence analysis in a more efficient manner than the reliance on intuition. Its second function was to provide a way to reduce the occurrence of and mitigate the impact of cognitive biases in intelligence analysis. By using the principle of eliminative induction rather than enumerative induction, ACH theoretically can provide a more efficient system for establishing epistemic justification for beliefs. However, to do this it needs to employ a theoretically viable scoring system to capture the degree of epistemic justification provided to each hypothesis by relevant available information. To fulfil its second function, ACH also needs to provide a suitably adapted theoretically valid method for establishing epistemic justification that can cope with the additional epistemic complexity that intelligence likely faces in belief acquisition. Whilst this is entirely possible, there is no indication that current guidance on ACH fulfils this requirement.

Intelligence, Bias and Belief Acquisition: A Theoretical Perspective

In the first part of this book, I have sought to address two questions. The first was: is belief acquisition in intelligence a unique epistemological act? Answering this question provides an essential theoretical framework for examining the effect of cognitive biases on the process of belief acquisition in intelligence. If belief acquisition in intelligence differs by either nature or degree from belief acquisition in non-intelligence contexts, then it is rational to infer that belief acquisition in intelligence could be affected in a different way by cognitive bias to belief acquisition in non-intelligence contexts.

I argue that the nature of intelligence is the covert pursuit of justified beliefs. Further, I argue that although intelligence is necessarily defined as an act of belief acquisition, belief acquisition in intelligence analysis differs in nature from belief acquisition in non-intelligence contexts. This is because intelligence has one necessary characteristic that separates it as an act of belief acquisition from non-intelligence: it is a covert act. This necessary characteristic has a significant implication for the question of whether belief acquisition in intelligence is impacted differently by cognitive bias from belief acquisition in non-intelligence contexts. The covert nature of intelligence provides a theoretical basis for arguing that that belief acquisition in intelligence is likely to be subject to a higher degree of epistemic complexity. This takes three forms: (1) establishing the epistemic quality of available information; (2) establishing epistemic justification where available information is not comprehensive; and (3) drawing in part or in total from information collected by an epistemically unreliable method. These forms of epistemic complexity could arguably place greater strain on human cognitive information-processing capabilities. It is therefore theoretically valid to argue that belief acquisition in intelligence is likely to be more vulnerable to cognitive bias. This has significant implications for approaches to mitigating cognitive bias in intelligence. It implies that mitigation should be primarily concerned with significantly reducing the cognitive strain in determining epistemic justification for beliefs, thereby reducing reliance on cognitive biases.

The second question that the first part of the book has attempted to answer is: does ACH provide a theoretically valid framework for establishing epistemic justification? As the predominant form of structured analytical method that is recommended for intelligence analysis, and the only structured analytical method that covers the whole process of belief acquisition,[21] the validity of the science part of the art versus science debate comes down to the ability of the ACH method to mitigate cognitive bias, or to mitigate epistemic complexity. An examination of the ACH method, and the multiple scoring systems that have been utilised in ACH to rank information sought to determine whether ACH provides any mechanisms to: (1) reduce epistemic complexity and cognitive strain, thereby reducing the risk of cognitive bias; (2) to prevent or reduce cognitive bias from impacting the ACH process, and, if these first mechanisms are not forthcoming; (3) to make cognitive biases visible to external examination.

To date, versions of ACH have utilised four separate information ranking systems: consistency of information, diagnostic value of information, subjective Bayesianism and credibility of information.

For any of these ranking systems to reduce epistemic complexity they have to fulfil multiple requirements. The first is to provide a theoretically valid method for establishing the epistemic justification that a piece of information provides to a given hypothesis. This method should draw from one or more of the strongest contenders within the philosophical field of epistemology, which are the theories of evidentialism, reliabilism and infallibilism. The method for establishing epistemic justification must be able to identify necessary epistemic justification, and sufficient epistemic justification. Further, the identification of sufficient justification must take into account the higher degree of complexity in identifying the epistemic justification of intelligence information. The second requirement is that the method needs to account for both partial and total epistemic justification. To do this, the method must be capable of being applied to individual premises of a hypothesis rather than the composite hypothesis. The third requirement is that the method is capable of being applied as a dual-ranking system, to determine the epistemic justification for believing an individual piece of intelligence information to be true, and to determine the degree of epistemic justification that individual pieces of intelligence information provide to a given hypothesis. I argue that none of the four information ranking systems that have been recommended to date in ACH can provide all three key requirements. As such, current forms of ACH neither provide theoretically valid methods to determine epistemic justification, nor offer a way to cope with epistemic complexity in belief acquisition.

The design of ACH was inspired by the scientific methodology of eliminative induction, which focuses on seeking disconfirming evidence for hypotheses as opposed to confirming evidence. However, ACH contains no mechanisms that would theoretically prevent subconscious cognitive bias from affecting the information ranking process, and eliminative induction is not theoretically less vulnerable to being subject to cognitive bias than enumerative induction. As such, ACH currently offers no mechanisms to reduce the likelihood of the occurrence of cognitive bias in intelligence. Further, whilst ACH was designed to make the occurrence of cognitive bias visible to external review, it lacks the key mechanisms that would allow this to occur. To make cognitive bias visible, ACH has to record how different pieces of information affect the degree to which an individual believes that each hypothesis is true or false. Without recording the relative impact of individual pieces of information on degree of belief, ACH offers no mechanism that could be used to detect the occurrence of cognitive bias. As such, ACH offers no mechanisms to make the occurrence of cognitive bias visible.

From a theoretical standpoint, ACH offers no mechanisms to mitigate the risk of cognitive bias in intelligence. Alternative approaches should therefore be sought for recommendation to intelligence communities while new versions of ACH are developed. However, this argument needs to be validated from an empirical standpoint. The second part of the book seeks to provide this. To validate the theoretical component I argued for in Part 1, the following needs to be determined from an empirical standpoint: (1) that no version of ACH provides a statistically significant difference in either the likelihood of occurrence of cognitive bias in intelligence, or the impact of cognitive bias on the analytical conclusions acquired through the ACH process; and (2) that alternative approaches have been shown to have a statistically significant reduction on the likelihood of occurrence of cognitive biases.

It is not possible for me to provide a comprehensive empirical validation for both these requirements here. ACH is an umbrella technique that can be adapted using multiple methods of ranking information and overall score calculation. Further, dozens of different cognitive biases have been identified in the social sciences. To date, there has been very little research into the efficacy of ACH in mitigating the impact of cognitive bias in intelligence. There is currently only one study that looks at the efficacy of structured analytical methods in mitigating cognitive bias or serial position effects in an intelligence analysis scenario (Cheikes et al. 2004). However, this study only tested one information ranking system that has been utilised in ACH, and only two types of cognitive bias. It is not possible to provide sufficient experimental research within the scope of this book alone to supplement the significant gaps in available research. To do so, multiple experiments would have to be conducted to pair all four information ranking systems of ACH with all identified cognitive biases. However, the research presented here can build upon previous research. A central part of this book therefore seeks to extend the research conducted by Cheikes et al. (2004) into the efficacy of ACH in mitigating cognitive biases in an intelligence scenario. To achieve this, a study was conducted in 2016 examining the efficacy of the version of ACH taught by the Cabinet Office to the United Kingdom's intelligence community in significantly reducing the likelihood of the occurrence of cognitive bias or mitigating the impact of cognitive bias on analytical judgements. The study built upon research by Cheikes et al. (2004) by testing a version of ACH that used two scoring systems – credibility of information and diagnostic value of information – and testing this version of ACH against both confirmation bias and serial position effects. Part 2 of the book will begin by presenting the results of this study.

The empirical component of the book will also provide an examination of alternative methods that may have an ability to reduce the likelihood of occurrence of cognitive biases that can be empirically demonstrated. A meta-analysis of experimental research was conducted to examine whether analytical conditions are associated with a statistically significantly higher or lower proportion of confirmation bias or serial position effects. The meta-analysis also identified whether there are any significant differences in the proportion of participants who exhibited these biases under different analytical conditions between belief adjustment conducted in an intelligence scenario and belief adjustment conducted in non-intelligence scenarios. In this capacity, the meta-analysis provides an empirical validation to the theoretical argument that belief acquisition in intelligence analysis is likely to be more susceptible to cognitive bias, as well as exploring the evidential basis for alternative approaches to mitigating the risk of cognitive bias in intelligence.

Notes

1. Some training manuals from Western intelligence services recommend using a matrix to organise and rank information, but this is more of a general guidance than a structured methodology for evaluating a hypothesis or hypotheses.

2. Subjective Bayesianism is sometimes recommended as an analytical method for evaluating hypotheses in intelligence analysis. However, this method was not originally developed for use in intelligence.

3. Some may argue that scientific approaches were being employed before the ancient Greeks, for example the ancient Babylonians who approached astronomy with the application of mathematics. However, the Babylonian method lacked an underpinning systematic theory to explain natural phenomena.

4. Aristotle, *Posterior Analytics*.

5. Ibid.

6. *Abduction* in both its original and contemporary interpretations form the cornerstone of scientific method (Boyd 1981, 1984; Harré 1986, 1988; Lipton 1991, 2004; Psillos 1999). Abduction is a type of inductive inference that assigns a primary role to explanatory consideration. Abduction is commonly referred to as 'inference to the best explanation'. Abductive inferences are in fact not a type of logical argument form, as the premises do not logically entail the conclusions. Abductive inferences can only stand as conditional truth-values for any proposition. The original concept of abduction was developed by Peirce (1931–58). Peirce proposed that abduction was a non-deductive logical inference that was applied to the stage of generating explanatory hypotheses in scientific inquiry. However, it has since been shown that Peirce's concept of abduction is not logical in any strict sense (Douven 2011). Peirce's writings make no mention as to selection of the best hypothesis. However, this is the principal notion behind the contemporary understanding of abduction: that it selects the best hypothesis to fit a set of facts. Although abduction is ubiquitous in various academic subjects, no one has yet managed to provide a definition of the term.

7. Most of the attempts to develop methods to knowledge of the world through a formal process of enquiry or research in the natural sciences revolve around trying to extend logical systems to the physical world: to remove, or ignore, the metaphysical neutrality of logic.

8. Consistency of information, diagnostic value of information and credibility of information have been adapted to both semantic (ordinal) scoring systems and integer scoring systems.

9. It has been argued that the scoring system of consistency of information stands as a measurement of the logical validity of each hypothesis included in ACH (Jones 2017). However, consistency of information does not stand as a mechanism for identifying the logical validity of argument forms. This is conducted by processes of formal logic,

either in the form of truth-tables or truth-trees. To complete this, propositions must be broken down into an argument structure, identifying the predicates involved and the logical connections between the predicates. The logical formula of the proposition, when analysed as an argument form, is then examined for logical validity. Logical validity is determined whereby an argument is valid if, and only if, it takes a logical form whereby it is impossible for the premises to be true but the conclusion to be false. Consistency of information is an attempt to identify whether an argument is sound: that it corresponds with an independent reality. Logical validity cannot be used as a mechanism to determine the soundness of an argument.

10. Although it is often attributed to Aristotle's *Metaphysics*, Plato in *Sophist* also put similar arguments forward. Medieval philosophers distinguished between a metaphysical and a semantic interpretation of the correspondence theory of truth. Thomas Aquinas famously argued for the metaphysical interpretation of the theory: 'a judgement is said to be true when it confirms to the external reality' (Aquinas 1265–74). Aquinas's theory allowed for truth to apply to both thoughts and objects. Aquinas argued that a thought is true because it confirms to an external reality, but that an object is true because it conforms to a thought (David 2013). The semantic interpretation of the correspondence theory of truth developed by medieval philosophers is a shortened version of Aristotle's argument, which emphasises that a sentence or proposition is true if it signifies. However, they were unclear about what a true sentence signifies to be true (Ockham 1323).

11. Russell (1918) and Wittgenstein (1921) later modified this theory into logical atomism. Logical atomism posits that the world contains objective facts which correspond to a set of logical facts (or 'atoms') that cannot be broken down. For further details on Russell's theory of logical atomism see Klement (2016). For further details of Wittgenstein's theory of logical atomism, see Proops (2013).

12. Both correspondence and coherence theories of truth argue that the truth of a proposition is a property that can be analysed by the truth-conditions that each proposition has (Young 2013).

13. Several philosophers have argued that a restricted notion of entailment based on a relationship of relevance is required (Restall 1996). For the existence of an object X to entail the necessary truth of P, X surely must at least be relevant to the truth of P. There must be some principle or criterion of relevance between a truth and what makes the truth true. However, it has been argued that the notion of relevance is just as ubiquitous as the notion of entailment (Goodman 1961).

14. Both the coherence and correspondence of truth theories are subject to regress. If the truth of a proposition P is correspondent or coherent to a set of propositions Q and R, or with an objective reality X, then we can ask: what set of propositions do Q and R cohere to, to make the set true by coherence, and what objective reality does X correspond to, to make it true by correspondence? This process could go on AD infinitum unless you are prepared to argue that there is a set of basic facts or true propositions that can be taken as foundational without having to provide proof.

15. This scoring system was used by the United Kingdom Cabinet Office in the version of ACH that was taught to intelligence analysts between 2016 and 2017.

16. Deductive logic is largely concerned with first-order logic. Classical logic is a system where a language is given a deductive system to be able to identify arguments that follow a valid logical form in that language. By doing so, classical logic identifies truth-conditions within languages (Shapiro 2013).

17. In this capacity, inductive inferences are ampliative: they can be used to amplify an experience or to generalise it. Induction can be used to generalise empirical knowledge. Deduction, by comparison, is explicative. Deduction orders our knowledge rather than adding to it (Vickers 2014).

18. Subjective Bayesianism could be interpreted as an attempt to identify the relative probability that a hypothesis is true compared with other hypotheses. However, probability cannot be applied in this manner as truth is in no way probable. Probability requires that a predicted outcome has the capacity to be one of several options. However, a truth doesn't have the capacity to be anything but true.

19. Frequentism is structurally similar to classical probability; however it only considers occurrences that have actually happened, rather than all possible occurrences, including future occurrences.

20. Bayes' logic provides a simple calculation for identifying conditional probabilities. For further reading see Joyce (2016).

21. It has been argued that subjective Bayesianism could also provide both stages of belief acquisition: the development of hypotheses and the evaluation of hypotheses. However, it may not be an explicit requirement of the process of subjective Bayesianism to generate as many hypotheses as possible. This is a specific requirement of the original ACH design.

PART 2

Intelligence, Bias and Belief Acquisition: An Empirical Perspective

3 The Efficacy of ACH in Mitigating Serial Position Effects and Confirmation Bias in an Intelligence Analysis Scenario[1]

To put ACH to the test in an experimental setting, a study was conducted in 2016 to see whether using ACH in an intelligence analysis task has a mitigating effect on the cognitive biases of confirmation bias and serial position effects. The study was facilitated by the United Kingdom's Professional Heads of Intelligence Analysis (PHIA) team, based at the Cabinet Office. The study tested the version of the ACH method taught by the PHIA to the UK's intelligence community between 2016 and 2017.[2] Participants were recruited from staff and the student body at King's College London (KCL), and from multiple departments and organisations within the UK government intelligence community.

Procedure

The study used a 2x2 factorial design with four experimental conditions.[3] Participants completed an analytical task in one of the four research conditions, providing the results via a questionnaire. Participants were required to conduct an intelligence assessment on whether the Pakistan-based Islamist terrorist group Lashkar-e-Tayyiba (LeT) was attempting to develop or acquire biological weapons for use in terrorist attacks. The assessment was based on open source background information on LeT and the production of anthrax, and six fictional intelligence reports. The scenario was an adapted version of the intelligence case regarding the development of biological and nuclear weapons by Saddam Hussein's regime in Iraq, prior to 2003. The scenario was developed in this way to ensure that it had ecological validity: that it represented a realistic intelligence analysis task. The adaption of this intelligence case drew principally upon information provided in the 2005 US government official review into weapons of mass destruction (WMD) in Iraq by the Commission on the Intelligence Capabilities of the United States Regarding Weapons of Mass Destruction. Part of the report's remit included an investigation into the accuracy of intelligence on Iraqi WMD up to March 2003. The report provided a sufficient level of detail to allow a suitably adapted version of the intelligence case to be provided. Some additional details were also obtained from Drogin (2008).[4] All information used to create the fictional intelligence scenario was taken from open source. (See Appendix for details of the Iraq WMD intelligence case, and how it was adapted for the study.)

The scenario included six fictional intelligence reports, four of which were of direct diagnostic value to a hypothesis (three reports supported the truth of hypothesis 1, and one supported the truth of hypothesis 2). The other two reports were in isolation diagnostically neutral but contained information that could be interpreted as giving weight to either hypothesis when combined with information from other intelligence reports. Like the Iraq case study regarding biological weapons activity, the overall intelligence case was weighted towards the hypothesis that LeT was actively attempting to acquire or develop biological weapons for terrorist purposes. However, legitimate reasons to doubt the intelligence claiming that LeT was attempting to develop biological weapons were present within the total body of information provided. Further, the intelligence that supported the alternative hypothesis – that LeT was not attempting to acquire or develop biological weapons – could be validly interpreted as an effort by LeT to conceal their activities.

Participants were informed that they would be role-playing the part of an intelligence analyst working in the Joint Intelligence Organisation (JIO) at the Cabinet Office in London and were responsible for providing assessments on national security issues that relate to the following countries: Pakistan, India, Afghanistan, Bangladesh, Sri Lanka, Bhutan and Nepal.[5] The participants were told that they had been asked for an assessment on the status of the biological weapons threat from LeT. Participants were required to provide a written assessment that need not be more than 500 words. The participants were informed that the specific exam question to answer was: 'Is LeT attempting to acquire OR develop biological weapons for use in terrorist attacks?', and that this was a true-or-false question that could only have two working hypotheses, either:

> Hypothesis 1: LeT is attempting to acquire or develop biological weapons for use in terrorist attacks, or:
> Hypothesis 2: LeT is not attempting to acquire or develop biological weapons for use in terrorist attacks.

The participants were given three hours in which to review the available intelligence and background information against these two working hypotheses and provide an assessment as to which one they believed to be true.[6]

Different types of information were collected from participants via a questionnaire. Participants were instructed to provide a score of their degree of belief that each of the hypotheses is true or false,[7] as well as an assessment of the credibility of information and diagnostic value of information for each intelligence report they read. Participants were also instructed to provide a short justification for the credibility of information scores that they gave and were informed that there were no right or wrong answers.[8]

There were two different orders in which the intelligence reports were provided to participants.[9] These were designed to allow a replication of the Iraq WMD case study, whereby information from intelligence source 'Curveball' was received first. However, the serial orders differed as to what point in the order of information inconsistent information was processed: towards the end, as was the case in the Iraq WMD case, or towards the beginning.[10]

The two ACH research groups were provided with a two-hour training session on the ACH method. This training session was the same as the one delivered by the PHIA across the UK intelligence community between 2016 and 2017.[11] The basic steps of the ACH method taught by the PHIA are as follows:

1. Develop a set of hypotheses.
2. Make a list of evidence and assumptions.
3. Construct a matrix listing the hypotheses along the top and evidence and assumptions along the side. Score each piece of evidence or each assumption for how diagnostic it is against each of the hypotheses in the set.
4. Refine the matrix.
5. Draw initial conclusions about the hypothesis and reject any that you consider refuted.
6. Consider how sensitive each hypothesis is to key pieces of evidence and consider the possibility of deception.
7. Report the conclusions of the ACH.
8. Identify future collection opportunities and intelligence gaps.

The ACH version delivered by the PHIA to the ACH group uses diagnostic value as the scoring system. Participants were also asked to provide assessments of credibility. However, the credibility scores were not used to calculate the overall ACH scores, and no guidance was provided on how credibility of information should be determined.[12]

A total of thirty-nine participants participated in the study from both staff and students within KCL, and from multiple departments within the British government.[13] Of these, thirty-two were recruited from KCL, and seven from UK government departments.[14]

Results

Final Assessments

Of the thirty-nine participants, twenty-seven (69.23 per cent) participants' final degree of belief scores favoured hypothesis 1 (that LeT was attempting to acquire or develop biological weapons for use in terrorist attacks), ten (25.64 per cent) favoured hypothesis 2 (that LeT was not attempting to acquire or develop biological weapons for use in terrorist attacks) and two (5.13 per cent) were neutral between each of the two hypotheses. There was no statistically significant difference in the final assessments between the four research groups.[15] Neither the serial order nor ACH had a statistically significant effect.[16]

Serial Position Effects

Participants were required to provide a total of seven degree of belief scores. The first score was provided after participants had read the background information on LeT.[17] The background information was diagnostically neutral to the exam question. The second score was provided after the first intelligence report had been processed. The remaining five scores were provided after each of the five subsequent intelligence reports had been processed. As such, the scores tracked the changes in the participant's degree of belief throughout the analytical task, allowing a measurement of belief adjustment. Belief adjustment was measured by the mean number of points (out of 100) by which the participant's degree of belief changed between each score. For the first degree of belief score collected (point A on the X axis in Figure 3.1), degree of belief change was measured as the difference between the first degree of belief scores provided, and a neutral degree of belief score (50 points allocated to each hypothesis).[18]

Serial position effects were measured in two ways. The first was by identifying the highest degree of belief change for each participant. Participants whose highest degree of belief change was recorded after processing the first two pieces of information in the series or the last two pieces of information in the series were considered as possible candidates for exhibiting a serial position effect. The highest overall degree of belief change score was compared with the highest degree of belief change score at the opposite end of the serial order. A difference of >5 points in degree of belief change between the highest recorded degree of overall belief change was used to identify a serial position effect of primacy or recency. A difference of <5 points of belief change was used to indicate no serial position effects. By this system of measurement, twenty-five participants demonstrated behaviour consistent with primacy (64.10 per cent), 10 demonstrated no serial order effects (25.64 per cent) and four demonstrated behaviour consistent with recency (10.26 per cent).

The second method of testing serial position effects was by analysis of the mean degree of belief change for all participants throughout the analytical task. Serial position effects were measured by comparing the difference between the highest degree of mean belief change prior to the midway point of information processing (point D in Figure 3.1) and the highest degree of belief change after the mid-point of information processing. Primacy was measured as the highest degree of mean belief change prior to the mid-point being greater than the highest point of mean degree of belief change after the mid-point by >5 points. Recency was measured as the highest degree of mean belief change after the mid-point being greater than the highest point of mean degree of belief change prior to the mid-point and the highest point of mean degree change after the mid-point by >5 points. No serial position effects were measured by the difference between the highest point of mean degree change prior to the mid-point and after the mid-point being <5 points.

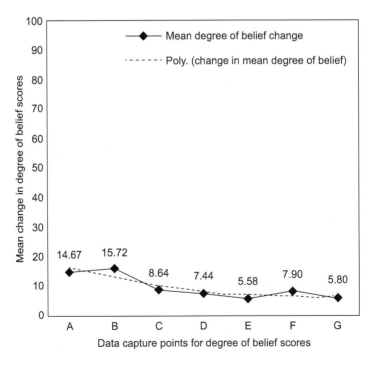

Figure 3.1 Mean degree of belief change during information processing.

Figure 3.1 clearly shows a serial position curve consistent with primacy. The information processed at the beginning of the analytical task (points A and B on the X axis) had a higher impact on belief adjustment than information processed towards the end of the analytical task. The mean belief adjustment for the first two scores were 14.67 (point A on the X axis), and 15.72 (point B on the X axis). Mean belief adjustment did not reach higher than 8.64 for the last five out of seven points in the serial order (points C to G on the X axis). There was a larger mean degree of belief adjustment at the beginning of the serial order than at the end.

These combined measurements for serial position effects indicate a primacy effect. The proportion of participants who exhibited primacy was statistically significantly higher than the proportion that exhibited no serial position effects (one-sample t-test of proportions, $p = .0085$).[19] There was no statistically significant difference between the proportion of participants who exhibited no serial position effects and the proportion that exhibited recency (one sample t-test of proportions, $p = 1.054$).[20] Two-way ANOVA tests for points A and B resulted in no statistically significant differences between the research groups. The primacy effect was comparable for all research sub-groups.[21]

Confirmation Bias

Confirmation bias was assessed by qualitative analysis of the scores provided by each participant for degree of belief, credibility of information and diagnostic value of information. The following criteria were used to identify behaviour consistent with confirmation bias:

1. Diagnostic value assessments are being directionally affected or amplified in line with the belief held by the participant.
2. Credibility assessments are being directionally affected or amplified in line with the belief held by the participant.
3. Degree of belief is being increased substantially towards a favoured hypothesis on the back of information ranked by the participant as being of low credibility.
4. The assignment of a high credibility score to objectively questionable intelligence is in line with strong degree of belief held by the participant.

113

5. High degree of belief is not being adjusted lower when contradicting information is rated as being of medium or high credibility by the participant.

Behaviour consistent with confirmation bias was exhibited by eight participants (21 per cent of the total number of participants).[22] A one-sample t-test of proportions was conducted to establish whether there was a statistically significant difference between the proportion of participants who exhibited confirmation bias and those that did not. The proportion of participants who exhibited no confirmation bias was statistically significantly higher than the proportion who exhibited confirmation bias (t-statistic was not significant at the .05 critical alpha level, $t(38) = 4.446$, $p = < .001$). Of the participants who exhibited behaviour consistent with confirmation bias, four participants were in the ACH condition, and four were in the non-ACH condition. As such, there could be no statistically significant difference between the proportion that exhibited confirmation bias in the ACH condition and the non-ACH condition.[23] This indicates that ACH has no mitigating impact on confirmation bias.

Degree of Belief Scores

The rationales participants provided for their degree of belief scores were examined using qualitative analysis. Fifty individual influencing factors of belief were identified (see Appendix for full details). Of the fifty influencing factors, nineteen (38 per cent) related to establishing the epistemic justification for believing the intelligence information to be true or false; fourteen (28 per cent) concerned LeT's capability to develop/acquire biological warfare (BW) agents or conduct terrorist operations; sixteen (32 per cent) concerned LeT's intent to develop/acquire BW agents or conduct terrorist operations; and one (2 per cent) concerned the risk of failing to consider the possibility that hypothesis 1 (the worst-case scenario) was true. Of the fifty influencing factors, thirteen (26 per cent) were relevant to identifying the answer to the exam question (to establishing the epistemic credibility of believing each hypothesis to be true or false), and thirty-seven (74 per cent) were not relevant to identifying the answer to the exam question. Most irrelevant factors were cited by participants after reading the background report, indicating that despite having no diagnostic value to either hypothesis, the background reports influenced participants' belief formation.

A two-way ANOVA test was conducted to see if analytic condition and serial order had any impact on the degree to which participants' belief scores were influenced by relevant factors cited in their belief score rationales (Figure 3.2).[24] Participants in the ACH condition were statistically significantly more likely to be influenced by relevant factors for establishing the answer to the exam question (and epistemic credibility) than the non-ACH condition.[25]

Diagnostic Value Assessments

Diagnostic value assessments were broadly consistent across the four research groups. Multinomial logistic regression tests were

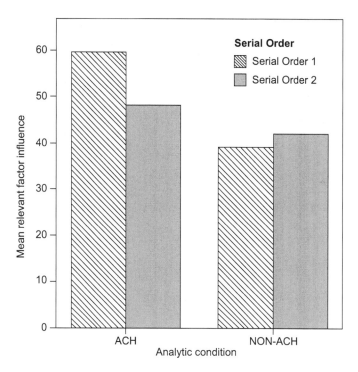

Figure 3.2 Two-way ANOVA: degree of influence on belief score from non-epistemically relevant factors.

performed to identify if there were statistically significant differences between the research group's diagnostic value of information scores for each of the six intelligence reports.[26] Only one report out of six yielded statistically significant results. For intelligence report 3, participants in the non-ACH + serial order 1 condition were more likely to score 'unknown' against hypothesis 2 than the other research groups ($p = < .0005$).[27] As this result was not repeated for the additional five intelligence reports, it probably reflects individual differences, which can have a disproportionate impact for small sample sizes.

Credibility Assessments

Multinomial logistic regression was conducted to identify if the independent variables of analytic condition and serial order had statistically significant effects on the credibility of information scores for each of the six intelligence reports.[28] Only one of the six intelligence reports yielded statistically significant results.[29] Both ACH research groups were statistically significantly more likely to provide an 'unknown' credibility score than both the non-ACH research groups for intelligence report 1 ($p = < .0005$).[30] However, as these results were not replicated for the other five intelligence reports, it is likely that the results were due to individual differences.

Qualitative analysis was conducted on the rationales that participants provided to explain their credibility scores. A wide variety of reasons behind credibility of information assessments were provided. The rationales cited by the largest proportions of participants were: motivations to lie or the possibility of deception (74.36 per cent); the reliability of sources in the sourcing chain (56.41 per cent); and consistency with what the participant(s) already believed true from prior reporting (53.84 per cent). On several occasions, a single rationale for credibility assessment was used by different participants for assigning different credibility scores. This included a single rationale being cited for scoring high and for scoring low credibility. There are also polarised assessments on the same issue: for intelligence report 2 some participants claimed that the information provided was too vague, whereas others claimed it was very specific; some participants claimed that the information was consistent with previous reporting, whereas others claimed it was inconsistent.

A total of 53.84 per cent of participants were influenced by factors that were not relevant or theoretically appropriate for establishing the epistemic justification for believing in a hypothesis. These non-epistemically relevant factors were: the classification of the intelligence report; the consistency of information with an analyst's prior beliefs; the consistency of information with prior reporting; the level of access the source had to the information; the level of detail provided in the report; the level of trust that the agent runners had in the source; the level of trust that the participants had for the intelligence provider; the nature of the relationship between the sub-sources; and the opinion that the information required an expert analysis or interpretation. There was no statistically significant difference between the proportion of participants who cited non-epistemically relevant factors compared with the proportion of participants who cited epistemically relevant factors.[31] The type of rationales provided by participants and the range of the proportion of participants who cited each rationale for the intelligence reports are listed below. (See Appendix for the rationales used to assess the credibility of each of the six intelligence reports.)

When judging the credibility of reporting that derives from humans (HUMINT and SIGINT) the rationales cited by the highest proportions of participants were: whether the source(s) involved were assessed to have motivation to lie (74.36 per cent of participants); the perceived reliability of the source(s) in the reporting chain (56.41 per cent); and consistency of newly received information with prior beliefs held by the participant (53.84 per cent of participants). The consistency of information with prior beliefs was cited by more participants than consistency of information with prior reporting (23.08 per cent of participants). This difference is of statistical significance.[32] The difference between the proportion of participants who cited motivation to lie or the possibility of deception was also statistically significantly higher than the proportion of participants who cited consistency of information with prior reporting as rationales for credibility assessments.[33] There was no statistically significant difference between

Table 3.1 Proportion of participants that cited rationales for judging credibility for each of the six intelligence reports.

Rationale	Proportion of participants that cited rationale	Intelligence report that had highest citation	Intelligence type that had highest citation
Ability to verify the information	7.69%	Intelligence report 6	HUMINT
Classification of intelligence report	2.65%	Intelligence report 3	HUMINT
Collection method/Sourcing chain	43.59%	Intelligence report 4	GEOINT
Concerns over source validation	28.21%	Intelligence report 3	SIGINT
Consistency of information with analysts' beliefs	53.84%	Intelligence report 2	HUMINT
Consistency of information with prior reporting	30.76%	Intelligence report 1	SIGINT
Diagnostic value of information	40.03%	Intelligence report 4	GEOINT
Epistemological status or quality of information	12.81%	Intelligence report 6	HUMINT
Information out of date	5.13%	Intelligence report 2	HUMINT
Intelligence provider agency unidentified	10.25%	Intelligence report 1	HUMINT
Internal consistency of the claim	2.56%	Intelligence report 2	HUMINT
Lack of independent corroboration	12.82%	Intelligence report 5	SIGINT
Level of access to the information	7.69%	Intelligence report 6	HUMINT
Level of detail provided	35.89%	Intelligence report 1	HUMINT
Level of trust agent runners have in source	38.46%	Intelligence report 3	HUMINT
Level of trust in intelligence provider	17.95%	Intelligence report 6	HUMINT
Motivations/Possibility of deception	74.36%	Intelligence report 5	SIGINT
Plausibility of information	7.69%	Intelligence report 1	HUMINT
Relationship between sub-sources	25.64%	Intelligence report 5	SIGINT
Reliability of source(s) in sourcing chain	56.41%	Intelligence report 6	HUMINT
Requires subject matter expertise to interpret claim	7.69%	Intelligence report 4	GEOINT
Whether the ultimate source is identified/known	15.38%	Intelligence report 1	HUMINT

the proportion that cited motivation to lie or the possibility of deception as a rationale compared with either the perceived reliability of the sourcing chain or consistency of information with previous reporting.[34] When judging the credibility of GEOINT, participants were most influenced by judgements of the reliability of the collection method (43.59 per cent of participants) and whether the information had diagnostic value for either of the two hypotheses (40.03 per cent).

The following rationales were cited most regularly in assessments of credibility of information for multiple intelligence reports: collection method/sourcing chain; consistency of information with prior beliefs; consistency of information with prior reporting; level of sources' access to information; level of detail provided; level of trust in the intelligence provider; motivations/possibility of deception; and reliability of source(s) in sourcing chain. Participants were more likely to consider motivation to lie by human sources when the report provided some level of detail about the human source (for example identity, affiliation and reasons for providing the information). However, when very few or no details of the human source were provided, participants were more influenced by consistency of the newly received information with prior reporting, prior knowledge or prior beliefs held by the participant. Further, participants were more likely to consider motivation to lie when the report directly contradicted prior reporting that supported beliefs already held by the analyst.

Discussion and Conclusions

The Efficacy of ACH in Mitigating SPE or Confirmation Bias

There was a statistically significant primacy effect, which affected 64.10 per cent of participants. Neither the different serial orders of the information nor the application of ACH had a statistically significant impact on the proportion of participants who exhibited primacy. These results indicate that the primacy effect was not caused by a specific piece of intelligence, or a specific order in which the information was presented. It indicates instead that there was a force towards forming a belief in the initial stages of information processing, and that this initially formed belief was unlikely to be subject to revision over the course of the belief acquisition process. The results also indicate that ACH did not have a mitigating effect on the likelihood that serial position effects would occur.[35] Whilst the results of the study do not comprehensively disprove the hypothesis that ACH has no ability to reduce the risk of serial position effects or confirmation bias affecting belief acquisition, they indicate that ACH has no meaningful mitigating effect.

Behaviour consistent with confirmation bias was exhibited by 21 per cent of participants. However, the proportion that exhibited no confirmation bias was statistically significantly higher than the proportion that did. This indicates that confirmation bias is less likely to occur during belief acquisition than serial position effects. There were no statistically significant differences in the proportions of participants who exhibited confirmation bias across the four research groups. This indicates that one or more analytical conditions that were shared across the research groups resulted in a reduced risk of confirmation bias and an increased risk of either serial position effects in general, or the specific serial position effect of primacy. These results also indicate that ACH did not reduce the likelihood that confirmation bias will occur in intelligence analysis.

The ability of ACH to mitigate cognitive biases depends on the ability of the scoring systems that ACH employs to process information to be unaffected by these biases. There was no indication that serial position effects had any impact on the ACH process: in terms of influencing either the credibility of information scores or the diagnostic value of information scores. However, the use of ACH did not prevent belief acquisition being influenced by serial position effects. Participants exhibited confirmation bias in their use of the ACH scoring system, in both their credibility of information and diagnostic value of information assessments. Further, there was no statistically significant difference between the ACH and non-ACH groups in the proportions that exhibited confirmation bias in credibility of information or diagnostic value of information assessments. This indicates that the ACH scoring systems of credibility of information and diagnostic value of information are not inherently free from being affected by confirmation bias, and that the application of ACH using these two scoring systems does not mitigate the impact of confirmation bias on analytical judgements derived using ACH. The study tested two of the four scoring systems that are used in variations of the ACH technique: credibility of information and diagnostic value. This study did not test the scoring systems of consistency of information or the application of base rate probability values to information (subjective Bayesianism). To provide a comprehensive test of the efficacy of ACH in mitigating bias, additional research that tests these scoring systems is required.

The results of the study were consistent with the results of the study conducted by Cheikes et al. (2004). The scoring system used in the study by Cheikes et al. (2004) was diagnostic value of information.[36] Credibility assessments of information were not recorded as part of the research procedure. The analytical task was taken from a real-life scenario of an explosion that occurred on the USS *Iowa* battleship on 19 April 1989. The participants were required to assess the relative likelihood for three hypothesised causes of the explosion. The study included sixty pieces of information.[37] The participants were asked to score the degree to which each piece of information supported the three hypotheses. The cause of the explosion on the USS *Iowa* has not been determined. As such, all three hypotheses are viable, and each has a body of supporting evidence (Schwoebel 1999; Thompson 1999). The Cheikes et al. (2004) study was designed to identify the primacy effect (referred to in the study as anchoring bias, or focalism).[38] A primacy effect was identified. However, there was no indication that ACH provided any mitigation against the primacy effect. The study found that there was a strong weighting effect, and participants gave stronger evidence ratings to hypotheses with higher confidence ratings. Although not explicitly described as such in the study, this behaviour is consistent with confirmation bias. However, ACH had no mitigating effect on this weighting effect, and therefore no effect on confirmation bias.[39]

Final Assessments and Degree of Belief

The majority of participants believed that hypothesis 1, that LeT was attempting to develop or acquire biological weapons for use in terrorist attacks, had more epistemic justification for believing to be true than the alternative hypothesis. This result was consistent across all research groups. These results, combined with the significant primacy affect that occurred in the first part of the information processing phase of belief acquisition, suggests a force towards forming an initial belief, or focal hypothesis, early on in an analytical process. The primacy effect observed in the study occurred after participants read the background report, and intelligence report 1. Whilst the background report was diagnostically neutral between the two hypotheses, intelligence report 1 was diagnostically weighted towards supporting the truth of hypothesis 1, and not hypothesis 2. There was no statistically significant difference between the four research groups in terms of: the point at which the observed primacy effect occurred; the degree of impact that the observed primacy effect had on belief formation; the initially favoured hypothesis; the finally favoured hypotheses; and the final degree of belief scores. This indicates that for all the research groups, primacy happened at approximately the same point in the information processing phase and had an approximately consistent degree of impact on belief formation, and that this led to the formation of an initial focal hypothesis that was maintained throughout the information processing stage.

The rationales provided for degree of belief scores revealed that most participants were influenced by factors that were not relevant to establishing the epistemic justification for believing each of the hypotheses to be true. Most of these non-epistemically relevant factors were cited after reading the background report. However, the impact on belief adjustment of the subsequently processed intelligence was predominantly based on epistemically relevant factors. The background report was diagnostically neutral between the hypotheses: it contained no current information on LeT activities, so any influence this had on belief adjustment would be irrelevant by default to establishing the epistemic justification for any beliefs formed. These results also support the indication that participants were subject to a force towards forming an initial focal hypothesis early on in an analytical task. It is reasonable to infer that a force towards forming an initial focal hypothesis resulted in the development of the initial belief anchor being influenced by non-epistemically irrelevant information. This indicates that serial position effects can negatively influence the ability to judge the epistemic value of information and that in analytical tasks where the initially processed information is non-diagnostic, there is a higher risk of acquired beliefs being influenced by non-epistemically relevant factors.

The results also indicate that ACH reduced the influence of non-epistemically relevant factors when forming beliefs. It is likely that this was a result of instructing participants to apply diagnostic reasoning or assessments of the credibility of information when processing information against the two hypotheses (despite not providing advice on how to assess credibility). The diagnostic value of information scores was broadly consistent across the four research groups. There was little disagreement in terms of the diagnostic value of each of the intelligence reports. These results are consistent with the results of Cheikes et al. (2004). Taken together, the results of both studies indicate that individuals do not have significant divergence in their understanding or assessment of the diagnostic value of information. The combination of these results provides reasonable evidence that ACH offers an advantage over the use of intuition alone in the acquisition of epistemically justified beliefs: whilst it doesn't make people better at identifying the diagnostic value of information, by instructing people to judge the diagnostic value of information and credibility of information as part of the processing of information it reduces the risk that beliefs will be influenced by irrelevant factors. However, this benefit has only been identified in versions of ACH that use diagnostic value as part of the scoring system or ask people to identify the credibility of information. The design of the study was insufficient to identify which of these two prior instructions for information processing had more influence over the relevance of factors for judging epistemic complexity.

Assessments of Credibility

The results of the study indicate that people are influenced by a wide range of factors in making judgements of credibility, or epistemic justification, of information. The results indicate that there will be a degree of variance in rationales used to judge credibility between different people, and that some rationales can be applied in a polar manner. Further, the results also indicate inconsistency among participants' understanding of consistency of information and degree of detail that information provides. This indicates that consistency can be interpreted in different ways. Further, it indicates that assessment of the degree of detail that information provides is open to subjectivity. The results also indicate that individuals are likely to be influenced by both relevant and non-relevant factors in assessing the epistemic justification that information provides to a belief. These results combined with the results for the rationales that influenced participants' degree of belief scores indicate that both belief and judgements of credibility can be influenced by non-epistemically relevant factors.

The most cited factors that influence assessments of credibility of information provided by human sources were the possible motivation of the individual providing the information to lie or engage in deception, the reliability of the sources in the sourcing chain through which the information was collected and the consistency of the information with a participant's prior beliefs. Consistency of information was more likely to be used as a rationale in measurement against prior beliefs that are held by the participant over consistency of information measured against a body of prior intelligence reporting. In comparison, when assessing the credibility of information that was not derived from human sources, participants were most influenced by judgements of the reliability of the collection method, and whether the information had diagnostic value for either of the two hypotheses. The results indicate that the motivation to lie or the possibility of deception are most likely to be considered in assessing credibility of information derived from human source reporting when information contradicts beliefs that are held by the analyst. This indicates that the possibility of deception is less likely to be considered for information that is consistent with an individual's prior beliefs or favoured hypothesis. This could indicate that the rigour applied to judgements of credibility of information will differ between being applied to information that does not fit with a favoured hypothesis and to information that does. This implies that judgements of credibility are susceptible to the impact of confirmation bias.

The results also have significant epistemological implications. They indicate that the primary concern of participants in establishing epistemic justifications for beliefs that derive from human sources in an intelligence context is the possibility of deception. However, the factor of the coherence of new information with a participant's prior beliefs also had a high frequency of citations. This indicates that judgements of epistemic justification for information derived from human sources are likely to be informed by theoretically invalid methods. However, judgements of epistemic justification of information that does not derive from human sources is likely to be informed by theoretically valid methods. Combined, these results indicate that epistemic complexity in intelligence is primarily concerned with establishing epistemic justification for information that derives from human sources. This could indicate that determining the epistemic justification for information derived from human sources in an intelligence context, where deception is a plausible risk, is more difficult that determining epistemic justification for information that does not derive from human sources. Further, the results indicate that the possibility of deception by human sources is less likely to be considered when determining the epistemic value of the claims that they make when little information is provided about the human sources. This implies that human source reporting that provides little background information about the human source that provided it is likely to be subject to less epistemic rigour in information processing, resulting in a greater likelihood of beliefs being formed with insufficient epistemic justification.

The results of the study are consistent with some research findings into the factors that influence judgements of the credibility of information. Research by Jungermann et al. (1996) found that participants were most likely to judge the trustworthiness of a source of information by perceived levels of honesty and competence. Further, Peters et al. (1997) found that judgements of credibility of sources of information were determined by three factors: (1) perceptions of knowledge and expertise; (2) perceptions of openness and honesty; and (3) perceptions of concern and care. The factor of the perceived concern or care from the individual providing the information is consistent with the results of research by Frewer et al.

(1996), who found that individuals who were perceived to have moderate accountability were perceived to be more trustworthy sources of information. This factor was not cited as a rationale that influences judgements of credibility by participants in the study. However, this may be due to the specific context of the analytical tasks in question. Both studies by Peters et al. (1997) and Frewer et al. (1996) were based on situations that involved the communication of risk, where some of the sources of information had a formal role of being accountable for risk management. However, the analytical situation used in this study was based on the assessment of a national security threat. None of the sources of information had a formal role of being accountable for the mitigation of national security threats. Comparison of the results with wider research on the topic indicates that perception of honesty and trustworthiness are significant influencing factors when judging the credibility of information from human sources. However, the research does not support previous research findings that suggested that a key influencing factor for judgements of credibility of information is the consistency of information provided by the same source.

*   *   *

This study is not without limitations. The measurement of serial position effects is a contentious issue in social sciences, and different studies use different ways of identifying whether they have occurred. The methods I have used may not be consistent with other studies on the subject. Further, the number of participants who volunteered for the study was relatively small. However, these limitations are not sufficient to invalidate the results.[40] The study showed that serial position effects have a significant impact on belief acquisition, with the majority of participants exhibiting primacy. The results of the experiment can be validly interpreted as indicating that primacy was the result of a force towards the formation of a focal hypothesis early on in the information processing phase. Confirmation bias affected a minority of participants. The use of ACH in reaching analytical judgements had no mitigating effect on the likelihood of occurrence of either serial position effects or confirmation bias and had no mitigation against the impact of confirmation bias on the information ranking systems of credibility of information and diagnostic value of information used to rank information in ACH. There was no indication that serial position effects had an impact on the ACH process; however this did not prevent them from influencing belief formation when using ACH. The experiment showed that the version of ACH taught by the PHIA to the UK's intelligence community between 2016 and 2017 has no efficacy in mitigating the impact of confirmation bias or serial position effects on belief acquisition in an intelligence context.

The experiment demonstrated that belief acquisition and judgements of the epistemic value (credibility) of information are influenced by factors that have no relevance in determining the epistemic justification that intelligence information provides for believing a hypothesis to be true. Further, the risk of belief acquisition in intelligence being influenced by non-epistemically relevant factors was higher when processing information derived from human sources, and when initially processed information is non-diagnostic. The higher risk of influence of non-epistemically relevant factors in belief acquisition occurring through initial information being of no diagnostic value was probably the result of the primacy effect. However, ACH had a reducing impact on this influence, indicating that the specific use of diagnostic reasoning or the explicit instructions to judge the credibility of information when processing information reduces the influence of non-relevant factors when forming beliefs.

The experiment provided some support for the theory that ACH offers no mechanisms to mitigate the risk of cognitive bias in intelligence. However, the current body of experimental research into the efficacy of ACH to mitigate the risk of cognitive bias in intelligence has only examined the efficacy of ACH in mitigating the risk of serial position effects and confirmation bias. Many more cognitive biases have been identified in the social sciences. To provide a comprehensive experimental validation of the efficacy of ACH to mitigate the risk of cognitive bias, all forms of ACH must be put to the test against all known cognitive bias types. Further, the efficacy of two of the four information ranking systems used in current versions of ACH, subjective Bayesianism and consistency of information, in mitigating either the impact or the likelihood of occurrence of confirmation bias or serial position effects has yet to be subject to experimental validation.

The experiment provides some support for the theory that, due to the covert nature of intelligence, the acquisition of justified beliefs in intelligence faces additional epistemic complexity. When establishing the epistemic justification for judging the credibility of intelligence information from human sources, and in establishing what degree of epistemic justification this information gave to competing hypotheses, participants were primarily influenced by whether the human source that provided the information had a motive to engage in deception. This has been identified as a factor that that is highly likely to be encountered in intelligence, and one that is arguably a direct result of the covert nature of belief acquisition in intelligence.

However, the experiment was not able to examine whether the likelihood of occurrence of serial position effects and confirmation bias was likely to have been influenced by any of the several factors under which the experiment was conducted that were not subject to control measures. It is possible that either the majority primacy effect was caused or exacerbated, or that the minority confirmation bias effect was caused or reduced by additional experimental factors. To establish if this was likely to be the case, the results of the study were compared with the results of additional studies into serial position effects and confirmation bias. The next two chapters will provide meta-analysis of available research into each bias, examining the evidential basis for alternative approaches to mitigating the risk of cognitive bias in intelligence, and providing empirical validation to the theoretical argument that belief acquisition in intelligence analysis is likely to be more susceptible to cognitive bias.

Notes

1. A version of this chapter was published as an article in the *Journal of Intelligence and National Security* in October 2018 (https://doi.org/10.1080/02684527.2018.1534640).

2. The study was designed with the statistical power of 0.05:78 to have a high probability of detecting if either serial order or ACH conditions had a minimum effect size of 0.8 or above on confirmation bias and/or serial position effects. Observed effect size (Cohen's d) = 0.8, probability level 0.05, observed power: 0.78034989. This means that the chance of type 1 error is 5 per cent and the chance of type 2 error is 32 per cent. Observed effect size (Cohen's d) = 0.7, probability level 0.05, observed power: 0.68121420. Observed effect size (Cohen's-d) = 0.5, probability level 0.05, observed power 0.44691462. Observed effect size (Cohen's d) = 0.3, probability level 0.05, observed power: 0.23025184. Previous research into the efficacy of ACH in mitigating cognitive biases has failed to detect an effect of ACH. As such, the effect size for this study had to be subjectively determined. A minimum effect of 0.8 is a large effect size. Setting an effect size of this magnitude is appropriate in determining whether ACH can effectively mitigate the risk of cognitive biases in intelligence analysis. The mitigation of cognitive biases is an essential part of the design of ACH, either by preventing the occurrence of cognitive bias or by preventing biases from having an impact on belief acquisition. The purpose of mitigation is to lessen the severity of a phenomenon. For ACH to provide to lessen the severity of the risk that intelligence analysis is subject to cognitive biases, it must have the ability to substantially reduce the likelihood of occurrence or the impact of cognitive bias on belief acquisition. If ACH had the ability to reduce the risk of cognitive bias, but the effect was either moderate or small, its impact, whilst offering a palliative, arguably cannot be considered a sufficient mitigation of cognitive bias for ACH to be adopted as a standard practice to intelligence analysis in place of intuition.

3. There were two between-subject factors (independent variables), each with two levels. These were analytic condition (ACH and non-ACH) and the serial order of the information processed (with two different serial orders). There were three dependent variables: degree of belief (represented on a numerical scale of 0–100), diagnostic value of information, measured by five categories (not applicable; unknown; if true supports the truth of the hypothesis; if true does not support the truth of the hypothesis; and if true necessarily disproves the hypothesis) and credibility of information measured by four categories (unknown, low, medium and high).

4. The 2004 House of Commons official review of the intelligence on weapons of mass destruction was also reviewed. However, it supplied

no additional information on the intelligence case not already provided by the US official review and Drogin (2008).

5. Participants were informed that their day-to-day job involved reading intelligence reports and open source information (news articles,
academic studies and so on) related to their region and writing
assessments on specific exam questions set by the Joint Intelligence
Committee (JIC) or the Prime Minister's National Security Office
(NSO).

6. Participants were informed that step-by-step instructions were
included in their answer booklets, and that it was important that
they follow these instructions exactly. Participants were informed
that these instructions would tell them when to read each specific
intelligence or background report, and that it was important that
they read the reports in the exact order laid out in the exam booklet
instructions. Participants were informed that the instructions were
designed to record how their belief of which hypothesis was more
likely to be true changed after reading each intelligence report provided, and on what basis it changed.

7. For scoring degree of belief, participants had to divide a total of 100
points between the two hypotheses. The number of points allocated
to a hypothesis indicated how strongly a participant believed it to be
true or false. The following example was provided for how the scoring system worked: 'If you are 100 per cent sure that hypothesis 1
is true, and hypothesis 2 is false, you would allocate hypothesis
1: 100 points, and hypothesis 2: 0 points. If you have no (or a neutral)
degree of believe that either hypothesis is true or false, you would
allocate 50 points to each. The more points you allocate to a hypothesis, the higher the strength of your belief that it is true.' Participants
were instructed to provide a short rationale for their scores, and
informed that there was no right or wrong score for any of the intelligence. Participants were instructed to provide the first score after
reading the background information, and to provide an updated
score after reading each of the six intelligence reports.

8. Participants were informed that there was no right or wrong answer
to the overall exam question, and that the study was concerned
only with how participants came to their final decision and what
influenced their belief. Finally, participants were informed that they
would be asked to provide some personal information: their age,
their gender and whether they had prior experience as an intelligence
analyst (in a yes or no answer format). Participants were informed
that this step of the study was entirely voluntary, and that if they did

not wish to provide some or any of this information, they did not need to do so. This was a stipulation made by KCL Research Ethics Committee.

9. In designing the two serial orders, a compromise was made between preserving the ecological validity of the intelligence scenario on which the study was based and the limitation on the number of serial orders that could be tested. The two different serial orders were as follows: (1) serial order 1: background report, intelligence report 1, intelligence report 2, intelligence report 6, intelligence report 4, intelligence report 5 and intelligence report 3; (2) serial order 2: background report, intelligence report 1, intelligence report 5, intelligence report 2, intelligence report 4, intelligence report 3 and intelligence report 6.

10. This design is not without limitation. A genuine balance of diagnostic support for either hypothesis could not be established without losing the ecological validity of the case study. The information was heavily skewed towards supporting one hypothesis over another in the real event. However, the degree of this proportion was softened in the study: four reports had clear diagnostic value for hypotheses, and three of these had diagnostic support for hypothesis 1 rather than hypothesis 2. Further, some of the information in the Iraq WMD case study was genuinely not diagnostic for either hypothesis 1 or hypothesis 2. This was also reflected in the study, with two intelligence reports that had neutral diagnostic value for the hypotheses (in addition to the background report, which was also of neutral diagnostic value).

11. The ACH groups were instructed that they were required to use the structured analytical method ACH to produce their answers. The ACH groups were told that the instructions in the answer booklet would look different from the ACH process demonstrated in the training session, and that the process was altered slightly to record how the participant's degree of belief changed throughout the analytical process, without it being influenced by the ACH scoring process. The ACH groups were also informed that their degree of belief as to which of the hypotheses was more likely to be true did not have to reflect their ACH final scores. The questionnaires for the ACH groups were set out differently from the non-ACH groups. For the ACH groups, a credibility and diagnostic value of information score was produced after reading each report, and at the same stage as providing a degree of belief score. For the non-ACH group, scores for credibility and diagnostic value were provided after the intelligence reports had been

processed. This was to prevent the credibility and diagnostic value assessments from having a competing effect on the degree of belief scores, and to ensure that the collection of degree of belief scores was as close as possible to an intuitive process. Regarding the final written assessment, the ACH groups were told that their assessment should present the cases for both hypotheses and which of the two was the stronger, as deemed by the ACH method. Participants were also told to include the limitations of the available intelligence, and what intelligence gaps there were if they were deemed appropriate.

12. Ethical approval for the study was granted by the KCL War Studies Group Research Ethics Panel on 23 July 2015, reference number LRS 14/15-0813.

13. A significantly large number of individuals were invited to participate in the study. The recruitment of British Government participants was managed by the Professional Heads of Intelligence Analysis team in the Cabinet Office. The following departments agreed to disseminate the recruitment advertisement: the Metropolitan Police, the Cabinet Office, the Home Office, the National Crime Agency and the UK Border Agency.

14. Participants were randomly allocated to research groups. Twenty participants were in the ACH condition, and nineteen were in the non-ACH condition. Research group 1 (ACH plus serial order 1) comprised nine participants. Research group 2 (ACH plus serial order 2) comprised eleven participants. Research group 3 (non-ACH plus serial order 1) comprised eleven participants. Research group 4 (non-ACH plus serial order 2) comprised eight participants.

15. Multinomial logistic regression tests were performed to identify if there were any statistically significant differences between the hypotheses favoured by the final degree of belief scores of each of the four research groups. The multinomial logistic tests were run at a 95 per cent confidence interval. The tests used the research group as an independent nominal variable and the final assessment as the dependent nominal variable. Tests were run using three separate measurements of the final hypothesis selection: degree of belief for all sub-groups, analytic condition (degree of belief for the non-ACH group versus ACH results for the ACH groups), and ACH scores for all sub-groups (ACH scores were calculated for non-ACH groups using the diagnostic value and credibility of information scores provided at the end of the procedure). Test information for degree of belief: two outliers were detected by inspection of boxplots. Multinomial logical regression tests are designed for

data samples that contain no outliers. If outliers are included in the test, then there is a chance that the results may be invalid. Multinomial logical regression tests were performed at a 95 per cent confidence interval for the sample containing outliers, and a sample with the outliers removed. Neither of these samples had multicollinearity, but neither of these samples had goodness of fit. The results of the multinomial logical regression tests were consistent for each of the samples tested: there were no statistically significant differences between the research sub-groups. Test information for analytic condition: Three outliers were detected by inspection of boxplots. Multinomial logical regression tests were performed at a 95 per cent confidence interval for the sample containing outliers, and a sample with the outliers removed. Neither of these samples had multicollinearity. The sample containing outliers had goodness of fit, but the sample with outliers removed did not have goodness of fit. The results of the multinomial logical regression tests were consistent for each of the samples tested: there were no statistically significant differences between the research sub-groups. Test information for ACH scores: this was tested using multinomial logical regression tests at a 95 per cent confidence interval on three separate measurements of the final hypothesis selection: degree of belief for all sub-groups, analytic condition (degree of belief for the non-ACH groups versus ACH results for the ACH groups) and ACH scores for all sub-groups (ACH scores calculated for non-ACH groups using diagnostic value and credibility scores provided). Four outliers were detected by inspection of boxplots. Multinomial logical regression tests were performed at a 95 per cent confidence interval for the sample containing outliers, and a sample with the outliers removed. Neither of these samples had multicollinearity, but nor did either of them have goodness of fit. The results of the multinomial logical regression tests were consistent for each of the samples tested: there were no statistically significant differences between the research sub-groups. The tests detected a comparatively large number of outliers. This was due to the ordinal nature of the factors involved, and the relatively small sample size for each research group. There were no statistically significant differences between research groups regarding which hypothesis was more likely to be finally favoured.

16. A two-way ANOVA was conducted to examine the effect of analytical condition and serial order on the final degree of belief scores. Data are mean ± standard error unless otherwise stated. Residual analysis was

performed to test for the assumptions of the two-way ANOVA. Outliers were assessed by inspection of a boxplot. Normality was assessed using Shapiro-Wilk's normality test for each cell of the design. The Shapiro-Wilk test of normality is recommended for experiments that have fewer than fifty participants (<50). Homogeneity of variance was assessed by Levene's test for equality of variances. There was homogeneity of variances ($p = .05$). There were no outliers, and residuals were normally distributed. The interaction effect between analytic condition and serial order was not statistically significant, $F(1, 35) = .658$, $p = .423$, partial $\eta2 = .018$. There was no statistically significant main effect of analytic condition on belief adjustment for either of the serial orders, $F(1,35) = .050$, $p = .825$, partial $\eta2 = .001$. There was no statistically significant main effect of serial order on belief adjustment for either the ACH or the non-ACH conditions, $F(1,35) = .182$, $p = .672$, partial $\eta2 = .005$.

17. The Bayesian prior for each participant was set before any information was processed as uninformative priors. A Bayesian prior expresses the degree of belief of an individual between different outcomes before any information has been processed. Uninformative priors reflect a balance among outcomes before information has been taken into account. For the study, the uninformative priors were set at 50/50 division of degree of belief scores allocated between hypothesis 1 and hypothesis 2.

18. As the points system for degree of belief change was measured on a 0–100 scale, the mean degree of belief change can be taken as a percentage of belief adjustment at each point of measurement.

19. A one-sample t-test between proportions was performed to determine whether there was a significant difference between the proportion of participants exhibiting primacy and the proportion exhibiting no serial position effects. The t-statistic was significant at the .05 critical alpha level, $t(38) = 2.774$, $p = .0085$.

20. A one-sample t-test between proportions was performed to determine whether there was a significant difference between the proportion of participants exhibiting recency and the proportion exhibiting no serial position effects. The t-statistic was not significant at the .05 critical alpha level, $t(38) = 1.659$, $p = 1.054$.

21. A two-way ANOVA was conducted to identify whether there were any statistically significant differences in the primacy effect between the four research groups. The two-way ANOVA examined the effect of the independent variables of analytical condition and serial order on belief adjustment. A separate test was conducted examining

belief adjustment at point A and point B. Data are mean ± standard error unless otherwise stated. Due to the comparatively small sample size of each of the four research groups, outliers were detected in some instances. Including outliers in a two-way ANOVA tests runs the risk of limiting the validity of the test results. However, as the sample sizes for each research group were comparatively small, removing the outliers would significantly compromise the representativeness of the samples. As such, where samples contained outliers, comparison tests were run on the total sample and a sample with the outliers removed. There was no statistically significant difference in the primacy effect exhibited by the four research groups at point A in the belief adjustment process. The interaction effect between analytic condition and serial order was not statistically significant, $F(1, 35) = .414$, $p = .524$, partial $\eta 2 = .012$. There was no statistically significant main effect of analytic condition on belief adjustment for either of the serial orders, $F(1,35) = .029$, $p = .865$, partial $\eta 2 = .001$. There was no statistically significant main effect of serial order on belief adjustment for either the ACH or the non-ACH conditions, $F(1,35) = .181$, $p = .673$, partial $\eta 2 = .005$. Residual analysis was performed to test for the assumptions of the two-way ANOVA. Outliers were assessed by inspection of a boxplot. Homogeneity of variance was assessed by Levene's test for equality of variances, $p = .310$. Normality was assessed using Shapiro-Wilk's normality test for each cell of the design. There were no outliers. There was homogeneity of variances ($p = .05$). Residuals were normally distributed for three out of the four cells of the design ($p > .05$). One cell, the ACH + serial order 2 condition was not normally distributed ($p = .007$) and was moderately positively skewed. A square root transformation was attempted. However, this resulted in two cells being not normally distributed. As such, the ANOVA was conducted on the untransformed data. ANOVA is considered to be fairly robust to deviations from normality (Maxwell and Delaney 2004). There was no statistically significant difference in the primacy effect exhibited by the four research groups at point B in the belief adjustment process. Residual analysis was performed to test for the assumptions of the two-way ANOVA. Outliers were assessed by inspection of a boxplot. Outliers were as assessed as being greater than three box-lengths from the edge of the box in a boxplot. Homogeneity of variance was assessed by Levene's test for equality of variances. Normality was assessed using Shapiro-Wilk's normality test for each cell of the design. There were seven outliers. Comparison tests were run on a sample containing the outliers, and on a sample with the outliers removed. The results presented are from the test run on the total sample, containing outliers. There was homogeneity of variances ($p = .147$). Residuals were normally distributed for three out of the four cells of the design ($p > .05$). One group was not normally distributed. As the distribution for all groups was not the same shape, the data could not be transformed. As such, the two-way ANOVA was conducted on the untransformed data. The interaction effect between analytic condition and serial order was not statistically significant $F(1, 35) = .569$, $p = .456$, partial η2 = .016. There was no statistically significant main effect of analytic condition on belief adjustment scores, $F(1, 35) = 1.23$, $p = .274$, partial η2 = .034. There was no statistically significant main effect of serial order on degree of belief adjustment score, $F(1, 35) = .001$, $p = .073$, partial η2 = .000. A comparison test was conducted on the sample with the seven outliers removed. The main effects results were consistent. The interaction effects for serial order were consistent. The interaction effect for analytic condition did have a statistically significant result: the ACH groups had a higher degree of belief change than the non-ACH groups. For the sample with outliers removed, the assumption of homogeneity of variances was violated ($p = .012$). Residuals were normally distributed for three out of the four cells of the design ($p > .05$). One cell, the ACH + serial order 2 condition, was not normally distributed ($p = .007$) and had positive kurtosis. A square root transformation was attempted. However, this did not result in a normal distribution. As such, the two-way ANOVA was conducted on the untransformed data. The interaction effect between analytic condition and serial order was not statistically significant $F(1, 28) = .864$, $p = .361$, partial η2 = .030. There was no statistically significant main effect of serial order on degree of belief change score, $F(1, 35) = .001$, $p = .073$, partial η2 = .000. Therefore, an analysis of the main effect for analytical condition and serial orders were performed. All pairwise comparisons were run where reported 95 per cent confidence intervals and p-values are Bonferroni-adjusted. There was no statistically significant main effect of serial order on degree of belief change score, $F(1, 35) = .001$, $p = .073$, partial η2 = .000. There was a statistically significant main effect of analytic condition on belief adjustment scores, $F(1, 28) = 62.60$, $p = < .0005$, partial η2 = .691. Data are mean ± standard error, unless otherwise stated. The unweighted marginal means for degree of belief change scores were 5.83 ± 1.31 for ACH and 19.53 ± 1.12 for non-ACH, respectively.

The non-ACH condition was associated with a mean degree of belief change score 13.69 (95 per cent CI, 10.15 to 17.24) points higher than the ACH condition, a statistically significant difference, $p = < .0005$. However, as the sample with the outliers removed was highly likely to be unrepresentative of the total sample, the results from the full sample will be accepted instead.

22. 20.51 per cent.

23. A two-sample t-test between proportions was performed to determine whether there was a significant difference between non-ACH and ACH samples with respect to the proportion who had the attribute confirmation bias. The t-statistic was not significant at the .05 critical alpha level, $t(37) = 0.081$, $p = .9357$.

24. The test had to be conducted with a sample that contained outliers. The outliers were caused by the ordinal nature of the variables and the relatively small sample sizes of the research groups. This may have impacted the validity of the two-way ANOVA but retained the integrity of the sample.

25. Data are mean ± standard error, unless otherwise stated. There was no statistically significant interaction between analytic condition and serial order for 'relevant factor influence', $F(1, 35) = 2.68$, $p = .111$, partial $\eta2 = .071$. There was no statistically significant main effect for serial order on 'relevant factor influence', $F(1, 35) = 1.04$, $p = .315$, partial $\eta2 = .029$. There was a statistically significant main effect for analytic condition on 'relevant factor influence', $F(1, 35) = 10.20$, $p = .003$, partial $\eta2 = .226$. The marginal means for the 'relevant factor influence' score was 54.06 ± 2.93 for ACH and 40.57 ± 3.04 for non-ACH, a statistically significant mean difference of 13.49 (95 per cent CI, 4.91 to 22.06), $p = .003$. The dependent variable was the percentage of influence from relevant variables (out of 100) (categorical and continuous variable). The independent variables were analytic condition and serial order (both nominal variables). There was independence of observations (between-subjects design). Five outliers were identified by inspection of boxplots. Removing these would significantly impair the quality of the sample. As such, no comparison tests were conducted. The two-way ANOVA was conducted on a sample containing outliers. The data was normally distributed (Shapiro-Wilk's, $p = > 0.5$). There was homogeneity of variance ($p = .599$, Levene's test for equality of variances).

26. One participant in the sample provided split category answers. As the multinomial logistic regression test assumes that all categories in the nominal and ordinal variables are mutually exclusive, this

participant's results were not included. Due to the ordinal nature of variables involved, and the relatively small sample sizes of the research groups, a comparatively large number of outliers were detected in isolated cases. The following intelligence reports had no statistically significant differences in the diagnostic scores between the four research groups: intelligence report 1, intelligence report 2, intelligence report 4, intelligence report 5 and intelligence report 6. For intelligence report 1 there was no need to conduct a multinomial logical regression test, as all answers were the same. There were therefore no statistically significant differences between the research groups. For intelligence report 2 there was no need to conduct a multinomial logical regression test, as all but one of the participants provided identical diagnostic value scores. The one participant that provided a different score ranked intelligence report 2 as 'unknown'. There was therefore no statistically significant differences between the four research groups. For intelligence report 4, three outliers were identified by inspection of boxplots. As such, a comparison test was performed on the original sample containing the three outliers and a sample with the three outliers removed. For the sample containing outliers, there was no multicollinearity, but no goodness of fit. The results showed no statistically significant differences between the research groups. The results were consistent for the sample with outliers removed. For intelligence report 5, one outlier was detected by inspection of boxplots. As such, a comparison test was performed on the original sample containing the outlier and on a sample with the outlier removed. For the sample containing the outlier, there was no multicollinearity and goodness of fit. The results showed no statistically significant differences between the research groups. The results were consistent for the test performed on the sample with the outlier removed. For intelligence report 6, two outliers were detected by inspection of boxplots. As such, a comparison test was performed on the original sample containing the two outliers, and a sample with the two outliers removed. For the sample with outliers included, there was no multicollinearity but no goodness of fit. There were no statistically significant results between the research groups. For the sample with the outliers removed, there was no multicollinearity, but no goodness of fit. ACH + serial order 1 and non-ACH + serial order 1 were more likely to score 'unknown' ($p = < .0005$). However, as the sample with outlier removed compromised the integrity of the data, the results for the multinomial logical regression test performed on the sample with the outliers included will be accepted: there were no statistically significant differences between the research groups.

27. Two outliers were detected by inspection of boxplots. As such, a comparison test was performed on the original sample containing the two outliers and on a sample with the two outliers removed. For the sample with outliers included, there was no multicollinearity and there was goodness of fit. Non-ACH + serial order 1 and non-ACH + serial order 2 were more likely to rank as unknown and not applicable than other sub-groups (p = < .0005). For the sample with the two outliers removed: there was no multicollinearity and there was goodness of fit. Non-ACH + serial order 1 was more likely to score 'unknown' than the other sub-groups (p = < .0005). As the sample with outlier removed compromised the integrity of the data, the results for the multinomial logical regression test performed on the sample with the outliers included will be accepted: the non-ACH + serial order 1 research group was more likely to score intelligence report 3 as of 'unknown' diagnostic value for hypothesis 2 than other research groups.

28. The tests were conducted at a 95 per cent confidence interval. Four participants in the sample provided split category answers, and one participant only provided a score for five out of six reports. As such, they were removed from the sample for the multinomial logistic regression test. The multinomial logistic regression test assumes that all categories in the nominal and ordinal variables are mutually exclusive. As such, these tests were performed using a sample of thirty-four participants out of thirty-nine.

29. The following reports did not result in statistically significant differences between the research groups: intelligence report 2, intelligence report 3, intelligence report 4, intelligence report 2 and intelligence report 6. For intelligence report 2, there were no outliers, no multicollinearity and no goodness of fit. For intelligence report 3, six outliers were identified by inspection of boxplots. Comparison tests were conducted on a sample with the outliers included and a sample with the outliers removed. There was no multicollinearity, but no goodness of fit for both the sample containing the six outliers and the sample with the six outliers removed. For intelligence report 4, two outliers were identified by inspection of boxplots. Comparison tests were conducted on a sample with the outliers included and a sample with the outliers removed. There was no multicollinearity, but no goodness of fit for both the sample containing the two outliers and the sample with the two outliers removed. For

intelligence report 5, two outliers were identified by inspection of boxplots. Comparison tests were conducted on a sample with the outliers included and a sample with the outliers removed. There was no multicollinearity, but no goodness of fit for both the sample containing the two outliers and the sample with the two outliers removed. For intelligence report 6, three outliers were identified by inspection of boxplots. Comparison tests were conducted on a sample with the outliers included and a sample with the outliers removed. There was no multicollinearity, but no goodness of fit for both the sample containing the three outliers and the sample with the three outliers removed.

30. The original sample contained two outliers. A multinomial logical regression was conducted on the sample with the outliers included, for comparison against the multinomial logical regression conducted on the sample with the outliers removed. When the sample contained outliers, the ACH sub-groups (for both serial orders) were statistically more likely to score 'unknown' credibility than the non-ACH sub-groups ($p = < .0005$). When the outliers were removed, the ACH + serial order 2 were statistically more likely to score 'unknown' credibility than other sub-groups ($p = < .0005$). As the removal of the outliers probably degraded the representativeness of the sample, the results for the multinomial logical regression tests conducted on the sample containing outliers will be accepted.

31. A one-sample t-test between proportions was performed to determine whether there was a significant difference between the proportion of participants who cited relevant rationales for credibility assessments and the proportion of participants who cited non-relevant rationales for credibility assessments. The t-statistic was not significant at the .05 critical alpha level, $t(38) = 0.481, p = .6332$.

32. A one-sample t-test between proportions was performed to determine whether there was a significant difference between the proportion of participants who cited consistency of information with prior beliefs and the proportion that cited consistency of information with prior reporting as rationales for credibility assessments. The t-statistic was significant at the .05 critical alpha level, $t(38) = 2.339, p = .0247$.

33. A one-sample t-test between proportions was performed to determine whether there was a significant difference between the proportion of participants who cited motivation to lie/possibility of deception and the proportion that cited consistency of information with prior reporting as rationales for credibility assessments. The t-statistic was significant at the .05 critical alpha level, $t(38) = 3.797, p = .0005$.

34. A one-sample t-test between proportions was performed to determine whether there was a significant difference between the proportion of participants who cited motivation to lie/possibility of deception and the proportion that cited consistency of information with prior beliefs as rationales for credibility assessments. The t-statistic was not significant at the .05 critical alpha level, $t(38) = 1.151$, $p = .2570$. A one-sample t-test between proportions was performed to determine whether there was a significant difference between the proportion of participants who cited motivation to lie/possibility of deception and the proportion that cited perceived reliability of source(s) in the reporting chain as rationales for credibility assessments. The t-statistic was not significant at the .05 critical alpha level, $t(38) = 0.993$, $p = .3272$.

35. The study carries the risk that the lack of statistically significant effect of ACH or serial order was the result of a type II error. The study was designed to identify a substantial effect size of serial order or ACH. However, if either serial order or ACH conditions had an effect lower than 0.8 (a moderate or small effect), this would not have been detected by the statistical analysis. To establish whether ACH has a moderate or small effect on serial position effects or confirmation bias, the study would need to be repeated with a larger sample size. Multiple published studies into serial position effects and confirmation bias have included sample sizes of below fifty participants. Key examples include: Cheikes et al. (2004), Koslowski and Maqueda (1993), Wason (1960), Tolcott et al. (1989), Perrin et al. (2001), Anderson (1965b, 1973a), Anderson and Barrios (1961) and Asch (1946). However, it does not follow that these studies lacked sufficient statistical power.

36. The study used the same ACH procedure as used by Folker (2000).

37. The sixty pieces of information included mechanical information, electronic information, psychological diagnoses of crew members and conflicting expert testimonies.

38. Cheikes et al. (2004) described the primacy effect as a form of confirmation bias, manifesting in a weighting effect. However, the effect is more consistent with primacy. Confirmation bias would manifest separately from primacy, although confirmation bias could plausibly be the result of a primacy effect.

39. The version of ACH taught by the PHIA uses a semantic scoring scale for diagnostic value, whereas the version used by Cheikes et al. (2004) used an integer scale. However, the two versions are compatible and therefore the results of the two studies are comparable.

40. The study has four specific limitations. The first limitation is that there are conflicting views regarding the measurement criteria to establish serial position effects. Several researchers have measured serial position effects by establishing whether information received at either the beginning or end of a serial order resulted in a disproportionate impact on the formation of beliefs (Nisbett and Ross 1980; Peterson and DuCharme 1967; Ross and Lepper 1980; Pennington and Hastie 1993). However, Hogarth and Einhorn (1992) use the following stipulation in measuring serial order effects: there are two pieces of evidence A and B. Some participants receive information in the order of A-B; others receive information in the order B-A. An order affect occurs when opinions after A-B are different from B-A. The results of the study show that most participants were disproportionately influenced by information processed at the beginning of a series of information compared with the end of a series of information. This was consistent for both serial orders. This is consistent with a significant primacy effect according to measurement criteria for serial position effects employed by Nisbett and Ross (1980), Peterson and DuCharme (1967), Ross and Lepper (1980), and Pennington and Hastie (1986). However, the results do not meet the criteria used by Hogarth and Einhorn (1992) to measure serial order effects. This is because a primacy effect was measured after participants had processed the background information, and intelligence report 1. Whilst the same information was presented to different participants in substantively different serial orders, the background information and the first intelligence report processed were in the same positions in both serial order 1 and serial order 2. However, this arguably does not invalidate the classification of the results as a serial position effect. Primacy is understood in psychology as the idea that items presented first in a series of information are more influential than items presented in the middle or at the end of a series of information (Nugent 2013). However, it does not follow that in all ecologically valid analytical scenarios the items presented first will necessarily result in a specific belief, and that this belief will be markedly different when the information is presented in the opposite order. Serial order effects can be detected in experiments where there is a clearly contrasting diagnostic value of information in the first half of a serial order compared with a second. Reversing the order tends to result in different, opposing beliefs being exhibited in conjunction with a serial position effect. However, other studies that examine serial position effects employ more complex scenarios, where diagnostic value is more intermixed and in some places

neutral or open to interpretation. As such, measurements for serial order effects cannot apply as a blanket measurement for serial position effects. Hogarth and Einhorn did not stipulate in what manner beliefs had to be different between serial orders to qualify as a serial order effect. It is not clear if this refers to the overall proposition that the participants believe to be true, or differences in degree of strength in beliefs. I argue that a better method for measuring a genuine serial position effect is that substantively different serial orders result in most participants exhibiting the same serial position effect. The validity of classification of the results as genuine serial position effects can be tested by examining whether there was consistency among participants exhibiting primacy or recency regarding what piece of information corresponded with the recorded serial position effect. If there were consistency between a specific serial position effect and a specific piece of information, then this would indicate that the results were caused by the contents of the specific piece of information, and not the position that the information was processed in. This was not the case for the participants who exhibited recency. There was no consistent pattern concerning which intelligence report corresponded with the degree of belief score at which the recency effect was recorded. Of the four participants who exhibited behaviour consistent with a recency effect, two exhibited the effect after processing intelligence report 5, one exhibited the effect after processing intelligence report 3 and one exhibited the effect after processing intelligence report 6. Similarly, there was no consistent pattern for participants who exhibited behaviour consistent with primacy. Of the twenty-five participants who exhibited behaviour consistent with primacy, eleven participants had the effect recorded after processing the background report, thirteen after processing intelligence report 1 and one after processing both. This does not indicate that the observed behaviours consistent with serial position were the result of the content of a specific piece of information. The results indicate that the observed serial position effects were therefore genuine. The second limitation concerns the ecological validity of the results. Most participants who agreed to participate in the study were recruited from KCL. In comparison, only a small proportion of participants from the UK intelligence community volunteered for the study. Participants were asked to supply information regarding whether they had prior experience of intelligence analysis in a yes/no format. Due to ethical regulations stipulated by KCL, the provision of this information was optional. However, an insufficient number of participants provided this information to allow analysis as to whether prior experience in intelligence analysis was a contributing factor in the results. Additional studies into serial position effects and cognitive bias in intelligence analysis have drawn participants exclusively from practising intelligence analysts (Cheikes et al. 2004; Tolcott et al. 1989). The study results could not be compared with the results of these studies to identify if prior experience in intelligence analysis could have an influence on the likelihood that an analyst will be affected by cognitive biases. The third limitation of the study concerns the lack of analysis into the possible contributing factors of age and gender in either serial position effects or confirmation bias. This personal information was requested from the participants as part of the questionnaire. Due to ethical regulations, the provision of this information was also optional. An insufficient number of participants provided this information to allow analysis as to whether either were contributing factors in the results. The fourth limitation of the study concerns the number of serial order sequences tested. Due to ethical constraints on the volume of participants who could be recruited, it was only feasible to test two serial orders out of forty-nine possible variations. To test all forty-nine variations with a between-subjects design would have required a substantial number of participants to achieve statistically significant results. The first intelligence report processed was the same for each of the two serial orders. This was necessary to provide background information about the assessment topic at the beginning of the analytical task. The study does not therefore provide an indication as to whether a primacy effect would have occurred or would have been of different magnitude for all the other combinations in which the information could have been processed. It would be reasonable to assume that it would be unlikely for an intelligence analyst to begin processing intelligence reporting for an analytical task without first having gained some background information on the subject. It is therefore reasonable to conclude that this limitation is unlikely to reduce the ecological validity of the results. However, the results of the study could indicate that prior knowledge of a subject could have a disproportionate influence on assessments of the current status of a subject, even if there is no necessary epistemic connection between the two.

4 Predicting Serial Position Effects[1]

Serial position effects are a group of cognitive biases that refer to the different ways beliefs are influenced by the sequence in which that the information is presented or processed. The two principal serial position effects are primacy and recency. Primacy is the phenomenon whereby information processed at the beginning of a series of information has a disproportionately high impact on an individual's belief acquisition or adjustment process. In contrast, recency is the phenomenon whereby information processed at the end of a series of information has a disproportionately high impact on the belief acquisition or adjustment process.

Following the identification of serial position effects as a cognitive bias by the psychologist Solomon Asch in 1946, a substantial body of research has been accumulated that shows that serial position effects have an impact on the way in which people acquire and adapt their beliefs. Studies into serial position effects have used varying combinations of experimental conditions, including the type of information on which the analysis is based, the nature of the analytical task, the complexity of the analytical task, the volume of information that is processed and the mode in which participants were asked to respond. However, researchers disagree as to which type of serial position effect is most prevalent, what impact different analytical conditions have and what the underlying cause(s) of serial position effects are. Most theories that have been proposed to explain and predict serial position effects have been based on a limited proportion of available research and are often focused narrowly on a specific type of cognitive task. To date, the most comprehensive meta-analysis of available research on serial position effects has been provided by

Hogarth and Einhorn (1992).[2] Hogarth and Einhorn combined findings of fifty-seven published studies on serial position effects between 1950 and 1992. This meta-analysis was used to develop a single model to explain how individuals adjust their beliefs on the receipt of new information. Their Belief-Adjustments Model (BAM) offered not only to account for the results of available research into the impact of analytical conditions on serial position effects, but to provide a way of predicting serial position effects in analytical tasks. Since its publication, the BAM has had significant influence as a predictive model for serial position effects in belief adjustment.

The studies on which the BAM is based mostly involved trait hypothesis-testing paradigms (Cheikes et al. 2004). Trait hypothesis-testing paradigms involve providing participants with a description of an individual and asking them to identify character traits that the individual possesses. The research on which the BAM was based did not include studies that offered a realistic emulation of an intelligence analysis scenario. As such, a new meta-analysis was conducted to address this gap in the data, to allow a comparison between the impact of serial position effects on non-intelligence analysis tasks and intelligence analysis tasks. An additional twenty-seven studies into serial position effects that provided sufficient information to include in a meta-analysis were identified by reviewing academic journals and available literature.[3] However, of these additional studies, only a small proportion were conducted that attempted to replicate the results of research into serial position effects in intelligence analysis scenarios. The meta-analysis included a total of eighty-one published studies.[4] The non-intelligence sample comprised 12,673 participants. By comparison, the intelligence sample comprised 292 participants.[5]

The meta-analysis examined serial position effects in each sample under eleven specific experimental conditions. Five of these conditions were examined in the meta-analysis conducted by Hogarth and Einhorn (1992) in development of the BAM: the response mode used to complete the analysis; the volume of information processed; the type of analytical task; the complexity of the task; and the consistency of the information. Six additional experimental conditions were included: reliance on recall; time pressure;

accountability; familiarity with the task; the type of information; and hypothesis testing instructions. The classification criteria for each of these experimental conditions are outlined below.[6]

Experimental Conditions

Response Mode

A body of research shows that judgements are affected by the way they are produced (Einhorn and Hogarth 1981; Goldstein and Einhorn 1987). Hogarth and Einhorn (1992) distinguished two common modes in which judgements are produced in relevant research: step-by-step (SbS), where participants are asked to express their beliefs after processing each new piece of information, and end-of-series (EoS), where participants are asked to express their belief after processing all the information. Hogarth and Einhorn (1992) argued that, when analysis is conducted using a SbS process, an individual will adjust his or her opinion incrementally according to each piece of information processed. However, when analysis is conducted using an EoS process, the initial belief will be adjusted by the aggregate impact of the succeeding evidence. The EoS process is therefore characterised by a single adjustment reflecting a net aggregate impact of the available information on the initial belief. Further, if an analyst is required to provide a series of updated assessments as more and more information is received, it will necessarily result in analysis being conducted in a SbS process, rather than an EoS process. However, if an analyst is asked to present a single final analysis, he or she could feasibly conduct the analysis either in a SbS process or in an EoS process (Hogarth and Einhorn 1992).

An examination of the research into serial position effects highlighted two separate response modes that had been classified by Hogarth and Einhorn (1992) in the category of SbS. Some studies split the information to be processed into blocks of information and required participants to provide an assessment after processing each block.[7] This is not strictly consistent with Hogarth and Einhorn's classification of the SbS response mode. As such, for the meta-analysis, SbS was split into two sub-categories: step-by-step interval and step-by-step continuous. Step-by-step continuous (SbS-C) follows Hogarth and Einhorn's original classification for the SbS response mode, whereby belief adjustments are made after each piece of successive information is processed. Step-by-step interval (SbS-I) is where belief adjustments are made after processing blocks of information. Studies conducted using non-intelligence analysis scenarios have predominantly used an EoS response mode. However, most studies conducted using an intelligence analysis scenario used a SbS-C response mode.[8]

Length of Series

Length of series refers to the volume of information that is processed in an analytical task. This factor was divided into two sub-categories: short length of series and long length of series. A short series of information includes fewer than six individual pieces of information, and a long series of information includes six or more individual pieces of information.[9] What constitutes a single piece of information is subject to interpretation. Some studies required participants to respond to a series of single words, whereas other studies required participants to read several paragraphs which contained multiple propositions. As a rule of measurement for the meta-analysis, depending on the research design of the study in question, a single unit of information was taken as either a single word or a single proposition (declarative sentence), or approximate equivalences from empirical information. Studies conducted using non-intelligence analysis scenarios are approximately evenly split between those that included a short series of information and those that included a long series of information using this classification. However, studies conducted using intelligence analysis scenarios have predominantly been conducted using short series of information conditions.[10]

Task Type

The factor of task type has traditionally been split into two categories: evaluation and estimation. Hogarth and Einhorn (1992) argued that information is encoded either relative to the current level of belief or in an absolute manner. When people undertake evaluation tasks, information is encoded as either positive or negative in relation to the hypothesis being considered. In evaluation tasks, evidence is considered as bipolar relative to the hypothesis, either as disconfirming or confirming a hypothesis (Lopes 1982). Whereas information is processed by addition for evaluation tasks, estimation tasks involve the assessment of a moving average. Hogarth and Einhorn further argued that these two different approaches to updating beliefs are affected by the sequence in which information is received. For example, a participant is conducting an analytical task using a SbS-C process. The participant receives two pieces of information that support his or her current belief. However, one of the pieces of information, X, is of stronger diagnostic value than the other piece of information, Y. X has a diagnostic score of +2 and Y has a diagnostic score of +1. If the participant is conducting an evaluation and receives the information in an increasing order of diagnostic value (weak-strong), Y followed by X, then the participant's belief will be revised using a process of addition, adding to his or her belief by a total of +3. If the participant is conducting an evaluation and receives the information in a decreasing order of diagnostic value (strong-weak), then the belief will still be revised by an addition of +3. However, this will not be the same if the subject is conducting an estimation. Let's say that the participant is conducting an estimation and the degree of strength of his or her currently held belief is scored as 5 (using a unipolar scale). The participant receives two pieces of information, A and B. A has a diagnostic value of 6 and B has a diagnostic value of 9. If the participant receives A and B in a weak-strong order, the belief will be positively adjusted, as 6 is greater than 5, and 9 is greater than the average of 6 combined with 5. However, if the participant receives the information in a strong weak order, then the adjustment of the belief, though positive, will not be on as great a scale of increase as the weak-strong order. This is because whilst 9 is greater than 5, 6 is not greater than the average of 9 combined with 5. As such, the participant's belief will be positively revised in conducting an estimation irrespective of the order in which the information is received; however, the positive revision will be greater if the information is received in the weak-strong order.

But when do people use a process of estimation to revise their beliefs in analysis over evaluation? Hogarth and Einhorn (1992) argued that this is affected by two considerations. The first is the scales used in the judgement process. Evaluation tasks require a true-false assessment, whereas an estimation involves a 'how much?' assessment. The second consideration is how compatible the information is with estimation versus evaluation (Tversky et al. 1988). Research has indicated that in evaluation, information is interpreted as being marked for one hypothesis versus another and interpreted directionally as either positive or negative (Lopes 1982). As such, the use of evaluation over estimation will depend on the nature of the assessment (a true or false answer or an estimation on a continuous scale), and the extent to which the information available is more consistent with an estimation (a unipolar scale) or evaluation (a bipolar scale) (Hogarth and Einhorn 1992).

The meta-analysis uses this classification of evaluation and estimation as two task types. However, an expansion was made for the Hogarth and Einhorn classification of estimation to include assessments of probability. Whilst a calculation of mathematical probability can be expressed on a numerical unipolar scale, it can be argued that, strictly speaking, probability is neither an estimation nor an evaluation. The estimation process described by the BAM is a process of averaging, whereas calculating probability is a process of determining a ratio. However, it has a closer similarity to estimation than to evaluation. In addition, a third category of task type was included in the meta-analysis. Some studies into serial position effects required participants to conduct an analytical task that involved both estimation and evaluation, according to Hogarth and Einhorn's classification. As such, the category of estimation and evaluation was included. Both studies that involve non-intelligence analysis tasks and studies that involve intelligence analysis have largely focused on estimation tasks. In comparison, very few studies focused on analytical situations that involve both estimation and evaluation.[11]

Task Complexity

The complexity of the analytical task has been shown to have an impact on belief acquisition and adjustment. The way in which people process information reflects the level of complexity of the task. As complexity increases, people resort to simpler cognitive processes to ease cognitive strain (Payne et al. 1990). Hogarth and Einhorn (1992) define complexity based on the types of information that must be processed for an analytical task. Complexity is also assumed to increase both as the volume of information to process increases and when the individual has a lack of familiarity with the task. Tasks can be split into two levels: simple and complex. Simple tasks are those that involve small amounts of information, usually of a simple nature (such as single adjectives to describe personality traits) and do not require prior skill or specific knowledge. Complex tasks are those that involve large amounts of information and require specific skills or prior knowledge (such as probability calculations). This includes the processing of information that is more complex, such as multiple propositions instead of single words, and the processing of numerical data. Most studies into serial position effects, for both intelligence analysis and non-intelligence analysis scenarios, have involved simple tasks.[12]

Consistency of Information

The factor of consistency of information is split into two categories: consistent information and inconsistent information. Consistent information occurs when all the information processed in an analytical task is internally consistent, supports either the same hypothesis in evaluation tasks, or provides the same directional weighting to an estimation. Inconsistent information occurs when information is not internally consistent, different pieces of information support different hypotheses, or the information provides different directional weightings for an evaluation process. Most studies, for both intelligence analysis and non-intelligence analysis scenarios, have been under inconsistent information conditions.[13]

Reliance on Recall

Reliance on recall refers to whether participants had constant access to all the information they had received or had to rely on memory for recalling the items of information. Reliance on recall refers to conditions where participants rely on memory for information processing, and no reliance on recall refers to conditions where participants have access to all the information they receive and are not therefore reliant on memory for information processing. Studies conducted using non-intelligence analysis scenarios were approximately evenly split between reliance on recall and no reliance on recall conditions.[14] However, all studies conducted using intelligence analysis scenarios have used no reliance on recall conditions.[15]

Time Pressure

Analytical tasks vary in terms of the amount of time in which they need to be conducted. Some analytical tasks have long or unlimited time frames for completion, whereas others may be required to be completed within very short time periods. The factor of time pressure was split into two categories: time pressure and no time pressure. Time pressure conditions were categorised as those where participants were given little time to adequately process the volume of information they were given or to complete complex tasks. These typically comprised studies where analytical decisions were required to be made within a deliberately brief time frame. This categorisation is necessarily subjective, and will depend on several additional factors, including the volume of information required to be processed in a task, the complexity of the task and the level of familiarity that a participant has with the task. Most studies into serial position effects in non-intelligence analysis scenarios have used time-pressured conditions, whereas most studies using an intelligence analysis scenario have not used time-pressured conditions.[16]

Accountability

Multiple studies have been conducted that look at the impact of accountability on serial position effects. These studies have used a variety of methods for inducing a sense of accountability, which have been separated into six different categories. The first category is the offer of financial incentives for correct analysis.[17] The second is the claim that participants' results would be published (Jones et al. 1968, experiment 3). Third is the requirement for participants to undergo a recall test after conducting analysis, where participants were informed that they would be tested before they began the analytical task.[18] The fourth category is the requirement for participants to undergo a recall test after conducting analysis, where participants were informed midway through their analytical task that they would be tested.[19] Fifth is the requirement for participants to justify their assessments, and informing participants of this prior to information processing.[20] The sixth category is the claim that results would be taken as an indication of a participant's intelligence quotient (IQ).[21] In this capacity, accountability refers to conditions where there was an incentive for the participant either to provide an accurate answer (such as reward or punishment) or to apply extra attention or rigour (such as the requirement to conduct a recall test on information processed during the analytical task), or conditions where the final assessments or analysis provided by the participant to a third party would be in some way attributed to the participant. In comparison, non-accountability refers to conditions where participants had no incentive to provide correct answers or pay additional attention or rigour to analysis, and their final analysis or assessment was provided to a third party in anonymity. Accountability is a significantly under-represented factor in studies into serial position effects in both non-intelligence scenario and intelligence analysis scenario research.[22]

Familiarity with Task

Task familiarity refers to the level of prior specialist knowledge, experience, or skills that are required for an individual to complete an analytical task. Some analytical tasks require no prior skills, experience, or specialist knowledge to complete. Examples of such analytical tasks that have been used in serial position research include estimating the length of a stick (Weiss and Anderson 1969); forming beliefs about an individual from a description of his or her personality or behaviour traits (Anderson and Jacobson 1965; Jones and Goethals 1972; Levin and Schmidt 1969; Mayo and Crockett 1964; Riskey 1979); forming an impression of competing statements (Miller and Campbell 1959; Schultz 1963; Cromwell 1950; Janis and Feierabend 1957; Lund 1925; Hovland and Mandell 1957); spotting patterns between visual stimuli (Feldman and Bernstein 1977); basic probability assessments (Peterson and DuCharme 1967); acting as a member of a jury in a criminal trial

(Anderson 1959; Carlson and Russo 2001; Rosnow et al. 1966; Weld and Roff 1938); estimating an average of a sequence of numbers (Anderson 1964a); and assessing the likely cause of specific incidents (Cheikes et al. 2004). In comparison, examples of tasks that require prior skills, specialist knowledge, or expertise that have been used in experimental research include providing tuition to high school students (Allen and Feldman 1974); analysing information regarding complex topics (for example Lana 1961); operating aircraft simulation equipment (Perrin et al. 2001); operating missile defence systems (Entin et al. 1997); role-playing as a military intelligence officer (Dale 1968; Entin et al. 1989; Tolcott et al. 1989); and accountancy (Dillard et al. 1991; Koch et al. 1989; Tubbs et al. 1990). The familiarity of task factor was split into three categories: familiarity with task, no familiarity with task and familiarity with task not required. Familiarity with task encompasses analytical tasks that require specific prior skills, knowledge, or experience to complete the task with competence, in which the participants had the requisite skills, knowledge, or experience. No familiarity with task encompasses analytical tasks that require specific prior skills, knowledge, or experience to complete the task with competence, in which the participants did not have the requisite skills, knowledge, or experience to complete the task with competence. Familiarity with task not required encompasses tasks that do not require specific prior knowledge, skills, or experience to complete with competence.

Type of Information

Type of information refers to the source of justification and knowledge from which the analytical task derives. This factor is split into five categories: a priori, authority, empirical (or a posteriori), testimony and mixed information types. As no empirical research into serial position effects included introspection or memory as a source of information, these were not included as a separate category of sources of knowledge and justification. A priori refers to information that has been derived purely from a process of reasoning, such as mathematical data. This falls within the epistemological category of reason as a source of justification or knowledge. Empirical encompasses information that has been derived through perception or physical observation by mechanical devices. This falls under the epistemological category of perception as a source of knowledge or justification. Testimony refers to claims that have been made by another individual about the truth or falsity of a proposition or event. An additional category of authority was included to distinguish information that has been provided by someone judged or perceived to be an expert witness or authoritative source. This allows a distinction of reliability to be included to testimony provided by expert witnesses. Mixed information refers to a body of information derived from more than one of the above source types (a priori, authority, empirical and testimony). Most studies that used non-intelligence analysis scenarios were derived purely from testimony, and only a small proportion were derived from mixed information.[23] In comparison, most studies using an intelligence analysis scenario were derived purely from empirical information.[24]

Hypothesis Testing Instructions (ACH)

Two studies in the intelligence analysis sample applied explicit hypothesis testing instructions to examine their impact on serial position effects. These studies applied a version of the ACH method, which combines the instructions to disconfirm hypotheses with the consideration of more than one hypothesis. Most studies in the intelligence analysis sample and all of the studies in the non-intelligence analysis sample had no hypothesis testing instructions. As such, hypothesis testing instruction strategies are significantly under-represented in available research.

Meta-Analysis Methodology

The methodology for the meta-analysis used two types of statistical tests in combination with qualitative analysis. Two-sample t-tests of proportions were used to identify if there were statistically significant differences between the proportions of participants exhibiting all types of serial position effects for each sub-factor compared against the overall sample. One-sample t-tests of proportions were used to identify if there were statistically significant majority results for the individual serial position effects of recency and primacy. Qualitative analysis was then employed to identify which of the statistically significant differences were likely to have been caused by moderator variables (where one analytical condition factor affects a second factor). This process allowed the identification of the variables that were most likely to have a causal effect on serial position effects, and where genuine causal effects attributable to specific analytical conditions differed between the intelligence analysis and non-intelligence analysis samples. Moderator variable effects were identified by consistent high or low proportions of participants being in a moderator variable condition.[25] For example, if all participants in short series of information series conditions exhibited primacy, but all these participants were also all in time-pressured conditions, time pressure and short series of information would both be viable candidates for having a moderator effect on primacy. Multinomial logistic regression tests were then used to predict the likelihood of occurrence of individual serial position effects from the factors that were identified as corresponding with a statistically significantly higher or lower risk.[26] The meta-analysis process involved multiple comparisons tests.[27] As such, a Bonferroni correction has been applied to the results. The Bonferroni correction for the serial position effect meta-analysis sets the benchmark for statistical significance at $p = < .004$.[28] This is a particularly conservative benchmark for establishing statistically significant results.

This approach is a significant methodological divergence from the meta-analysis conducted by Hogarth and Einhorn (1992). First, whilst Hogarth and Einhorn classified each study as a single entity, with a singular serial position effect result, my meta-analysis has accounted for the participants in each study who did not exhibit the majority effect. Second, instead of looking for visually identifiable patterns between the majority result of each study, the meta-analysis sought to identify statistically significant differences for each serial position effect. This was achieved by totalling the number of all participants in a specific analytical condition, rather than assigning individual studies as a single, equal unit of measurement.

The meta-analysis included a third serial position effect in addition to primacy and recency. Whilst these are the two most prevalent serial position effects that have been identified and discussed in subsequent research, a handful of studies into serial position effects exhibit a phenomenon whereby participants exhibit both primacy and recency within a single analytical task (that information at the beginning and at the end of a series have a disproportionately high impact on belief adjustment).[29] However, little has been done in currently available research to discuss or examine this phenomenon, or to acknowledge it as an alternative serial position effect in addition to primacy and recency. This additional serial position effect will be referred to as bracketing.

Whilst this methodology has the strengths (and the inevitable limitations) of statistical analysis, and an expansion of both the types of serial position effects that have been exhibited in available research, and the number of analytical factors for analysis, it is not without limitations. The first limitation is that the studies of which the meta-analysis is based used inconsistent methods for measuring serial position effects. For example, studies that looked at impression formation asked participants to rank the impression they had formed of a fictional person on a numerical scale after being provided with an adjective that described the fictional individual (Asch 1946; Anderson and Barrios 1961), whereas studies that focused on assessment of aircraft using Patriot missile defence simulators required participants to rank the probability that an approaching aircraft was friendly or hostile (Adelman et al. 1996; Adelman and Bresnick 1992). Whilst all methods used some form of numerical scaling to measure the impact of information processed on belief formation, the scales and measurements were not consistent. Another associated issue is that different researchers are likely to have applied different measurements to identify what scores counted as primacy and recency. Primacy and recency record disproportionate influences in belief. However, how significant the influence on belief needs to be to count as disproportionate is open to interpretation. The second limitation concerns data classification. Most studies included in the meta-analysis presented results as a mean degree of belief identified using analysis of variance (ANOVA) but did not specify what proportion or number of participants exhibited a serial position effect and what proportion or number did not.[30] Further, several of the studies where multiple serial position effects were observed did not provide full details of the number or proportions of participants who exhibited primacy, recency and no serial position effects. For studies that presented results as a mean, the total number of participants was assigned to an overall majority result reported for the study. For studies where only two serial position effects were observed, a majority result was assigned 75 per cent of the total proportion of participants and 25 per cent was assigned to the minority effect. Where results were described as mixed, but no details of proportions provided, the number of participants was divided equally between the number of reported serial position effects. This means that the proportions of participants assigned to each serial position effect in the meta-analysis are highly unlikely to be accurate, but instead offer as reasonable an approximation as possible. This is a considerable, but unavoidable limitation of the meta-analysis methodology. However, the methodology used is likely to provide a reasonable representation of the data.

The third limitation is that the statistical methodology applied in the meta-analysis (multinomial logistic regression and t-tests) cannot be used to test for interaction effects or moderator variables. This is another unavoidable limitation. Any analytical task will be conducted under a large number of variables. It is unfeasible for experimental research to measure each of these factors in a way that would allow the accurate identification of relational effects through statistical methods. As such, likely moderator variables were instead identified by qualitative analysis of the data. The effect of moderator variables is a significant, but unavoidable issue.

The final limitation of the meta-analysis is the comparative size of the intelligence analysis sample compared with the non-intelligence analysis sample. Only eight studies were identified that conducted research into ecologically valid (realistic) intelligence analysis scenarios. Most of these experiments used military intelligence scenarios informed by technical information (for example, air defence simulations analysing the movement of aircraft). Currently available research into serial position effects and intelligence analysis is therefore not representative of all types of intelligence analysis scenarios. In the face of these limitations, the following meta-analysis cannot be taken as an accurate account of how different factors affect serial position effects, or of the differences in this impact between intelligence analysis and non-intelligence analysis. However, it can arguably provide a reasonable indication as to how different factors impact serial position effects, whether differences in impact between intelligence and non-intelligence contexts are likely to exist, and, if so, where such differences may lie.[31] The results of the meta-analysis are summarised below.

Results and Discussion

The first observation that can be drawn from the meta-analysis is that serial position effects are highly prevalent in analytical tasks. Of the non-intelligence analysis sample, 86.8 per cent of participants exhibited serial position effects. Of the intelligence analysis sample, 70.89 per cent of participants exhibited serial position effects.[32] This may indicate that intelligence analysis is marginally less susceptible to serial position effects than non-intelligence analysis. However, due to the comparatively small sample size for the intelligence analysis sample, this indication can only be tentative. The second observation is that for the non-intelligence analysis sample the predominant serial position effect was primacy (49 per cent of participants).[33] However, whilst the predominant serial position effect for the intelligence analysis sample was recency (37.33 per cent of participants), there was no statistically significant difference between the proportion that exhibited recency and the proportion that exhibited primacy (33.62 per cent of participants).[34]

There was no statistically significant difference between the proportion of participants who exhibited no serial position effects in the ACH condition (hypothesis testing instructions of disconfirm hypotheses + consider multiple hypotheses) compared with the wider intelligence analysis sample ($t(322) = 1.238, p = .2166$). There was also no statistically significant difference between the proportion of participants who exhibited no serial position effects in the no hypothesis testing instructions compared with the wider intelligence-analysis sample ($t(550) = 0.328, p = .7427$). This indicates that ACH has no mitigating effect on serial position effects.

In the non-intelligence analysis sample, the meta-analysis indicated that the following factors have a reducing influence on the occurrence of serial position effects: short series of information (t(18846) = 8.274, p = < .001), not reliant on recall (t(18628) = 4.499, p = < .001) and recall test (participants informed pre-information processing) (t(13604) = 15.913, p = < .001).[35] The meta-analysis also indicated that long series of information (t(19169) = 14.379, p = < .001), reliance on recall (t(19070) = 10.425, p = < .001), a priori information (t(353) = 2.153, p = < .001) and testimony information (t(18168) = 19.080, p = < .001) are factors that increase the likelihood of the occurrence of serial position effects.[36]

In the intelligence analysis sample, the meta-analysis indicated that the factors of empirical information and complex tasks possibly lower the risk of the occurrence of serial position effects.[37] The meta-analysis indicated that the following factors possibly increase the likelihood of occurrence of serial position effects: long series of information, evaluation tasks, time pressure, no familiarity with task and mixed information.[38] No factors were associated with a statistically significant majority of participants exhibiting no serial position effects. The only factor that was associated with 100 per cent of participants in no serial position effects was the requirement to justify analysis (participants informed pre-information processing). However, this result was only observed in the non-intelligence sample. Further, the result represents a very small fragment of the overall non-intelligence analysis sample: only thirty-six participants (0.28 per cent of the non-intelligence analysis sample).

There was no consistency between the intelligence analysis and non-intelligence analysis samples regarding viable factors for having a reducing impact on the likelihood of occurrence of serial position effects. However, there was some consistency between the intelligence analysis and non-intelligence analysis samples regarding viable factors for having an amplifying impact on the likelihood of occurrence of serial position effects. The factor of long series of information was consistent between the two samples. This could indicate that there are genuine differences in the way that serial position effects impact intelligence analysis compared with non-intelligence analysis. However, these differences could be explained by the fact the intelligence analysis sample was of a substantially smaller size than the non-intelligence analysis sample, making it much more vulnerable to the impact of individual differences. There were no cases in the intelligence analysis sample that were in conditions where information was exclusively a priori, or exclusively testimony, or in conditions where participants were required to conduct a recall test (participants informed pre-information processing). As such, the results for these conditions could not be compared between the two samples.

Given the similarity in the impact of long series of information between both samples, and the limitations in the sample size and number of factors included in the intelligence sample, the meta-analysis results for the non-intelligence analysis sample are judged the strongest indicators of factors that may have a causational impact on the likelihood of occurrence of serial position effects in both non-intelligence analysis and intelligence analysis. The meta-analysis results indicate that processing of six or more pieces of information probably has an amplifying impact on the likelihood that serial position effects will occur. The results also tentatively indicate that processing fewer than six pieces of information have a reducing effect on the likelihood that serial position effects will occur. The results indicate that memory has a significant impact on serial position effects. Tasks that required participants to not be reliant on memory for processing information, that required participants to make greater effort to commit information to memory, or that involved a small volume of information to process were all associated with reduced proportions of serial position effects. In comparison, tasks that required processing a large volume of information were associated with an increased proportion of serial position effects.

* * *

The following nineteen factors were associated with a statistically significant majority, or 100 per cent of participants exhibiting primacy in the non-intelligence analysis sample: EoS, SbS-I, long series of information, estimation, estimation and evaluation, simple tasks, inconsistent, reliant on recall, time pressure, no time pressure, financial reward, performance made public, performance as an indicator of IQ, non-accountability, familiarity with task not applicable, a priori information, authority information, empirical information and testimony information. There is no consistent pattern of high associations between these variables and either a long series of information condition or a reliance on recall condition.[39] As such, there is no indication that either condition had a moderator variable effect. All nineteen factors are therefore possible candidates for having an amplifying effect on the likelihood that primacy will occur in an analytical task. However, as primacy was the predominant serial position effect, some or none of these associations may be the result of a causal relationship. This is exemplified by both the factors of time pressure and non time pressure being associated with a statistically significant majority of primacy.

The following factors were associated with a statistically significant majority, or 100 per cent of participants exhibiting recency in the non-intelligence analysis sample: SbS-C, short, evaluation, complex, not reliant on recall, familiar with task, not familiar with task, mixed information and recall test (participants informed mid-information processing). There is no consistent pattern of high association between these variables and either a short series of information condition, or a not reliant on recall condition. As such, there is no indication that either condition had a moderator variable effect.[40] All ten factors are therefore viable candidates for having an amplifying effect on the likelihood that recency will occur in an analytical task. As recency was the minority serial position effect, there is a lower likelihood that some or none of these associations may be the result of a causal relationship in comparison with the factors that were associated with a majority result for primacy.

The following factors were associated with a statistically significant majority, or 100 per cent of participants exhibiting primacy in the intelligence analysis sample: long series of information, and evaluation tasks. Both factors were suitably represented within the sample to examine for possible moderator variable effects. However, there was 100 per cent association between the two factors. As such, moderator variable analysis could not be conducted. Both factors are therefore viable candidates for having an amplifying effect on the likelihood of the occurrence of primacy in an intelligence analysis task, and both are possible candidates for having a moderator variable effect. No factors were associated with a statistically significant majority of participants exhibiting recency in the intelligence analysis sample.

The only similarity between the intelligence analysis sample and the non-intelligence sample was that the condition of a long series of information was associated with a statistically significant majority of participants exhibiting primacy.[41] In contrast, the short series of information condition was associated with a statistically significant majority of participants exhibiting recency in the non-intelligence analysis sample.[42] The short series of information condition was associated with a majority result of recency in the intelligence analysis sample. However, the result was not of statistical significance ($p = .034$). Taken together, these results indicate that length of series is likely to have an effect on the likelihood of the occurrence of primacy and recency in an analytical task.

The analytical factors that have been identified as likely to have a causal impact on serial position effects account for the difference in the overall proportions of participants who exhibited serial position effects between the intelligence and non-intelligence samples. The intelligence sample had a statistically significantly lower proportion of participants who exhibited serial position effects and had a larger proportion of participants who exhibited recency compared with the non-intelligence sample, where primacy was the predominant serial position effect. A total of 69.18 per cent of participants in the intelligence sample were in short series of information conditions, a factor associated with both a reduced risk of serial position effects in general and a higher risk of recency. In comparison, the proportions of participants in long series of information conditions in the non-intelligence sample were approximately equal to the proportion of participants in short series of information conditions. The influence of volume of information accounts for the difference in proportions of participants exhibiting serial position effects between the two samples.

It is difficult to draw firm conclusions about the serial position effect of bracketing, as the number of recorded cases was very small (eighty-nine participants out of 12,673 in the non-intelligence analysis sample, and no recorded cases in the intelligence analysis sample). It is unclear if the low number of recorded cases is due to a genuine rarity of occurrence, or a lack of recording of the phenomenon in available research. However, all cases of bracketing were in long series of information and familiarity with task not required conditions. One or both of these variables therefore stand as viable for having a moderator variable effect, and account for all conditions in which bracketing was recorded as having a statistically significantly higher proportion.[43] However, further research is required to identify whether there was a moderator variable effect.

An Examination of Previous Serial Position Effects Prediction Models

Several theories and models have been advanced to explain and predict individual serial position effects. The following will be compared against the results of the meta-analysis: the BAM (Hogarth and Einhorn 1992); the belief inertia effect theory (Hogarth and Einhorn 1992); the temporal relevance theory (Jones and Goethals 1972); and the processing cessation theory (Newtson and Rindner 1979).

BAM

Hogarth and Einhorn (1992) made multiple predictions about serial position effects in the BAM. The first prediction concerned the factor of response mode. They predicted that when estimations are conducted using a SbS-C process, where all information is consistent (either positive or negative), then the analysis will not be affected by serial position effects. However, if the evidence is mixed, and presented in a mixed order, the analysis will be affected by recency (unless all diagnostic evidence is ignored). Recency will have the largest impact where there is both strong positive and strong negative evidence, and there is a high sensitivity to evidence.[44] Hogarth and Einhorn's predictions regarding estimations drawing from consistent information in a SbS-C response mode are consistent with the meta-analysis. There were 472 participants in SbS-C response modes, conducting estimation tasks drawing from consistent information. Of these, 89 per cent exhibited no serial position effects, a statistically significant difference compared with the participants who did exhibit serial position effects (p = < .001).[45] Hogarth and Einhorn's predictions regarding tasks drawing from inconsistent information are also supported by the data. A total of 2,622 participants were in SbS-C response modes, conducting estimation tasks drawing from inconsistent information. Of these, 50 per cent exhibited recency and 42 per cent exhibited primacy. This difference is of statistical significance (p = < .001).[46]

Hogarth and Einhorn predicted that when estimations or evaluations are conducted using an EoS process, if the analyst has no prior belief on the subject before starting the analysis, the analyst's initial belief will always be derived from the first piece of information received, or as an amalgamation of the first few pieces of information received (if the first few pieces of information are consistent). The first, or first few pieces of information processed will be given greater weighting than the subsequent information. As such, EoS analysis will tend to result in primacy. In these circumstances, it will make no difference whether the evidence is consistent (either all supporting or all contradicting) or mixed. However, the sequence in which information is received (supportive of one hypothesis over another) will have a significant impact on the initial belief derived by the analyst. This is on the assumption that EoS will only be used when analysts are asked to conduct a specific piece of analysis after reading all the information (and they didn't know what the task was), and where the task is cognitively simple and involves a small volume of information. Out of all studies included in the meta-analysis, 3,537 participants were in simple task, short series of information and EoS response mode conditions. Of these, 51 per cent exhibited primacy and 37 per cent exhibited recency. This difference is of statistical significance (p = < .001).[47] This is consistent with Hogarth and Einhorn's predictions. However, whilst it suggests that there is a higher likelihood of primacy occurring in comparison to recency, it does not arguably indicate a tendency of primacy. Further, Hogarth and Einhorn's predictions regarding consistent versus inconsistent conditions are not supported by the meta-analysis data. Hogarth and Einhorn predicted that both inconsistent and consistent information would tend to result in primacy. A total of 3,059 participants were in EoS, simple, short series of information and inconsistent information conditions. Of these, 56 per cent exhibited primacy and 30 per cent exhibited recency, consistent with Hogarth and Einhorn's predictions (a statistically significant difference, $-=<.001$).[48] A total of 478 participants were in EoS, simple, short series of information and consistent information conditions. However, of these only 21 per cent exhibited primacy, whereas 79 per cent exhibited recency (a statistically significant difference: $p=<.001$).[49] This is inconsistent with Hogarth and Einhorn's predictions.

Of the conclusions that Hogarth and Einhorn made in their BAM, one is supported by available data. The BAM predicts that the long series of information will result in primacy, or a force towards primacy, and the short series of information will result in recency. The BAM predictions are consistent with the meta-analysis results. Hogarth and Einhorn (1992) hypothesised that as the number of pieces of information that need to be processed increases, two effects can occur. The first is that the participant can tire. The second is that beliefs become less sensitive to the impact of new information. This is because newly received information represents a comparatively small proportion of the information that the participant has already processed. Hogarth and Einhorn's prediction that EoS induces primacy whereas SbS-C induces recency is contradicted by different patterns in primacy and recency depending on the volume of information required to process in a task, whereby large volumes of information are most likely to result in primacy and small volumes of information tend to result in recency. Hogarth and Einhorn's prediction that primacy affects simple tasks that involve a large volume of information to process, irrespective if analysis is conducted SbS-C or by end of series, is supported by the data. However, the data also show that primacy affects 76 per cent of complex tasks that involve a large volume of information. This indicates that the factor of volume of information has a causal impact on serial position effects, but that task complexity or response mode do not.

Belief Inertia Effect Theory

The belief inertia effect was proposed by Hogarth and Einhorn (1992). They argued that the extent to which a single piece of information will result in the adjustment of one's beliefs will be dependent on individual variables that will be different from person to person. However, if people's beliefs are weakly held, then both supporting and contradictory evidence will have a greater impact than if the belief were strongly held. The more people become committed to a belief, the impact of both supporting and contradictory evidence will reduce. The longer the series of information, the lower the impact evidence will have on adjusting the participant's belief, irrespective of what the belief is, or whether the subsequent evidence is supporting or contradicting. This is due to the belief inertia effect and will inevitably lead to the effect of primacy in analysis. In accordance with the belief inertia theory, the predominance of primacy in conditions that require a long series of information is due to most people beginning with weakly held beliefs which are disproportionately impacted by information received at the beginning of the task and transform into strongly held beliefs, on which subsequent information has a lower influence. If the belief inertia effect theory is true, it follows that recency is unlikely to occur in long series of information conditions. The meta-analysis results are consistent with the latter of these predictions; only 26 per cent of participants in long series of information conditions exhibited recency. However, very few studies into serial position effects that were included in the meta-analysis underpinning the BAM, or the current meta-analysis, recorded the degree of participants' initial belief in hypotheses prior to the receipt of the first piece of information. As such, one key premise of the belief inertia model is currently untested.

Temporal Relevance Theory

Jones and Goethals (1972) argued that in some cases recency was the result of tasks in which the information presented refers to an object or situation that changes over time. As such, information received later in the task is presumed to have a higher temporal relevance, and therefore has a higher influence than information received early in the task. However, none of the participants who exhibited recency in the non-intelligence analysis sample were in experimental conditions where the subject or object being analysed changed its nature during the time in which the analysis was conducted. Further, out of the intelligence analysis sample, 55.67 per cent of participants who exhibited recency were in a temporal relevance scenario, and 44.33 per cent were not. This difference was not of statistical significance ($p = .0525$).[50] The meta-analysis therefore does not support the temporal relevance theory.

Processing Cessation Theory

Newtson and Rindner (1979) argued that the more pauses, or break points, there are in conducting a piece of analysis, the higher the likelihood of primacy. If their processing cessation theory is true, it would follow that the SbS-C response mode would have the highest likelihood of primacy occurring, and that the EoS would have the lowest likelihood of primacy occurring out of the three response modes examined under the meta-analysis. This theory is not supported by the meta-analysis data. For the non-intelligence analysis sample, 9.41 per cent of participants in SbS-C conditions exhibited primacy, compared with 57.37 per cent of participants in EoS conditions and 79.95 per cent of participants in SbS-I conditions. For the intelligence analysis sample, 43.24 per cent of participants in SbS-C conditions exhibited primacy, compared with 0 per cent in EoS conditions and 0 per cent in SbS-I conditions. The intelligence analysis sample data is consistent with the processing cessation theory. Whilst the sample sizes for participants in both EoS and SbS-I conditions in the intelligence analysis sample were very small, the non-intelligence sample, by far the largest sample of the two, is not. As such, this theory has limited support from the meta-analysis results.

* * *

Of these proposed explanations and prediction models of serial position effects, only some elements of the BAM offer valid explanations of serial position effects that are consistent with the results of current experimental research. However, the BAM only focuses on predicting the likelihood of different serial position effects occurring from a small number of analytical conditions and does not provide an account of the indicated impact of memory on serial position effects. There are some similarities between research into serial position effects on recall and serial position effects on belief acquisition and adjustment. Research has indicated that primacy is the predominant serial position effect or has a more pronounced effect on recall than recency (Henson 1998; Murdock 1968). Research has also indicated that volume of information has a greater impact on primacy than on recency (Henson 1998), and that the larger the volume of information required to process leads to an increase in primacy (Jahnke 1963; Robinson and Brown 1926). The similarities concerning the influence of memory between the meta-analysis into the impact of serial position effects on the acquisition and adjustment of beliefs when processing information, and the ability to recall a series of information, provide a consistent indication that memory is a key factor in determining serial position effects.

The Impact of Analytical Conditions on Serial Position Effects

There are multiple conclusions that can be tentatively drawn from the meta-analysis into serial position effects. The first is that serial position effects are highly likely to occur during analysis, meaning that belief acquisition is likely to be subject to chance to a significant degree. The second conclusion is that there is no compelling indication from currently available research that serial position effects have a different impact, and therefore pose different risks, for intelligence analysis tasks compared with non-intelligence analysis tasks. However, there are considerable gaps in available research into the effect of serial position effects in intelligence analysis scenarios under different analytical conditions. As such, it remains possible that there are legitimate differences in the way that serial position effects affect intelligence analysis compared with non-intelligence analysis.

The third conclusion is that the results provide an indication of what the conditions in which analysis is undertaken may contribute to a reduced risk of serial position effects occurring in both intelligence analysis and non-intelligence analysis. Tasks that involved processing fewer than six pieces of information or no reliance on recall for information processing, or that required participants to conduct a recall test where they were informed of this requirement prior to information processing were associated with a reduced risk of serial position effects. Tasks that involved the processing of more than six pieces of information, involved a reliance on recall to process information and drew exclusively from either a priori or testimony information were associated with an increased risk of serial position effects. Tasks that involved the processing of more than six pieces of information were associated with an increased likelihood of the occurrence of primacy, whereas tasks that involved the processing of fewer than six pieces of information were associated with an increased likelihood of the occurrence of recency.

The fourth conclusion concerns possible underlying causes or factors that may influence serial position effects. The meta-analysis indicates that memory plays a significant role in the overall risks of being subject to serial position effects during an analytical task. The meta-analysis results for serial position effects are consistent with some elements of Hogarth and Einhorn's BAM that seek to explain the causes of individual serial position effects in belief acquisition. However, this theory does not account for the results of the meta-analysis indicating that memory plays a significant role in both the overall risks and the prediction of individual serial position effects. The BAM also does not account for the meta-analysis results indicating that the type of information from which an analytical task derives may also have an impact on the overall risk of serial position effects.

The meta-analysis indicates that the most significant factors that influence serial position effects are memory, the volume of information required to be processed during belief acquisition and the type of information from which belief acquisition is derived. However, the meta-analysis also indicates that primacy is the predominant serial position effect. Based on the results of the meta-analysis, I propose an alternative model for the prediction of serial position effects. Most models that have been proposed to predict serial position effects assume that serial position effects in belief acquisition are solely caused by specific analytical conditions under which beliefs are acquired. I propose an alternative theory: that serial position effects are the result of the impact of specific analytical conditions on an underlying cognitive process. Further, I argue that the analytical conditions that have a causal impact on serial position effects are those that have a direct impact on the requirement to commit processed information to long-term memory. The role that memory plays in influencing serial position effects can theoretically account for both the factors of volume of information and type of information having a direct impact on the likelihood that serial position effects will occur. A high volume of information arguably places a greater reliance on long-term memory for synthesising and comparing individual pieces of information. Conversely, a low volume of information places less reliance on committing information to long-term memory for information processing. In addition, processing information from either of the information types of a priori and testimony would theoretically lead to a greater reliance on committing information to long-term memory. The vast majority of studies in the meta-analysis that derived exclusively from a priori information required participants to make mathematical calculations by processing different pieces of data. Mathematical calculations would arguably require a greater reliance on long-term memory to conduct over time, even if only drawing on a small volume of data, as a running total or average would need to be maintained and updated after processing each piece of information. In comparison, testimony information carries higher complexity in establishing the epistemic justification for believing it to be true. The epistemic credibility of each testimony needs to be determined before individual testimonies can be synthesised during information processing. However, part of the process of making judgements of epistemic justification for multiple testimonies concerning a single event or subject require comparison against one another to determine consistency. This arguably leads to a greater reliance on committing information processed to long-term memory.

I argue that there is an underlying cognitive process that underpins belief acquisition which produces a force towards forming a focal (or favoured) hypothesis in the initial stages of information processing. This underlying cognitive process results in a high likelihood of primacy occurring during belief acquisition. The risk of primacy occurring during belief acquisition is increased when the volume of information to process is more than six pieces of information; when an individual is reliant on long-term memory for processing information; and when individuals are not aware of an explicit requirement to commit processed information to long-term memory prior to beginning information processing. The following factors conversely lead to (1) a reduced likelihood of occurrence of serial position effects in general; (2) a reduced likelihood of the occurrence of primacy; and (3) an increased likelihood of the occurrence of recency when the volume of information to process is fewer than six pieces of information; when an individual is not reliant on long-term memory for processing information; and when an individual is aware of an explicit requirement to commit processed information to longer-term memory prior to beginning information processing. In this capacity, the primary cause for serial position effects impacting belief acquisition is an underlying force towards forming a focal hypothesis in the initial phase of information processing, and the secondary cause is the degree to which individuals are required to rely on long-term memory to process and synthesise information.

Notes

1. A summary version of Chapters 4 and 5 was published as a journal article in the *International Journal of Intelligence and Counter-Intelligence* 33 (2).
2. The use of the term 'meta-analysis' in this context, and throughout the book, does not follow the strict scientific interpretation of the term, which refers to statistical analysis of aggregate data. In this book, the term is used to refer to a comparison of different populations based on an aggregate of prior experimental research, to provide a theory or model to account for the existing data.
3. These additional studies were conducted between 1925 and 2004. A total of thirty-four studies were identified; however, eight of these provided insufficient detail to allow inclusion in meta-analysis: one study had inconclusive results, two studies did not explicitly state what the results were and four studies failed to provide the number of participants involved.

4. The eighty-one studies are: Adelman et al. (1993), Allen and Feldman (1974), Anderson (1964b, 1965, 1967a, 1968c, 1973a, 1973b), Anderson and Barrios (1961), Anderson and Farkas (1973), Anderson and Hubert (1963), Anderson and Jacobson (1965, 1968), Anderson and Norman (1964), Arnold et al. (2000), Asare (1992), Asch (1946), Ashton and Ashton (1988), Benassi (1982), Bossart and Di Vesta (1966), Butt and Campbell (1989), Carlson and Russo (2001), Cheikes et al. (2004), Crano (1977), Curley et al. (1988), Dale (1968), De Wit et al. (1989), Dillard et al. (1991), Dreben et al. (1979), Entin et al. (1997), Feldman and Bernstein (1977, 1978), Furnham (1986), Hendrick and Costantini (1970a, 1970b), Hendrick et al. (1973), Hogarth and Einhorn (1992), Hovland and Mandell (1957), Janis and Feierabend (1957), Jones et al. (1968), Koch et al. (1989), Lana (1961), Langer and Roth (1975), Levin (1976), Levin and Schmidt (1969, 1970), Levin et al. (1977), Lichtenstein and Srull (1987), Luchins (1957a, 1957b, 1958), Luchins and Luchins (1970, 1984, 1986), Lund (1925), Mayo and Crockett (1964), McAndrew (1981), Miller and Campbell (1959), Newtson and Rindner (1979), Parducci et al. (1968), Perrin et al. (2001), Peterson and DuCharme (1967), Pitz and Reinhold (1968), Pratz (1987), Riskey (1979), Roby (1967), Rosenbaum and Levin (1968), Rosnow et al. (1966), Schultz (1963), Serfaty et al. (1989), Shanteau (1970, 1972), Stewart (1965), Strange et al. (1978), Tesser (1968), Tetlock (1983), Tiwari (1978), Tolcott et al. (1989), Weiss and Anderson (1969), Whitesmith (2018), and Yates and Curley (1986).

5. The studies that comprised the intelligence samples are: Adelman et al. (1993), Cheikes et al. (2004), Entin et al. (1989, 1997), Perrin et al. (2001), Serfaty et al. (1989), Tolcott et al. (1989) and Whitesmith (2018). Studies were not included in the meta-analysis where specific analytical factors were unknown, or where insufficient information was provided to identify the proportion of participants who exhibited specific serial position effects. This means that some of the studies included in Hogarth and Einhorn's analysis are not included in mine.

6. Research conducted by Luchins (1957b) showed that the primacy effect exhibited by participants who were explicitly warned about the dangers of serial position effects before they began their analytical task was less severe than the primacy effect exhibited by the control group. In comparison, participants who were explicitly warned about the dangers of serial position effects midway through their analytical task exhibited recency. This research indicates that having

a conscious awareness of serial position effects may help reduce the degree of serial position effects. However, this control measure did not prevent serial position effects from occurring. Due to the paucity of available research that employed similar control measures, this factor was not reflected in the meta-analysis.

7. These studies are: Butt and Campbell (1989), Entin et al. (1989), Hovland and Mandell (1957), Jones et al. (1968), Lund (1925), Miller and Campbell (1959), Newtson and Rindner (1979), Pratz (1987) and Rosnow et al. (1966).

8. For the non-intelligence analysis sample, 67 per cent of participants were in EoS conditions, 23 per cent were in SbS-C conditions and 10 per cent were in SbS-I conditions. For the intelligence analysis sample, 76 per cent were in SbS-C conditions, 22 per cent were in EoS conditions and 2 per cent were in SbS-I conditions.

9. The measurements for each of these categories is not consistent with that used by Hogarth and Einhorn (1992), whereby a short series of information involved up to twelve pieces of information, and a long series of information involved seventeen or more pieces of information. The different categorisation method was based on the average volume of information that can be retained in the short-term memory. This approach was adopted due to the fact that in some studies into serial position effects participants relied on recall to process information, whereas in other studies participants did not have to rely on recall.

10. For the non-intelligence analysis sample, 51 per cent of participants were in long series of information conditions and 49 per cent were in short series of information conditions. For the intelligence analysis sample, 69 per cent were in short series of information conditions and 39 per cent were in long series of information conditions.

11. For the non-intelligence analysis sample, 71 per cent of participants were in estimation conditions, 26 per cent of participants were in evaluation conditions and 3 per cent were in estimation and evaluation conditions. For the intelligence analysis sample, 69 per cent of participants were in estimation conditions and 31 per cent were in evaluation conditions.

12. For the non-intelligence analysis sample, 84 per cent of participants were in simple task conditions and 64 per cent of participants in the intelligence analysis sample were in simple task conditions.

13. For the non-intelligence analysis sample, 92 per cent of participants were in inconsistent information conditions and 96 per cent of participants in the intelligence analysis sample were in inconsistent information conditions.

14. For the non-intelligence analysis sample, 52 per cent of participants were in reliance on recall conditions and 48 per cent of participants were in no reliance on recall conditions.

15. Only two studies in the meta-analysis have compared reliance on recall conditions against no reliance on recall conditions. Levin and Schmidt (1970) conducted an experiment into the formation of beliefs regarding personality traits. One research group was presented with trait adjectives one after another and had to rely on memory to process all information. A second research group was presented with all the trait adjectives at the same time and retained access to them during the analysis. Both groups exhibited recency. A similar methodology was used by Pitz and Reinhold (1968) involving three research groups. Like Levin and Schmidt (1970), all three research groups exhibited recency.

16. For the non-intelligence analysis sample, 79 per cent of participants were in time-pressured conditions. For the intelligence analysis sample, 20 per cent were in time-pressured conditions.

17. Jones et al. (1968) (experiments 1 and 2), and Pitz and Reinhold (1968).

18. Anderson and Hubert (1963) (experiment 1), Curley et al. (1988), Levin et al. (1977), Riskey (1979) (experiments 1 and 2), and Yates and Curley (1986).

19. Anderson and Hubert (1963) (experiment 2).

20. Tetlock (1983).

21. Feldman and Bernstein (1978), and Crano (1977).

22. For the non-intelligence analysis sample, 94 per cent of participants were in non-accountability conditions. For the intelligence analysis sample, 87 per cent of participants were in non-accountability conditions.

23. For the non-intelligence sample, 49 per cent of participants were in conditions that derived exclusively from testimony, 27 per cent of participants were in conditions that derived exclusively from empirical information, 10 per cent were in conditions that derived exclusively from a priori information, 9 per cent were in conditions that derived exclusively from authority information and 5 per cent were in conditions that derived from mixed information sources.

24. For the intelligence analysis sample, 64 per cent of participants were in conditions that derived exclusively from empirical information and 36 per cent were in conditions that drew from mixed information sources.

25. A high proportion was measured between 50 and 95 per cent. A low proportion was measured between 5 and 49 per cent.
26. Multinomial logistic regression is a model that predicts the probabilities of the different possible outcomes (serial position effects) of a categorically distributed dependent variable, given a set of independent variables.
27. Each analytical factor was tested separately against the same data samples. Each test utilised a null hypothesis following the form: X analytical condition had no impact on serial position effects.
28. Each analytical condition and its connected sub-variables have been taken as a family of statistical tests. As such, a separate Bonferroni compensation has been calculated for the serial position effect meta-analysis (which tested eleven analytical conditions), and the confirmation bias analysis (which tested thirteen analytical conditions). The Bonferroni compensations were calculated using $p = 0.05$ as the alpha (critical value for significance). The Bonferroni compensation is considered by some academics to be too conservative, running the risk of excluding genuinely statistically significant results. However, due to the low quality of the data on which the meta-analysis is based, a conservative standard for establishing statistical significance is appropriate.
29. Some participants were reported to have exhibited a mixture of both primacy and recency under repeated experimental conditions.
30. Out of the eighty-five studies, eighty (94 per cent) did not include this information.
31. The methodological approach for the meta-analysis has several advantages of the meta-analysis conducted by Hogarth and Einhorn (1992). Hogarth and Einhorn classified each study by the serial position effect that was exhibited by most participants. This methodology does not account for participants who exhibited opposing serial position effects, or the proportion of participants who exhibited no serial position effects. By attempting to capture the number of participants who exhibited each specific serial position effect and no serial position effects, my meta-analysis can indicate whether any analytical factors correspond with a higher or lower risk of serial position effects occurring. Second, by not taking the number of participants in each study into account, studies of varying participant numbers are given equal impact in Hogarth and Einhorn's method. This can easily lead to false analysis. If 80 per cent of studies were classified as primacy and 20 per cent of studies were classified as recency using Hogarth and Einhorn's method, this

gives the impression that primacy is the predominant serial position effect. However, if the total number of participants who exhibited recency was significantly higher than the number of participants who exhibited primacy, then this assumption would be invalid. Third, unlike Hogarth and Einhorn (1992), where studies included multiple experiments, experiments were all counted separately from one another. Further, where experiments included multiple research conditions each to be tested for a serial position effect, these were also recorded separately from one another. This allowed a more granular analysis of the identification of factors that could influence serial position effects. Finally, the meta-analysis also included the four experiments featured in Hogarth and Einhorn (1992). These experiments were not included in Hogarth and Einhorn's meta-analysis to develop the BAM.

32. The proportion of serial position effects was statistically significantly higher in the non-intelligence analysis sample ($p = < .001$). A two-sample t-test between proportions was performed to determine whether there was a significant difference between the proportion of participants exhibiting serial position effects and the proportion exhibiting no serial position effects. The t-statistic was significant at the .05 critical alpha level, $t(12963) = 7.851, p = < .001$.

33. The proportion that exhibited primacy was statistically significantly higher than the proportion that exhibited recency (37 per cent). A one-sample t-test between proportions was performed to determine whether there was a significant difference between the proportion of participants exhibiting primacy and the proportion exhibiting recency. The t-statistic was significant at the .05 critical alpha level, $t(12672) = 14.691, p = < .001$.

34. A one-sample t-test between proportions was performed to determine whether there was a significant difference between the proportion of participants exhibiting primacy and the proportion exhibiting recency. The t-statistic was not significant at the .05 critical alpha level, $t(291) = 0.753, p = .4518$.

35. The following factors were associated with a significantly lower proportion of participants exhibiting serial position effects in the non-intelligence analysis sample: SbS-C, short series of information, consistent information, no time pressure, no reliance on recall, no accountability, familiarity with task and recall test (participants informed pre-information processing). Of these factors, the following were suitably represented within the sample to examine for possible moderator variable effects: short series of information and no

reliance on recall. More than 50 per cent of the participants in the following conditions were also in both a short series of information condition and a no reliance on recall condition: step-by-step (continuous), consistent information, no time pressure and familiarity with task. However, consistent information only fell within the 50 to 55 per cent range of participants also being in a no reliance on recall condition. More than 50 per cent of the participants in the no accountability condition were in a short series of information condition; however, less than 50 per cent were also in a no reliance on recall condition. No conditions had more than 50 per cent of participants in a no reliance on recall condition and more than 50 per cent of participants in a short series of information condition. Less than 50 per cent of participants in the recall test (participants informed pre-information processing) condition were in both a short series of information condition and a no reliance on recall condition. Short series of information is a viable candidate for having a moderator variable effect. However, if short series of information did have a moderator effect, it either had no effect or minimal effect on the factors of not reliant on recall and recall test (participants informed pre-information processing). The following variables stand as possible factors that have a reducing effect on serial position effects, but the data do not provide as strong a case to reject the null hypotheses, as they could have been caused by the moderator variable effect of short series of information: SbS-C, consistent information, no time pressure, no accountability and familiarity with task.

36. Long series of information ($t(19169) = 14.379$, $p = < .001$), reliance on recall ($t(19070) = 10.425$, $p = < .001$), a priori information ($t(353) = 2.153$, $p = < .001$) and testimony information ($t(18168) = 19.080$, $p = < .001$). Long series of information is a viable candidate for having a moderator variable effect; however it is unlikely to have a moderator effect on the factors of reliant on recall, a priori information and testimony information. The following factors were associated with a significantly higher proportion of participants exhibiting serial position effects in the non-intelligence analysis sample: EoS, long series of information, estimation and evaluation tasks, inconsistent information, reliant on recall, time pressure, financial reward for correct analysis, performance as an indicator of IQ, recall test (participants informed mid-information processing), no familiarity with task, a priori information, testimony and mixed information. Of these factors, the following were suitably represented within the sample to examine for possible moderator variable

effects: long series of information and reliant on recall. More than 50 per cent of the participants in the following conditions were also in both long series of information and reliant on recall conditions: EoS, estimation and evaluation, inconsistent information, time pressure, financial reward, performance as an indicator of IQ, recall test (participants informed mid-information processing), no familiarity with task, a priori information and testimony information. However, a priori information and testimony information only fell within the 50 to 55 per cent range of participants also being in a long series of information condition. More than 50 per cent of the participants in the mixed information condition were in a long series of information condition; however, less than 50 per cent were also in a reliant on recall condition. Less than 50 per cent of participants in a reliant on recall condition were also in a long series of information condition. The following stand as possible factors that have an increasing effect on the likelihood of the occurrence of serial position effects: EoS, estimation and evaluation, inconsistent information, time pressure, financial reward for correct analysis, recall test (participants informed mid-information processing) and no familiarity with task. However, the relationship between these factors and an increased proportion of participants exhibiting serial position effects could have been the result of a moderator variable effect from the factor of long series of information.

37. Empirical information ($t(447) = 3.327$, $p = .0010$) and complex tasks ($t(395) = 4.035$, $p = < .001$). Of these factors, the following were suitably represented within the sample to examine for possible moderator variable effects: empirical information and complex tasks. More than 50 per cent of participants in familiar with task conditions were also in empirical conditions. Less than 50 per cent of participants in complex task conditions were also in empirical conditions. Less than 50 per cent of participants in empirical tasks, and in familiar with task conditions were also in complex task conditions. There was no indication that either empirical tasks or complex task conditions had moderator variable effects.

38. Long series of information ($t(380) = 3.454$, $p = .0006$), evaluation tasks ($t(380) = 3.454$, $p = .0006$), time pressure ($t(347) = 4.683$, $p = < .001$), no familiarity with task ($t(326) = 3.761$, $p = .0002$) and mixed information ($t(379) = 3.411$, $p = .0007$). Of these, the following factors were suitably represented within the sample to examine for possible moderator variable effects: long series of information, complex tasks, evaluation tasks and mixed information. More than

50 per cent of participants in mixed information conditions and evaluation conditions were also in a long information condition. Less than 50 per cent of participants in a complex task condition or a time-pressured condition were also in a long series of information condition. More than 50 per cent of participants in a long series of information, a no familiarity with task, or a mixed information condition were also in a complex task condition; however this range was only 50 to 55.56 per cent. More than 50 per cent of participants in long series of information conditions and in mixed information conditions were also in evaluation conditions. Less than 50 per cent of participants in complex task conditions, time-pressured conditions and no familiarity with task conditions were also in evaluation conditions. More than 50 per cent of participants in a long series of information conditions were also in a mixed information condition. Less than 50 per cent of participants in a complex, time-pressured or a no familiarity with task condition were also in a mixed information condition. The meta-analysis indicates that there is no strong indication that long series of information, evaluation tasks, or mixed information had moderator variable effects. As such, all five of the factors that were associated with an increased proportion of serial position effects in the intelligence analysis sample stand as viable factors for having an effect on serial position effects, increasing the likelihood of occurrence.

39. Of these factors, the following were suitably represented within the sample to examine for possible moderator variable effects: long series of information and reliant on recall. More than 50 per cent of each of the following factors were in both a long series of information condition and a reliant on recall condition: end-of-series, step-by-step (interval), simple, time pressure, financial reward, performance made public, performance as an indicator of IQ, familiarity with task not applicable, a priori information, empirical information and testimony information. More than 50 per cent of participants in each of the following factors were in a long series of information condition but had less than 50 per cent in a reliant on recall condition: estimation and evaluation, and authority information. More than 50 per cent of participants in each of the following factors were in a reliant on recall condition but had less than 50 per cent in a long series of information condition: estimation, inconsistent information and non-accountability. The factor of no time pressure had less than 50 per cent of participants in both a long series of information condition and a reliant on recall condition.

40. Of these factors, the following were suitably represented within the sample to examine for possible moderator variable effects: short series of information and not reliant on recall. More than 50 per cent of each of the following factors were in both a short series of information condition and a not reliant on recall condition: step-by-step (continuous), complex, consistent information and familiarity with task. There were no conditions in which more than 50 per cent of participants were in a short series of information condition but had less than 50 per cent in a not reliant on recall condition. More than 50 per cent of participants in each of the following factors were in a not reliant on recall condition but had less than 50 per cent in a short series of information condition: evaluation and mixed information. The following factors had less than 50 per cent of participants in both a short series of information condition and a not reliant on recall condition: no familiarity with task and recall test (participants informed mid-information processing).

41. For the non-intelligence analysis sample, the odds of primacy occurring over recency in a long series of information condition were 2.68 (95 per cent CI, .248 to .290) times that of a short series of information condition, a statistically significant effect, $Wald = 1045.043$, $p = < .001$. For the intelligence analysis sample, the odds of primacy occurring over recency in a long series of information condition were 42.549 (95 per cent CI, 17.467 to 103.648) times that of a short series of information condition, a statistically significant effect, $Wald = 68.169$, $p = < .001$.

42. The odds of recency occurring over primacy in a short series of information condition were 3.729 (95 per cent CI, 3.443 to 4.039) times that of a long series of information condition, a statistically significant effect, $Wald = 1045.043$, $p = < .001$.

43. For the non-intelligence sample, bracketing is more likely to occur than no serial position effects in a SbS(C) condition compared with an EoS condition. The odds of bracketing occurring over no serial position effects in a SbS(C) condition were 3.845 (95 per cent CI, 2.540 to 5.850) times that of an EoS condition, a statistically significant effect, $Wald = 40.175$, $p = < .001$. Bracketing is more likely to occur than no serial position effects in an evaluation task compared with an estimation task. The odds of bracketing occurring over no serial position effects in an evaluation condition were 1.924 (95 per cent CI, 1.314 to 2.817) times that of an estimation condition, a statistically significant effect, $Wald = 11.328$, $p = .001$. Bracketing is more likely to occur over no serial position effects in a complex task compared

with a simple task. The odds of bracketing occurring over no serial position effects in a complex task condition were .325 (95 per cent CI, .218 to .484) times that of a simple task condition, a statistically significant effect, $Wald = 30.518, p = < .001$. Bracketing is more likely to occur over no serial position effects in a task that is reliant on recall compared with a task that is not reliant on recall. The odds of bracketing occurring over no serial position effects in a reliance on recall condition were 2.890 (95 per cent CI, 1.980 to 4.219) times that of a non-reliance on recall condition, a statistically significant effect, $Wald = 30.230, p = < .001$. Bracketing is more likely to occur over no serial position effects in recall test (participants informed pre-information processing) conditions compared with non-accountability conditions. The odds of bracketing occurring over no serial position effects in recall test (participants informed pre-information processing) conditions were 2.979 (95 per cent CI, 1.929 to 4.599) times that of non-accountability conditions, a statistically significant effect, $Wald = 24.252, p = < .000$. Bracketing is more likely to occur over no serial position effects in a testimony information condition compared with a mixed information condition. The odds of bracketing occurring over no serial position effects in testimony information conditions were 8086207.143 (95 per cent CI, 5244251.915 to 12468269.45) times that of mixed information conditions, a statistically significant effect, $Wald = 5182.864, p = < .001$.

44. This is similar to a model proposed by Carlson and Dulany in 1988. Carlson and Dulany's model assumes that subjects 'revise belief on the basis of a cascaded reasoning process that combines beliefs about three premises – the association of a clue and a possible cause, and forward and backward implications of the clue – to revise belief in a causal hypothesis' Carlson and Dulany (1988).

45. A one-sample t-test between proportions was performed to determine whether there was a significant difference between the proportion of participants exhibiting serial position effects and the proportion exhibiting no serial position effects. The t-statistic was significant at the .05 critical alpha level, $t(471) = 27.080, p = < .001$.

46. A one-sample t-test between proportions was performed to determine whether there was a significant difference between the proportion of participants in these experimental conditions exhibiting primacy and the proportion exhibiting recency. The t-statistic was significant at the .05 critical alpha level, $t(2621) = 4.286, p = < .001$.

47. A one-sample t-test between proportions was performed to determine whether there was a significant difference between the proportion of

participants in these experimental conditions exhibiting primacy and the proportion exhibiting recency. The t-statistic was significant at the .05 critical alpha level, $t(3536) = 8.976, p = < .001$.

48. A one-sample t-test between proportions was performed to determine whether there was a significant difference between the proportion of participants in these experimental conditions exhibiting primacy and the proportion exhibiting recency. The t-statistic was significant at the .05 critical alpha level, $t(3058) = 16.154, p = < .001$.

49. A one-sample t-test between proportions was performed to determine whether there was a significant difference between the proportion of participants in these experimental conditions exhibiting primacy and the proportion exhibiting recency. The t-statistic was significant at the .05 critical alpha level, $t(477) = 15.566, p = < .001$.

50. A one-sample t-test between proportions was performed to determine whether there was a significant difference between the proportion of participants exhibiting recency in a temporal relevance scenario in the intelligence sample and the proportion exhibiting recency that were not in a temporal relevance scenario. The t-statistic was not significant at the .05 critical alpha level, $t(290) = 1.947, p = .0525$.

5 Predicting Confirmation Bias

Confirmation bias is the tendency to search for evidence that supports a preconceived or favoured theory, to interpret information to confirm a preconceived or favoured theory, or to ignore or unfairly discredit information that would disprove a preconceived or favoured theory. The term 'confirmation bias' has historically been used to describe other behaviours such as enumerative induction (Wason 1960); illusory correlation (Chapman and Chapman 1967); the inability to describe disconfirming evidence (Kuhn et al. 1988); and the inability to adequately consider alternative hypotheses (Koslowski and Maqueda 1993). Confirmation bias in its contemporary understanding has also been referred to by different names in the social sciences. These include pseudo-diagnosticity (Evans et al. 2002); primes (Galinsky and Moskowitz 2000); trait consistency bias (Hayden and Mischel 1976); and type-two error (Rosenhan 1973). 'Pseudo-diagnosticity' refers to the phenomenon whereby participants only consider evidence that favours a focal hypothesis as being diagnostic towards the focal hypothesis, and do not consider the diagnostic value that the evidence has for alternative hypotheses (Koslowski and Maqueda 1993).[1] The term 'type-two error' specifically refers to confirmation bias in the context of medical diagnosis, where medical physicians are more inclined to diagnose a healthy person as sick than a sick person as healthy.[2]

Confirmation bias has been the subject of less research than serial position effects. The meta-analysis for confirmation bias comprised a total of twenty studies and 1,940 participants.[3] This was divided into a non-intelligence analysis sample, which included seventeen studies and 1,816 participants,[4] and an intelligence analysis sample which included three studies and eighty-four participants.[5] Given the multiple instances of conflation of confirmation bias with a preference towards enumerative induction, only a portion of the available research on hypothesis testing strategies was suitable for inclusion in the meta-analysis. Studies included were those that looked at information selection in cases where participants had been induced to have a focal hypothesis (Wason 1960; Koslowski and Maqueda 1993; Evans et al. 2002; Mynatt et al. 1977; Doherty et al. 1996; Klayman and Ha 1989). The tendency to select information that confirms a focal hypothesis in this instance is taken to be a form of confirmation bias. Some studies examining hypothesis testing strategies also included alternative research conditions where participants were primed to consider multiple hypotheses, allowing comparison of the impact that the experimental factor of hypothesis testing priming may have on confirmation bias to be included in the meta-analysis. However, there is some controversy about whether hypothesis testing strategies can always effectively identify confirmation bias from a positive hypothesis testing strategy (Koslowski and Maqueda 1993). As such, studies that only required participants to develop an independent testing strategy by identifying what evidence they sought to complete the analysis but that did not require the participants to process this information were not included in the meta-analysis.[6] This is because without information as to how the participants processed evidence in an analytical task, it could not be determined whether the results are reflective of confirmation bias or enumerative induction.[7]

The meta-analysis into confirmation bias faces three limitations. The first of these concerns data classification. Four of the studies included in the meta-analysis analysed the results in terms of mean responses of participants, without providing details of the number of participants who exhibited behaviour consistent with confirmation bias (Moskowitz and Roman 1992; Foster et al. 1976; Lord et al. 1984 (experiment 1) and Ross et al. 1975). However, the details of these studies were sufficient to infer the approximate proportion of participants who exhibited confirmation bias. A similar classification system to that used in the serial position effects meta-analysis was applied to these studies. For studies that presented results as a mean, the total number of participants was assigned to an overall majority result reported for the study. For studies where a minority confirmation bias effect was observed, 25 per cent of participants were coded as having exhibited confirmation bias. Where results were described as mixed, but no details on proportions provided, the number of participants were divided equally between those who exhibited confirmation bias and those who did not. The proportion of studies that provided specific details of the proportion of participants who exhibited behaviour consistent with confirmation bias was larger for confirmation bias than for serial position effects. This means that the meta-analysis into confirmation bias, whilst based on a substantially smaller sample of participants, has greater statistical accuracy than the serial position effects meta-analysis.

The second limitation is the comparative size of the intelligence analysis sample compared with the non-intelligence analysis sample. Only three studies were identified that conducted research into realistic (ecologically valid) intelligence analysis scenarios. As with research into serial position effects, most of these experiments used military intelligence scenarios informed by technical information. As such, currently available research into confirmation bias in intelligence analysis is not representative of all types of intelligence analysis. Further, the limited research into confirmation bias in intelligence analysis scenarios severely limited the extent to which the intelligence analysis sample could be compared with the non-intelligence analysis scenario for individual research factors.[8]

The third limitation is that it can be difficult to distinguish between confirmation bias and the serial position effect of primacy. It is possible to exhibit both in an analytical task, and there may be interaction effects between the two biases. However, unless sufficient methods are used to measure each phenomenon it can be difficult to distinguish whether one or the other, or both, were present. Two studies that were used in the meta-analysis for serial position effects were also used in the confirmation bias meta-analysis because the behaviour of some participants was consistent with both primacy and confirmation bias (Whitesmith 2018; Cheikes et al. 2004). However only the methodology of one of these studies (Whitesmith 2018) was sufficient to clearly identify primacy from confirmation bias.[9] Given these limitations, the following meta-analysis cannot be taken as an accurate account of how different factors affect confirmation bias, or of the potential differences in this impact between intelligence analysis and non-intelligence analysis. However, it can arguably provide a strong indication as to whether such differences are likely to exist and, if they do exist, where such differences lie.

The meta-analysis examining confirmation bias examined thirteen specific experimental conditions. Eleven of these conditions were the same conditions examined in the meta-analysis used to examine serial position effects. However, two additional conditions were included to reflect specific control factors used in the research designs of multiple experiments into confirmation bias. These conditions are the diagnostic weighting of initial information, and the information selection instructions given to participants before conducting the analytical task. Details of these conditions are given below. In addition, a wider range of hypothesis testing instructions has been included in confirmation bias research than in research into serial position effects.

Two-sample t-tests were used to identify analytical factors that were associated with a statistically significantly higher or lower proportion of participants who exhibited confirmation bias compared with the mean of the specific sample.[10] The Bonferroni correction for the confirmation bias meta-analysis sets the benchmark for statistical significance at $p = < .003$.

Additional Experimental Conditions

Diagnostic Weighting of Initial Information

Several studies examined the impact of the diagnostic weighting of information processed at the beginning of an analytical task on confirmation bias and hypothesis testing strategies (Moskowitz and Roman 1992; Foster et al. 1976; Doherty et al. 1979; Higgins et al. 1977; Ross et al. 1975). These studies applied two experimental conditions: where the initially received information was diagnostically weighted towards a specific hypothesis, and where the information initially processed was diagnostically neutral between hypotheses. Studies that used non-intelligence analysis scenarios were split evenly between those in which the initial information received by participants was diagnostically weighted and those where the initial information was diagnostically neutral.[11] In comparison, all studies using an intelligence analysis scenario were derived from diagnostically neutral initial information conditions.

Information Selection Instructions

Some studies examined the impact of information selection instructions given to participants before beginning an analytical task (Evans et al. 2002; Mynatt et al. 1977; Doherty et al. 1996). Evans et al. (2002) examined the impact of instructing participants to select information that has the best diagnostic value in discriminating between two competing hypotheses. Other studies examined the impact of making explicit reference to a single hypothesis compared with multiple hypotheses prior to an analytical task (Mynatt et al. 1977; Doherty et al. 1996). All studies that applied experimental manipulations for information selection examined the ability of participants to identify information with diagnostic value. These experimental manipulations fall into three sub-categories. A single hypothesis manipulation refers to experimental conditions where explicit reference was made to a single hypothesis prior to participants beginning an analytical task. A multiple hypothesis manipulation refers to experimental conditions where explicit reference was made to more than one hypothesis prior to participants beginning an analytical task. No manipulation refers to experimental conditions where no information selection instructions were given to participants. Most studies in both the intelligence analysis and non-intelligence analysis samples did not employ information selection instruction manipulations.[12]

Hypothesis Testing Instructions

A handful of studies applied explicit hypothesis testing instructions to examine their impact on confirmation bias. A wider range of different hypothesis testing instructions were provided in the confirmation bias meta-analysis data than the serial position effects data. In one study, participants were instructed to be as objective as possible in their analysis (Lord et al. 1984). Ross et al. (1975) informed participants about confirmation bias and instructed them to avoid being subject to it. Some participants were instructed to seek to confirm their focal hypotheses whereas other participants were explicitly instructed to seek to disconfirm hypotheses (Mynatt et al. 1977). Lord et al. (1984) instructed participants to consider more than one hypothesis in their analysis. Other participants were instructed to test hypotheses by examining available information (Mynatt et al. 1977; Koslowski and Maqueda 1993). In the intelligence analysis sample, two studies applied a version of the ACH method (disconfirm hypotheses + consider multiple hypotheses).[13] Most studies in both the intelligence analysis sample and the non-intelligence analysis sample had no hypothesis testing instructions.[14] As such, hypothesis testing instruction strategies are significantly under-represented in available research.

Results and Discussion

The meta-analysis highlighted that both intelligence analysis and non-intelligence analysis are equally susceptible to confirmation bias.[15] For non-intelligence analysis, the most important factors that were likely to influence confirmation bias were the diagnostic weighting of initial information, type of information, hypothesis testing instructions, consistency of information and accountability.

The most viable conditions for having a reducing impact on the likelihood of occurrence of behaviour consistent with confirmation bias in the non-intelligence sample were consistent information and instructions to consider more than one hypothesis.[16] In comparison, the requirement to justify analysis (where participants were informed prior to information processing) is a possible candidate for having a reducing effect on the likelihood of occurrence of behaviour consistent with confirmation bias in intelligence analysis.[17]

The strongest conditions for being viable candidates for having an increasing effect on the likelihood of occurrence of behaviour consistent with confirmation bias in the non-intelligence sample were diagnostically weighted initial information and mixed information conditions.[18] The following factors stand as viable candidates for having an amplifying effect on the likelihood of occurrence of behaviour consistent with confirmation bias in intelligence analysis: simple tasks, time pressure, familiarity with task, non-accountability and multiple hypotheses manipulation in information selection instructions.[19]

There were no similarities between the intelligence analysis and non-intelligence analysis samples in terms of the analytical conditions that coincided with reduced or increased proportions of participants exhibiting confirmation bias. Whilst this indicates that there may be multiple viable factors that affect intelligence analysis differently from non-intelligence analysis, these results could be due to individual differences, the small sample size, or both. The intelligence analysis sample was very small: eighty-four participants. Individual differences are highly likely to have a disproportionate impact on small sample sizes. Given this consideration, and the fact that there was no statistical significance between the non-intelligence analysis and intelligence analysis samples in terms of the proportion of participants who exhibited confirmation bias, there is currently no compelling evidence of a difference between the intelligence analysis and non-intelligence analysis samples.

The results of the meta-analysis have implications for accountability manipulations and the use of ACH in attempting to mitigate the effect of confirmation bias in intelligence analysis. The results indicate that for non-intelligence analysis, most forms of accountability tested in social science research increase the risk of confirmation bias, and that no currently tested form of accountability coincides with a statistically significantly reduced risk of confirmation bias. For intelligence analysis, the risk of confirmation bias may be mitigated by requiring analysts to justify their assessments and making them aware of this before they begin an analytical task. For the intelligence analysis sample, 50 per cent of participants who were instructed to disconfirm hypotheses + consider multiple hypotheses (the ACH method) exhibited behaviour consistent with confirmation bias, compared with 71.15 per cent of participants who exhibited confirmation bias in no hypothesis testing instruction conditions. Whilst the application of ACH was associated with a lower proportion of participants exhibiting behaviour consistent with confirmation bias compared with the overall intelligence analysis sample, this difference was not of statistical significance ($p = .0545$). Further, the differences between the likelihood of confirmation bias occurring over no confirmation bias in disconfirm + consider multiple hypotheses (ACH) conditions compared with conditions in which participants were not given hypothesis testing instructions also failed to reach statistical significance. You are more likely to exhibit confirmation bias than no confirmation bias in a no hypothesis testing instructions condition compared with a disconfirm hypotheses + consider multiple hypotheses condition (ACH). However, the odds of confirmation bias occurring over no confirmation bias in a disconfirm hypotheses + consider multiple hypotheses condition are .405 (95 per cent CI, .162 to 1.014) times that of a no hypothesis testing instructions condition, a non-statistically significant effect, *Wald* $= 3.727$, $p = .054$. These results indicate that the application of the ACH method has no significant effect on confirmation bias in intelligence analysis tasks.

*   *   *

Whilst the results of the meta-analysis into confirmation bias suggest that there may be genuine areas of difference between the impact of analytical conditions on confirmation bias in intelligence analysis compared with non-intelligence analysis, the greater size and quality of data of the non-intelligence sample lends greater weight to the results taken from this sample over that of the intelligence analysis sample. As such, tentative conclusions of the confirmation bias meta-analysis will be drawn by looking at the strongest viable candidates in the non-intelligence analysis sample for analytical conditions that are likely to affect confirmation bias. The results indicate that the risk of confirmation bias may be increased by the analytical conditions of diagnostically weighted initial information and mixed information conditions. The results also indicate that the risk of confirmation bias may be decreased by the analytical conditions of consistent information, instructions to consider more than one hypothesis and no information selection manipulations.

An Examination of Previous Confirmation Bias Prediction Models

Three theories have been put forward as explanations of cognitive bias: the suspended focal hypothesis theory; the inability to identify diagnostic value of information theory; and the inadequate consideration of alternative hypotheses theory.

Suspended Focal Hypothesis Theory

Karmiloff-Smith and Inhelder (1974–5) argued that confirmation bias was the result of people clinging to an initial theory as a temporary step in a problem-solving process in which an initially formed focal hypothesis is held in temporary suspension while people process contradicting information. According to the suspended focal hypothesis theory, confirmation bias would occur because: (1) participants develop a hypothesis to explain initially processed information; (2) this hypothesis becomes the focal hypothesis; and (3) there is a time delay in revising the focal hypothesis during information processing while participants process disconfirming information. The theory implies that confirmation bias is only a temporary phenomenon in information processing and that its effect can be neutralised given sufficient time. In this capacity, confirmation bias is only strictly a cognitive bias if insufficient time is available when processing information. The suspended focal hypothesis theory has partial support from available research. Koslowski and Maqueda (1993) found that participants frequently treated focal hypotheses as working hypotheses to be refined in the light of further information. The suspended focal hypothesis theory cannot be directly tested by the meta-analysis, as few studies were designed to record the changes in degree of belief during information processing. However, the theory can be validly tested against the results of the meta-analysis in terms of the factor of consistency of information. The internally consistent information condition was associated with a lower proportion of participants exhibiting behaviour consistent with confirmation bias. The suspended focal hypothesis theory could be interpreted as being consistent with these results. If an initial hypothesis is developed to explain initially received information, then there will be less of a time delay in revising the hypothesis where subsequent information is consistent with the initial information, as there is no disconfirming information to process. As such, the suspended focal hypothesis theory would predict a lower proportion of confirmation bias in consistent information conditions. Diagnostically weighted initial information was associated with a higher proportion of participants exhibiting behaviour consistent with confirmation bias in both the non-intelligence analysis and intelligence analysis samples. This association supports the argument of a tendency to form of a focal hypothesis in the initial stages of analysis, implied by the suspended focal hypothesis theory. This early reinforcement of a focal hypothesis could lead to a decrease in focus given to considering alternative hypotheses. However, this result does not bear direct relevance to the suspended focal hypothesis theory as the factor only concerns the initial stages of information processing, rather than the full process.

The results concerning the processing of mixed information can also be interpreted as being consistent with the suspended focal hypothesis theory. Particular types of information could be interpreted as having a comparative epistemological value compared with others. For example, empirical information and a priori information could be intuitively interpreted as having higher epistemological value than testimony. Processing information that draws exclusively from one epistemological type of information may involve less cognitive strain, as less time or effort is required to compare epistemological value across multiple information types. However, processing information that includes multiple epistemological types may incur greater cognitive strain in weighting the epistemological value of certain types of information against others, and synthesising this with diagnostic value. As such, processing mixed information may contribute to the length of time it takes to revise an initially formed focal hypothesis against disconfirming information.

Inability to Identify Diagnostic Value of Information Theory

A second explanation of confirmation bias is that participants are not often able to accurately perceive or identify the diagnostic value of information (Koslowski and Maqueda 1993; Kuhn et al. 1988). This theory can be tested by available research. Two studies recorded participants' judgements of the diagnostic value that a series of information had to a set of competing hypotheses (Cheikes et al. 2004; Whitesmith 2018). In both these studies there was broad agreement between participants on the diagnostic value of information. However, whilst confirmation bias was exhibited by a large proportion of participants in the study by Cheikes et al. (2004), only a small proportion of participants in the study by Whitesmith (2018) exhibited behaviour consistent with confirmation bias. This does not indicate an association between judgements of diagnostic value and confirmation bias. If there was broad agreement over diagnostic value judgements in both studies, you would expect to see comparable proportions of participants exhibiting behaviour consistent with confirmation bias. As such, these studies do not provide strong support for a causal link between confirmation bias and the inability to identify diagnostic value.

The theory can also be tested against the confirmation bias meta-analysis. The inability to identify the diagnostic value of information would arguably predict no significant differences in the proportions of participants exhibiting behaviour consistent with confirmation bias between those in diagnostically weighted initial information conditions and those in diagnostically neutral initial information conditions. However, in the non-intelligence analysis sample, diagnostically weighted initial information was associated with a statistically significantly higher proportion of participants exhibiting behaviour consistent with confirmation bias, and diagnostically neutral initial information was associated with a statistically significantly lower proportion of participants exhibiting behaviour consistent with confirmation bias. As such, the inability to identify diagnostic value of information theory has little support from available research.

Inadequate Consideration of Alternative Hypotheses Theory

A third explanation for confirmation bias is that people do not adequately consider alternative hypotheses (Kuhn et al. 1988; Mynatt et al. 1977). This theory implies a disproportionate focus on a focal hypothesis. This theory can be supported by the meta-analysis results. The meta-analysis found that the condition where participants were instructed to consider more than one hypothesis was associated with a reduced likelihood of occurrence of confirmation bias. If participants make conscious effort to process information against more than one hypothesis, it follows that this may reduce the focus on a focal hypothesis, therefore reducing the risk of confirmation bias.

This theory also has support from research into hypotheses testing. Doherty and Hunter (2003) found that a focal hypothesis is likely to be judged in comparison to a small number of alternative hypotheses. As most current research into confirmation bias has not captured the focal hypotheses, changes in focal hypotheses of participants and the processing of information against alternative hypotheses, this theory cannot be directly tested by the meta-analysis. Like the suspended focal hypothesis theory, the results for diagnostic weighting of evidence support the implication of a tendency to form of a focal hypothesis in the initial stages of analysis. This early reinforcement of a focal hypothesis could lead to a decrease in time given to consideration of alternative hypotheses or reduce the influence of information that disconfirms or is inconsistent with the focal hypothesis compared with information that lends diagnostic support. However, the factor only concerns the initial stages of information processing rather than the full process, so it cannot provide a full test of the inability to adequately consider alternative hypotheses theory.

* * *

The suspended focal hypothesis theory, the inability to adequately consider alternative hypotheses theory and the inability to identify the diagnostic value of information theory are not mutually exclusive. All theories imply two shared characteristics that explain confirmation bias: (1) a focal hypothesis is formed in the initial stages of information processing; and (2) the focal hypothesis is maintained throughout the analytical task. However, the theories differ as to what causes the focal hypothesis to be maintained: a time delay in revising the focal hypothesis when processing information that does not diagnostically support the focal hypothesis;

an inability to perceive the diagnostic value that information provides to a focal hypothesis; and an ability to adequately consider alternative hypotheses. Of these, the theories of a time delay in hypothesis revision and the inability to adequately consider alternative hypotheses are partially supported by available research.

The shared premise of both these theories – that a focal hypothesis is formed in the initial stages of information processing – is consistent with the results of the meta-analysis concerning the possible impact of no information selection manipulations and diagnostically weighted initial information conditions. The condition where no explicit reference is made to participants of possible hypotheses prior to information processing was associated with a reduced risk of behaviour consistent with confirmation bias. It could be argued that making explicit references to possible hypotheses prior to information processing increases the likelihood of a focal hypothesis being formed in the initial stages of information processing, as it acts as a type of priming. The condition of not priming participants with possible answers to an analytical task prior to information processing has a converse effect of reducing the likelihood of participants forming a focal hypothesis in the initial stages of information. Likewise, diagnostic weighting of initial information was associated with an increased risk of behaviour consistent with confirmation bias. It could be argued that initial information being diagnostically weighted towards one hypothesis or set of hypotheses rather than others acts as a priming mechanism, increasing the likelihood that a focal hypothesis is developed in the initial stages of information processing.

The Impact of Analytical Conditions on Confirmation Bias

As with the results of the meta-analysis into serial position effects outlined, multiple conclusions can be tentatively drawn regarding confirmation bias. The first is that, similarly to serial position effects, confirmation bias is highly likely to occur during belief formation in an analytical task. Second is that, again, similarly to serial position effects, there is no compelling indication from currently available research that confirmation bias has a different impact, and therefore poses different risks, for intelligence analysis tasks compared with non-intelligence analysis tasks. However, there are considerable gaps in available research into the effect of confirmation bias in intelligence analysis scenarios under different analytical conditions, and it remains possible that there are legitimate differences in the way that confirmation bias affects intelligence analysis compared with non-intelligence analysis. This meta-analysis has helped to indicate where such differences may lie.

The third conclusion is that the results provide an indication of what conditions in which analysis is undertaken may contribute to a reduced risk of confirmation bias occurring. Tasks that involve internally consistent information, where individuals were requested to consider multiple hypotheses, and where explicit mention was made to multiple possible hypotheses prior to information processing, are associated with a reduced risk of confirmation bias. In comparison, tasks that involve diagnostically weighted initial information and tasks that derive from mixed types of information are associated with an increased risk of confirmation bias.

The fourth conclusion concerns possible underlying causes or factors that influence confirmation bias. The meta-analysis results provide support for, but cannot diagnostically differentiate between, the suspended focal hypothesis theory and the inability to adequately consider alternative hypotheses theory. However, these two theories are not mutually exclusive, and can theoretically be combined with the meta-analysis results to form a single theory to account for confirmation bias. I argue that, similarly to serial position effects, there is a subconscious tendency to form a focal hypothesis as early as possible in an analytical task. The following analytical conditions have an impact on the risk of confirmation bias: internal consistency of the information processed, the diagnostic weighting of information, the type of information processed, and priming effects through hypothesis testing instructions and information selection manipulations that are made prior to information processing. These factors directly influence the point at which a focal hypothesis is formed in the processing of information, leading it to be formed in initial stages of information processing as opposed to when all information available has been processed, and impede the hypothesis from being modified appropriately during information processing. These factors impact the risk of confirmation bias by: (1) priming the development of a focal hypothesis in the initial stages of information processing; and (2) increasing the cognitive effort required for the adequate consideration of information against alternative hypotheses, processing information of different epistemological types, or processing inconsistent information. The factor of processing information from mixed information types increases cognitive strain as different types of information have different degrees of epistemic quality. Not only will the degree of epistemic justification be more complicated to identify for information of mixed types but it will also need to be taken into account when individual pieces of information are compared against others to determine the cumulative degree of epistemic justification for both the focal and alternative hypotheses.

Intelligence, Bias and Belief Acquisition: An Empirical Perspective

In Part 2 of this book, I have sought to answer three questions. The first is: does ACH have a mitigating impact against confirmation bias or serial position effects in intelligence analysis? An experimental study was conducted into the efficacy of ACH in mitigating confirmation bias and serial position effects in an epistemologically valid intelligence scenario. The results indicate that ACH had no mitigating impact in significantly reducing the likelihood of occurrence of either confirmation bias or serial position effects. Further, the results indicate that ACH has no mitigating impact on confirmation bias impacting the ACH process itself. The results of the study are consistent with previous research into the efficacy of ACH in mitigating cognitive bias (Cheikes et al. 2004).

In addition to adding to the empirical validation for the efficacy of ACH in mitigating cognitive bias, the experimental study provided some support for the theoretical argument that belief acquisition in intelligence may face higher epistemic complexity than belief acquisition in non-intelligence contexts. The experiment demonstrated that belief acquisition and judgements of the credibility of information are influenced by factors that have no relevance in determining the epistemic justification of intelligence information, and that this risk is higher when processing information derived from human sources. The influence of non-relevant factors could be the result of greater difficulty in establishing epistemic justification. However, it does not follow from this that intelligence necessarily faces a higher degree of epistemic complexity than non-intelligence contexts. The higher degree of epistemic complexity is specifically linked to belief acquisition that involves processing information from mixed sources, or information that is derived in part or in total from human sources. However, it is reasonable to argue that there is likely to be an association between the proportion of information derived from human sources, and the degree of epistemic complexity encountered in belief acquisition. It is also reasonable to argue that intelligence will routinely involve information derived from human sources, and therefore carries a routine risk of involving higher epistemic complexity.

The second question I sought to answer is: what analytical conditions are associated with an increased or reduced risk of confirmation bias and serial position effects? Meta-analyses were conducted into experimental research on serial position effects and confirmation bias. These meta-analyses identified statistically significant associations between analytical conditions and higher or lower rates of each bias. Based on the results of the meta-analyses, I have proposed a new theoretical model to predict serial position effects and confirmation bias. I argue that serial position effects are the result of the impact of specific analytical conditions on an underlying cognitive process that produces a force towards forming a focal hypothesis as early as possible in an analytical task. The analytical conditions that have a causal impact on serial position effects are those that have a direct impact on the reliance on long-term memory to process information. The epistemic complexity of processing information derived from human sources (testimony) exacerbates the requirement on long-term memory to process information. However, information types can have different ways of exacerbating this risk that do not relate to epistemic complexity. Belief acquisition that involves mathematical calculations drawn from a priori information also increases the reliance on long-term memory for information processing.

I argue that confirmation bias is also caused by an underlying cognitive process that results in a tendency to form a focal hypothesis as early as possible in an analytical task. Further, the analytical conditions that have an impact on the risk of confirmation bias are those that directly influence the point at which a focal hypothesis is formed in the processing of information, leading it to be formed in the initial stages of information processing as opposed to when all information available has been processed, and prevent the hypothesis from being modified appropriately.

These models are theoretically linked. Both involve the formation of a focal hypothesis in the initial stages of information processing. The two biases stem from the same origin or underlying cognitive process, which results in a force towards the formation of an initial focal hypothesis. However, I argue that each form of bias is influenced by different analytical conditions under which belief acquisition occurs. The implications of this theory, if true, are that it is unlikely that there is a single approach or method by which the risk of all cognitive biases can be mitigated: different biases will require different approaches. However, the meta-analysis provides an indication that the risks of individual cognitive biases can be managed by manipulating the analytical conditions under which beliefs are acquired.

Both the experimental results and the meta-analysis provide support to the argument that ACH has no mitigating impact on confirmation bias or serial position effects. However, this is specifically within the context of using diagnostic value and credibility of information as information ranking systems. The experimental results also show that viable alternative approaches could be developed based on analytical conditions that correspond with a reduced likelihood of occurrence.

Notes

1. Pseudo-diagnosticity was first reported by Doherty et al. (1979) and has been replicated in several studies, including Fischoff and Beyth-Marom (1983), Mynatt et al. (1993), Doherty et al. (1996), and Covey and Lovie (1998).

2. Rosenhan (1973) argues that type-two error is due to the greater risk of misdiagnosing illness than health.
3. Six additional relevant studies for which the data could not be extracted or inferred for the meta-analysis include Galinsky and Moskowitz (2000), Evans and Lynch (1973), Hayden and Mischel (1976), Darley and Gross (1983), Langer and Abelson (1974), and Beattie and Baron (1988).
4. Carlson and Russo (2001), Wason (1960), Koslowski and Maqueda (1993), Evans et al. (2002), Mynatt et al. (1977), Doherty et al. (1996), Klayman and Ha (1989), Lord et al. (1980), Tetlock (1985), Moskowitz and Roman (1992), Bruner and Potter (1964), Foster et al. (1976), Rosenhan (1973), Doherty et al. (1979), Higgins et al. (1977), Lord et al. (1984) and Ross et al. (1975). The results of Carlson and Russo (2001) were included in both the serial position effects meta-analysis and the confirmation bias meta-analysis as they were consistent with both cognitive biases.
5. Cheikes et al. (2004), Tolcott et al. (1989) and Whitesmith (2018). Data from Cheikes et al. (2004), Tolcott et al. (1989) and White-smith (2018) were included in both the confirmation bias and the serial position effects meta-analysis. Both Cheikes et al. (2004) and Whitesmith (2018) tested for both serial position effects and confirmation bias (referred to as an 'anchoring heuristic' in Cheikes et al. (2004)). The results of Tolcott et al. (1989) were included in both the serial position effects meta-analysis and the confirmation bias meta-analysis as they were consistent with both cognitive biases.
6. Studies included were those that looked at information selection in cases where participants had been induced to have a focal hypothesis (Wason 1960; Koslowski and Maqueda 1993; Evans et al. 2002; Mynatt et al. 1977; Doherty et al. 1996; and Klayman and Ha 1989). The tendency to select information that confirms a focal hypothesis in this instance is taken to be a form of confirmation bias. Some studies examining hypothesis testing strategies also included alternative research conditions where participants were primed to consider multiple hypotheses, allowing comparison of the impact that the experimental factor of hypothesis-testing priming may have on confirmation bias to be included in the meta-analysis. However, there is some controversy about whether hypothesis testing strategies can always effectively identify confirmation bias from a positive hypothesis testing strategy (Koslowski and Maqueda 1993). As such, studies that only required participants to develop an independent testing strategy, by identifying what evidence they sought to complete the

analysis, but that did not require the participants to process this information were not included in the meta-analysis. These studies are: Beattie and Baron (1988), Cox and Griggs (1982), Devine et al. (1990), Klayman and Ha (1989), Skov and Sherman (1986), Taplin (1975), Kareev and Halberstadt (1993), Kareev et al. (1993), Lord et al. (1984) (experiment 2), Millward and Spoehr (1973), Mynatt et al. (1993), Mynatt et al. (1978), Snyder and Campbell (1981), Snyder and Cantor (1979), Snyder and Swann (1978), Strohmer and Newman (1983), Tweney et al. (1980), Whetherick (1962), and Yachanin and Tweney (1982).

7. Whilst the inclusion of Wason (1960) as a study that showed behaviour consistent with confirmation bias as opposed to positive hypothesis-testing strategies (or enumerative induction) has been challenged (Koslowski and Maqueda 1993; Whetherick 1962; Evans 2016), it has been included in the meta-analysis. This is because it is possible to identify behaviour of some participants in the study that is consistent with confirmation bias, and not enumerative induction. Three participants consistently sought to test their focal hypothesis despite consistent disconfirming evidence.

8. Comparisons of all sub-variables could only be completed for the factors of task complexity and time pressure. Most studies conducted using non-intelligence analysis scenarios were conducted using a long series of information (81.44 per cent). In comparison, all studies conducted using intelligence analysis scenarios were conducted using long series of information conditions. No studies included in the meta-analysis involved evaluation and estimation conditions. For the non-intelligence analysis sample, most studies were conducted using simple tasks (61.51 per cent). In comparison, studies using intelligence analysis scenarios were approximately evenly split between complex and simple task conditions (46 per cent in complex task conditions and 54 per cent in simple task conditions). For the non-intelligence analysis sample, most participants were in consistent information conditions (57.65 per cent). In comparison, all participants in the intelligence analysis sample were in inconsistent information conditions. For the non-intelligence analysis sample, most participants were in no reliance on recall conditions (66 per cent). In comparison, all participants in the intelligence analysis sample were in no reliance on recall conditions. Most studies into confirmation bias in both non-intelligence analysis (83.48 per cent) and intelligence analysis (75 per cent) scenarios have used non time-pressured conditions. Whereas research into intelligence studies are

approximately evenly divided between those that employed accountability conditions and those that did not, few studies conducted using non-intelligence scenarios have used accountability conditions (10.13 per cent of the sample). For both the intelligence analysis and non-intelligence samples, most participants were in no familiarity with task conditions. For the non-intelligence analysis sample, 5.29 per cent were in familiarity with task conditions, 8.37 per cent in no familiarity with task conditions and 86.34 per cent in familiarity with task not required conditions. For the intelligence analysis sample, 25 per cent were in familiarity with task conditions and 75 per cent in familiarity with task not required conditions. There were none in no familiarity with task conditions. As such, familiarity with task and no familiarity with task conditions are underrepresented in current research. Studies that used non-intelligence analysis scenarios were split relatively evenly across different type of information conditions. In the non-intelligence sample, 9.97 per cent of participants were in conditions that derived exclusively from a priori, 28.47 per cent of participants were in conditions that derived exclusively from authority, 19.71 per cent were in conditions that derived exclusively from empirical information, 31.06 per cent were in conditions that derived exclusively from testimony and 10.79 per cent were in conditions that derived from mixed information sources. In comparison, most studies using an intelligence analysis scenario were derived from mixed information (75 per cent). As such, single type of information categories, beyond empirical information, are not yet represented in research into intelligence analysis.

9. Cheikes et al. (2004) used insufficient methods to identify whether primacy or confirmation bias was exhibited. The bias effect identified is described as an anchoring heuristic. However, this is consistent with both primacy and confirmation bias.
10. As with the serial position effects meta-analysis, each analytical factor was tested separately against the same data samples. Each test utilised a null hypothesis following the form: X analytical condition had no impact on confirmation bias.
11. In the non-intelligence sample, 58.48 per cent of participants were in weighted conditions and 34.91 per cent in neutral conditions. A total of 6.61 per cent of participants were in conditions where the diagnostic value of initially processed information was unknown.
12. In the intelligence analysis sample, 29 per cent were in multiple hypotheses manipulation conditions and 71 per cent were in no manipulation conditions. In the non-intelligence sample, 84 per cent

of participants were in no manipulation conditions, 10 per cent were in single hypothesis manipulation condition and 6 per cent were in multiple hypothesis manipulation conditions.

13. Galinsky (1999), Lord et al. (1984), and Pyszczynski and Greenberg (1987) found that exposing participants to counterfactual or alternative hypotheses reduced confirmation bias. This factor was not consistently measured across all the confirmation bias studies. As such, it was not included as a separate factor in the meta-analysis.

14. For the non-intelligence analysis sample, 0.83 per cent of participants were in confirm hypotheses conditions, 0.83 per cent were in disconfirm hypotheses conditions, 2.2 per cent were in maximal objectivity conditions, 1.98 per cent in avoid confirmation bias conditions, 2.2 per cent were in consider multiple hypotheses conditions, 4.13 per cent were in test hypotheses conditions and 87.83 per cent were in no instructions conditions. For the intelligence analysis sample, 62 per cent of participants were in no instruction conditions and 38 per cent were in disconfirm and consider multiple hypotheses conditions.

15. There was no statistically significant difference between the proportion of participants who exhibited confirmation bias in the intelligence and the non-intelligence samples. For the non-intelligence analysis sample, 61.20 per cent of participants exhibited confirmation bias. For the intelligence analysis sample, 63.095 per cent of participants exhibited confirmation bias. A two-sample t-test between proportions was performed to determine whether there was a significant difference between the proportions exhibiting confirmation bias between the two samples. The t-statistic was not significant at the .05 critical alpha level, $t(1898) = 0.303$, $p = .7620$.

16. The following factors were associated with a significantly lower proportion of participants exhibiting behaviour consistent with confirmation bias in the non-intelligence analysis sample: SbS-C, short series of information, evaluation tasks, consistent information, time pressure, financial reward for correct analysis, non-accountability, empirical information, authority information, instructions to consider multiple hypotheses, instructions to test hypotheses, multiple hypotheses manipulation in information selection instructions and diagnostically neutral initial information. Of these factors, the following were suitably represented within the sample to examine for possible moderator variable effects: consistent information and diagnostically neutral initial information. More than 50 per cent of participants of each of the following factors were in both consistent

information and diagnostically neutral initial information conditions: step-by-step (continuous), financial reward for correct analysis, empirical information and instructions to test hypotheses. More
than 50 per cent of participants in each of the following factors were
in a consistent information condition but had less than 50 per cent in
a diagnostically neutral initial information condition: short series of
information, evaluation, time pressure, non-accountability, authority information and no hypothesis testing instructions. There were
no factors in which more than 50 per cent of participants were in a
diagnostically neutral initial information condition but had less than
50 per cent in a consistent information condition. The following
factor had less than 50 per cent of participants in both a consistent information condition and a diagnostically neutral information
condition: consider multiple hypotheses. The meta-analysis indicates
that consistent information is a viable candidate for having had a
moderator variable effect, but that it was unlikely to have had an
effect on conditions where participants are explicitly instructed to
consider more than one hypothesis. The following factors stand as
possible viable candidates for having a reducing effect: SbS-C, short
series of information, evaluation tasks, financial reward for correct
analysis, empirical information, authority information, instructions
to consider multiple hypotheses, instructions to test hypotheses,
multiple hypotheses manipulation in information selection instructions and diagnostically neutral initial information.

17. Moderator variable analysis could not be conducted as only one factor was associated with a statistically significantly lower proportion
of participants exhibiting behaviour consistent with confirmation
bias.

18. The following factors were associated with a significantly higher
proportion of participants exhibiting behaviour consistent with
confirmation bias in the non-intelligence analysis sample: estimation, inconsistent information, requirement to justify analysis (participants informed pre-information processing), perceived risk of
medical misdiagnosis, no familiarity with task, mixed information,
testimony information and diagnostically weighted initial information. The meta-analysis indicates that diagnostically weighted initial
information is a viable candidate for having a moderator variable
effect, but that it is unlikely to have had a moderator variable effect
on a mixed information condition. The analysis also indicates that
inconsistent information is unlikely to have had a moderator variable effect. Of these factors, the following were suitably represented

within the sample to examine for possible moderator variable effects: inconsistent and diagnostically weighted initial information. More than 50 per cent of each of the following factors were in both inconsistent information and diagnostically weighted initial information conditions: estimation tasks and no familiarity with task. More than 50 per cent of participants in a mixed information condition were in an inconsistent information condition but had less than 50 per cent in a diagnostically weighted initial information condition. More than 50 per cent of participants in each of the following factors were in a diagnostically weighted initial information condition but had less than 50 per cent in an inconsistent information condition: requirement to justify analysis (participants informed pre-information processing), perceived risk of medical misdiagnosis and testimony. No factors had less than 50 per cent of participants in both an inconsistent information condition and a diagnostically weighted information condition. The following factors also stand as possible viable candidates for having an amplifying effect: EoS, SBS-I, long series of information, estimation, inconsistent information, requirement to justify analysis (participants informed pre-information processing), perceived risk of medical misdiagnosis, familiarity with task and testimony information.

19. Of these factors, the following were suitably represented within the sample to examine for possible moderator variable effects: simple tasks and non-accountability. All factors had more than 50 per cent of participants in both simple task and non-accountability conditions. The meta-analysis indicated that neither simple task conditions nor non-accountability conditions had a moderator variable effect. Other factors were insufficiently represented within the sample to conduct moderator variable analysis.

6   Reducing the Risk of Cognitive Bias in Intelligence Analysis

A significant proportion of human cognition is spent on trying to anticipate danger in its varying forms from the world around us. The more that we can prepare for the likely threats we face, the better the chances we have of mitigating the damage that may be incurred. Intelligence has formed a significant part of this activity throughout human history. However, like many efforts of human understanding, acquiring justified beliefs in intelligence is by no means easy. Our cognitive faculties are fallible and prone to bias. Cognitive biases are both natural and inevitable. However, the potential costs of these phenomena in intelligence are much higher than in many other areas of intellectual enquiry. Cognitive biases have been identified as contributing factors to multiple intelligence failures in the twentieth and twenty-first centuries that have cumulatively led to significant loss of human life. Academic debate about how best to mitigate intelligence failures that are the result of cognitive bias has pitted two opposing solutions against one another: the reliance on intuition versus the use of structured analytical methods adapted from other academic fields.

The purpose of this book was to expand the debate regarding the best methods for reducing the occurrence or mitigating the impact of cognitive biases in intelligence analysis. I specifically sought to: aid in equalising the balance of empirical validation between the two opposing arguments for mitigating bias in intelligence studies; contribute to the validation of structural analytical methods as a way of mitigating bias in intelligence; and explore alternative ways to reduce or mitigate bias that can be supported by experimental research. In addition, I sought to contribute to the theoretical debate surrounding best practice for belief acquisition in intelligence by examining intelligence as an epistemological act. I have sought to answer five specific questions:

1. Is belief acquisition in intelligence a unique epistemological act?
2. Does ACH provide a theoretically valid framework for establishing epistemic justification?
3. Does ACH have a mitigating effect against the cognitive biases of confirmation bias or serial position effects?
4. Do serial position effects or confirmation bias affect intelligence analysis differently from non-intelligence analysis?
5. What analytical conditions are associated with an increased or decreased risk of confirmation bias and serial position effects?

In answering the first two questions I sought to establish a theoretical basis in which to ground my research into the impact of cognitive bias in belief acquisition and adjustment in intelligence analysis. There has been considerable disagreement in the field of intelligence studies as to what characteristics define intelligence as a unique concept. However, without a working definition, it is difficult to examine whether belief acquisition in intelligence would theoretically be impacted differently by cognitive bias compared with belief acquisition in a non-intelligence context. Various arguments have been put forward for suitable definitions of intelligence, with very few areas of agreement. However, the lack of agreement over a suitable definition for intelligence has not arisen because intelligence is a difficult concept or entity to define. The key issue that has led to a lack of agreement amongst academics is a misunderstanding of the correct methodological approaches to establishing a taxonomy. The correct methodology for establishing the essential nature of a concept or entity, and therefore its taxonomy, is to identify its necessary characteristics. I proposed that, of all the characteristics of intelligence suggested in existing academic definitions, the following stand as viable necessary conditions: that intelligence is a covert human behaviour, and that intelligence seeks to gain knowledge or justification for the beliefs of the individual engaged in intelligence. By combining these necessary conditions, I argue that the essential nature of intelligence is the covert pursuit of justified beliefs. In this capacity, the fundamental nature and purpose of intelligence is epistemological, that is, it is concerned with establishing knowledge, or justification for beliefs.

By examining leading theories from the philosophical field of epistemology and comparing these to the leading theories from the field of intelligence studies, I propose that, although intelligence draws upon the same sources and uses the same standards of gaining knowledge or justification for beliefs as any other type of epistemological endeavour, intelligence is a unique epistemological act. Intelligence differs in nature from belief acquisition in non-intelligence contexts by one necessary characteristic: it is a covert behaviour. This characteristic could plausibly result in intelligence involving greater epistemic complexity, and greater challenges for intelligence analysts in determining epistemic justification for their beliefs. This takes three forms: establishing the epistemic quality of available information, establishing epistemic justification where available information is not comprehensive and drawing in part or in total from information collected by an epistemically unreliable method. These forms of epistemic complexity could place greater strain on human cognitive information-processing capability. It is therefore theoretically valid to argue that belief acquisition in intelligence may be more vulnerable to cognitive bias. This theoretical position entails that mitigation of cognitive bias in intelligence should be primarily concerned with reducing the cognitive strain in determining epistemic justification for beliefs.

The theoretical basis I have proposed is not controversial. The taxonomy I have suggested – that intelligence is the covert pursuit of justified beliefs – is consistent with elements of most arguments that have been proposed for definitions of intelligence. Further, it is arguably more controversial to suggest that intelligence analysis requires unique methods of establishing knowledge or justified beliefs that cannot be used outside of the intelligence world. However, whilst my arguments are not controversial, it does not follow that they are right. If valid examples can be proposed in which intelligence does not seek to establish knowledge or justify beliefs, or where intelligence is not intended to be kept hidden from the subject of information collection, then my argument for a taxonomy of intelligence is automatically invalidated. Whilst my own efforts to generate such examples met with no success, it does not follow that such examples cannot be found. However, irrespective of whether this taxonomic theory meets with agreement within intelligence studies, my proposal for updating the methodological approach to establishing a taxonomy for intelligence should at least enable the debate to progress.

Legitimate contention may be found with my argument regarding the degree to which intelligence analysis may face greater challenges in establishing the epistemic justification or beliefs compared with other attempts to gain knowledge in non-intelligence situations. There are many circumstances in which attempts to establish the epistemic justification for beliefs may be subject to greater challenges than intelligence analysis. It cannot be easily established whether intelligence analysis holds a monopoly on epistemic complexity. As such, my stipulation that this may happen only on a case-by-case, rather than a wholesale, basis is a reasonable caveat.

In addition to providing key grounding for the research conducted as part of this book, this theoretical basis can help provide a wider foundation or contextual understanding for a sub-field of intelligence studies focusing on intelligence as an epistemological act. The limits of intelligence are intrinsically linked to the limits of knowledge. In this sense, intelligence failure is at least in part a problem of epistemology. If we are to understand the limits of our ability to be justified in the predictions we make about future threats, or interpretations of past or current events, it is necessary to develop an approach that is based on the most appropriate epistemological principles for this purpose. Whilst the prospect of learning lessons from the field of epistemology to improve intelligence analysis has been addressed in a small number of papers in intelligence studies, these have demonstrated a narrow understanding of the logical consequences and the weaknesses of some epistemological theories that have already been identified, and a narrow understanding of wider critical debate within the field of epistemology. By providing an account of the key arguments from epistemology regarding the sources of knowledge and mechanisms by which knowledge can be gained and by outlining the key strengths and limitations of these theories that have been put forward in epistemology, we can at the very least progress the debate in this area by improving the quality of contextual theoretical understanding of epistemological implications for intelligence from a philosophical viewpoint.

* * *

Despite the importance that the practice of intelligence analysis places on the mitigation of intelligence failures, little theoretical development has been attempted on best practice (or normative approaches) for reducing the risk of cognitive bias in intelligence analysis. Whilst some normative theories of intelligence analysis have been advanced, I argue that none of them are sufficiently theoretically robust to stand as practical or efficient solutions to mitigating cognitive biases.

Two normative theories of mitigating cognitive bias in intelligence analysis have been proposed in intelligence studies. The first is that intelligence analysis should be conducted in reliance on intuition. However, to rely on intuition is to reject the need for being justified in our belief that an argument is true. As knowledge requires demonstrable justification, this cannot be provided by intuition alone. Further, a significant body of research in the social sciences has demonstrated that to rely on intuition alone for mitigation of cognitive biases is not effective. The second normative theory of mitigating cognitive bias in intelligence is that structured analytical methods should be applied in intelligence analysis. Whilst there is a large volume of research that can be utilised to validate the first normative approach, there is very little research that has been conducted to validate the second. In answering the questions 'Does ACH provide a theoretically valid framework for establishing epistemic justification?' and 'Does ACH have a mitigating impact against confirmation bias or serial position effect in intelligence analysis?', I sought to build upon previous empirical validation for the argument that structured analytical methods are a more effective approach to mitigating bias in intelligence analysis compared with a reliance on intuition alone, and theoretical validation for ACH as an analytical method.

In answering these research questions, I used three separate research methodologies. The first examined the theoretical validity of ACH in providing mitigation for cognitive biases and in providing a system for establishing epistemic justification. The second examined the efficacy of ACH in mitigating the cognitive biases of confirmation bias and serial position effects in an experimental setting. The third utilised data from multiple studies to examine the available empirical evidence of ACH's efficacy in significantly reducing the likelihood of the occurrence of serial position effects and confirmation bias in belief acquisition. This research directly addressed a gap in validating the 'science' part of the art versus science debate, by expanding the research conducted by Cheikes et al. (2004) into the efficacy of ACH to cover additional scoring mechanisms used in the ACH process and to test ACH's efficacy of reducing the occurrence of or mitigating the impact of the cognitive bias of serial position effects.

An examination of the theoretical validity of ACH as an umbrella technique for mitigating confirmation bias and establishing epistemic justification identified several key weaknesses in the ACH design. The first weakness relates to the four central scoring systems used by ACH to process information. Information ranking systems in ACH need to provide a method of establishing epistemic justification that provides the required relationships of relevance, and necessity (or where this is unattainable, sufficiency), between a belief and truth. The leading theories within epistemology for how to provide this are: that the degree to which a belief is justified is the degree to which it fits the evidence available to the subject (evidentialism); that a belief is justified if it originates from a reliable cognitive method (reliabilism); and that a belief is justified if it cannot be defeated by counter-argument or contrary evidence (indefeasibilism). Information ranking systems in ACH should incorporate at least one of these approaches to stand as a theoretically rigorous method of establishing epistemic justification. Further, ACH should provide guidance on how these methods can be used to identify the epistemic justification provided by information that could have been the product of intentional deception or unintentionally imparted falsehoods. Information ranking systems in ACH also need to be able to distinguish between partial epistemic justification and total epistemic justification for multiple hypotheses as well as being able to identify the relative, and cumulative, degree of epistemic justification that each hypothesis has for being accepted as a justified belief. Finally, ACH needs to provide two levels of epistemic justification: the degree of epistemic justification for accepting each piece of intelligence information as a justified belief, and the degree of epistemic justification that each piece of intelligence information provides to the individual premises contained within a hypothesis. However, none of the four scoring systems used in ACH meet all these criteria. As such, ACH does not currently provide a theoretically valid framework for establishing justification for beliefs. The second weakness concerns the ability of ACH to allow cognitive biases to be identified by external review. ACH contains no mechanism to measure belief adjustment in response to the processing of individual pieces of information. As such, there is no theoretical reason why ACH would allow individuals to identify when cognitive biases have occurred. A third weakness is that there is no obvious reason why the scoring systems used in ACH or the approach of eliminative induction that is the central tenet of the ACH design would be invulnerable or significantly less susceptible to cognitive bias than intuition.

An experiment conducted using a version of ACH taught to the UK intelligence community by the Cabinet Office between 2016 and 2017, which used the scoring systems of diagnostic value of information and credibility of information, showed that ACH did not have a statistically significant impact on the proportion of participants who exhibited serial position effects or the proportion of participants who exhibited confirmation bias. ACH had no impact on belief acquisition and no reducing effect on the occurrence of confirmation bias. Further, confirmation bias affected the ways in which participants used the scoring systems of credibility of information and diagnostic value of information. As such, ACH did not prevent confirmation bias from affecting assessments made using the ACH process. ACH had no mitigating impact on the proportion of participants who exhibited serial position effects. However, there was no indication that serial order or serial order effects had an impact on the way in which people used the ACH scoring systems for credibility of information and consistency of information. The results of the experimental study are consistent with the results of existing published research examining the efficacy of ACH in mitigating confirmation bias (Cheikes et al. 2004). The results were also consistent with a wide body of research into the occurrence of serial position effects in non-intelligence analysis. Meta-analysis of currently available research into the efficacy of ACH in mitigating confirmation bias revealed that the ACH method, applied using either the credibility of information or the diagnostic value of information scoring systems, does not have a statistically significant mitigating impact on confirmation bias or serial position effects.

Based on the results of these three research approaches, I argue that there is no indication from current experimental research that ACH has a reducing impact on the cognitive biases of confirmation bias or serial position effects. However, this does not mean that ACH cannot reduce or provide mitigation for cognitive biases. The efficacy of ACH has only been tested against two forms of cognitive biases. Further, the efficacy of two of the scoring systems of consistency of information and subjective Bayesianism used in ACH in mitigating cognitive bias has not been subject to experimental validation. However, even if these scoring systems could be shown via experimental research to reduce or mitigate bias, they do not provide a theoretically valid mechanism for establishing the epistemic justification for hypotheses. Subjective Bayesianism provides no mechanism for connecting probability judgements with truth or identifying epistemic justification for beliefs, and consistency of information permits logical invalidity.

ACH cannot identify which hypotheses are more likely to be true, as truth is in no way probable. However, ACH can be used to gauge the degree of epistemic justification that respective hypotheses have. To do this, ACH needs to be modified, and to have restrictions placed on further modification. Information scoring systems used in ACH must provide a theoretically viable way to establish epistemic justification. In addition, judgements of the epistemic justification for believing individual pieces of information to be true must have an impact on the overall ACH score. Finally, guidance on how to judge the epistemic justification (or credibility) of information that is based on theoretically valid principles needs to be provided. The experimental study showed that participants' judgements of credibility of information ultimately derived from human sources can be influenced by non-epistemically relevant factors, but this risk can be reduced by instructing analysts to judge information for credibility or diagnostic value. Further, as I have demonstrated, guidance on judging the epistemic justification of information provided by publicly available intelligence analysis training manuals is not theoretically valid.

ACH is not without value to intelligence analysis: it can be used to enable challenge analysis, it can be used as a mechanism to identify intelligence gaps and it can be also used to identify the epistemic justification for competing hypotheses. However, to do this new information scoring systems need to be devised, there needs to be restrictions on the scoring systems used and adequate training needs to be provided on how to process information appropriately using the ACH method. Whilst there is no obvious reason why ACH would mitigate cognitive bias in an analytical task, it is possible that the efficacy of ACH could be demonstrated against other cognitive biases in experimental research. Further, even if experimental research into ACH using all four of its scoring systems demonstrates that it does not mitigate against any known cognitive bias, it does not follow that ACH cannot be adapted to do so. ACH is an umbrella method that has been adapted several times since its development. However, if a second purpose of ACH is to be able to establish epistemic justification for analytical judgements in intelligence, the scoring systems used must be those that are theoretically able to do so. As such, I propose that for ACH to be used to establish justification for beliefs, and to mitigate or reduce cognitive bias, its scoring systems must have the dual qualities of being theoretically able to establish epistemic justification and of having been proved by experimental research to have a mitigating or reducing impact on at least one type of cognitive bias.

In addition to contributing to the empirical validation of the efficacy of the ACH method in reducing or mitigating cognitive biases, the experimental research provided an insight into factors that influence judgements of credibility. The research indicates that people are influenced by a wide range of factors in forming beliefs and making judgements of the epistemic value of information, but that not all factors are relevant to establishing the degree of epistemic justification that information provides to belief acquisition.

215

The most cited factors that influence assessments of epistemic value of information derived from human sources were the possible motivation of the individual providing the information to lie or engage in deception, the reliability of the sources in the sourcing chain through which the information was collected and the consistency of the information with a participant's prior beliefs. Further, the results indicate that the motivation to lie or the possibility of deception is most likely to be considered in assessing the epistemic justification of information when information contradicts beliefs that are held by the participant. Further, the research indicates that the risk of beliefs being influenced by non-relevant factors is associated or increased when initially processed information is diagnostically neutral. This indicates that the risk of non-relevant factors influencing beliefs is linked to the underlying cognitive process that likely causes both confirmation bias and serial position effects: the force towards forming a focal hypothesis in initial stages of information processing. Comparison of the results with wider research on the topic indicates that perception of honesty is a significant influencing factor when judging the epistemic justification of information. However, there is no indication that judgements of the epistemic justification of information derived from non-human sources are influenced by non-epistemically relevant factors. This indicates that epistemic complexity in belief acquisition is primarily concerned with information derived from human sources. The experimental research also identified that there is likely to be a significant degree of individual difference in factors that influence assessments of epistemic justification of information, and that single factors can be applied both inconsistently and in a polar manner during a single act of belief acquisition.[1]

* * *

The questions 'do serial position effects or confirmation bias affect intelligence analysis differently compared with non-intelligence analysis?' and 'what analytical conditions are associated with an increased or reduced risk of confirmation bias and serial position effects?' were addressed by meta-analysis into serial position effects and confirmation bias. The results of the meta-analyses indicate that analytical conditions have an impact on the likelihood of occurrence of serial position effects and confirmation bias. However, the results do not offer a compelling indication that serial position effects or confirmation bias have a different impact or pose different risks for intelligence analysis tasks compared with non-intelligence analysis tasks. The meta-analysis revealed several analytical conditions that are likely to have an impact on confirmation bias and serial position effects. Tasks that involved the processing of more than six pieces of information, required a reliance on recall and were derived exclusively from a priori or testimony information were associated with an increased risk of serial position effects. Tasks that involved the processing of fewer than six pieces of information, involved no reliance on recall and involved the requirement to conduct a recall test where participants were informed of this requirement prior to information processing were associated with a reduced risk of serial position effects. Only one analytical factor demonstrated the potential to result in no serial position effects having a higher likelihood of occurrence than serial position effects: the requirement to justify analysis (where participants were informed prior to information processing). However, this effect was only observed in the non-intelligence analysis sample and represented a very small proportion of the overall sample (0.28 per cent). Tasks that involved processing more than six pieces of information were associated with an increased likelihood of primacy, whereas those that involved processing fewer than six pieces of information were associated with an increased likelihood of recency. Tasks that involve internally consistent information, instructions to consider more than one hypothesis and a multiple hypotheses information selection manipulation are associated with a reduced risk of confirmation bias. Tasks that involve diagnostically weighted initial information and information of mixed epistemological types are associated with an increased risk of confirmation bias.

Whilst the meta-analysis indicated that there may be some areas of difference between the intelligence and non-intelligence analysis samples, given the small sizes of the intelligence analysis samples in each of the meta-analyses, these results are more likely to have been the result of individual differences having a disproportionate impact. However, there are considerable gaps in available research into the effect of serial position effects and confirmation bias in intelligence analysis scenarios under different analytical conditions. As such, it remains possible that the differences highlighted between the non-intelligence analysis samples and the intelligence analysis samples are legitimate differences in the way that serial position effects and confirmation bias affect intelligence analysis compared with non-intelligence analysis. By highlighting where such differences may lie, the results of the meta-analysis can be used to inform further research.

The meta-analyses have several limitations, of which three are significant. The first limitation of the meta-analysis concerns data classification. There is no consistency in the measurement of serial position effects or confirmation bias in available research. What counts as confirmation bias or a serial position effect in one study may well have not been counted as such in another. Further, most serial position effect studies and a portion of confirmation bias studies used a mean degree of belief change for results, rather than explicitly stating the number of participants who exhibited these biases. Proportions of participants who exhibited serial position effects and confirmation bias were approximated as well as possible but are unlikely to be exact. This is not a significant issue for large sample sizes such as the serial position effects meta-analysis study, which included data for 12,673 participants. However, this issue is substantially more problematic for the intelligence samples, which were much smaller in size (the sample size for serial position effects was 292 and for confirmation bias eighty-four). The confirmation bias samples were substantially smaller than the samples for serial position effects. However, only a small number of studies did not provide exact numbers of participants who exhibited confirmation bias in experimental settings. Unfortunately, most studies in the intelligence sample for confirmation bias have this feature. As such, the results for the non-intelligence sample of the confirmation bias meta-analysis are arguably the most reliable, followed by the results for the non-intelligence analysis sample of the serial position effects and the results of the intelligence analysis sample for serial position effects. The results for the intelligence analysis sample for confirmation bias are the least likely to be reliable. Some of the results of the serial position effects meta-analysis are consistent with existing predictions models and meta-analyses. Some are also consistent with the findings of research into serial position effects in serial recall. This strengthens the case for the validity of the results. A related limitation is that association does not necessarily indicate a statistical correlation or causation. The results cannot therefore be a conclusive basis for identifying a causal relationship between analytical conditions and serial position effects or confirmation bias. The results of the meta-analysis for serial position effects are arguably a stronger case for causational relationships than the meta-analysis for confirmation bias, due to the higher volume of available research. However, the quality of data for the confirmation bias meta-analysis in the non-intelligence analysis sample allowed greater accuracy of the statistical tests.

The second limitation of the meta-analyses concerns methodology. The statistical tests used cannot identify interaction effects between different variables or conclusively identify moderator variable effects. Likely moderator variable effects were identified by qualitative analysis. This methodology is far from perfect. However, the limitations of the methodology reflect the limitations of the data available and the practical limitations on research. There is no available statistical method that could have provided a statistical account of interaction effects or moderator variables from available research given the large number of analytical condition variables. Whilst the methodology is not perfect, it is an arguable improvement on previous meta-analyses into serial position effects which relied purely on qualitative analysis and were based on a lower volume of research. The methodology used sought to take the proportion of participants into account when measuring the prevalence of serial position effects and confirmation bias and identify statistically significant differences. The methodology employed in the meta-analyses is arguably more robust than the purely qualitative approaches that have been used before. Whilst the imperfect classification of data necessarily reduces the validity of the results, the Bonferroni adjustment for multiple comparison tests provides a high degree of conservatism. This method is arguably a more robust indicator of differences and similarities than qualitative analysis alone. Previous meta-analysis into serial position effects took the results of all studies to have equal import and failed to take into account the variance of sample sizes. My methodology also included five new analytical factors that have not been considered in previous meta-analysis into serial position effects: reliance on recall, time pressure, accountability, type of information and familiarity with task. It also provided the first meta-analysis attempt to examine the impact of individual analytical factors into confirmation bias. The results of the meta-analysis are consistent with some of the predictions made by previous meta-analyses into serial position effects. However, previous meta-analyses only took a small number of variables into account. As I have provided the first substantial meta-analysis into the impact of analytical conditions on confirmation bias, there are no other works with which to compare the results.

The third significant limitation of the meta-analysis is that currently available research does not allow a comparison of the impact of all analytical conditions on serial position effects and confirmation bias, particularly between intelligence and non-intelligence analysis. These limitations restrict both the utility and the validity of the meta-analysis results. However, they are arguably unavoidable: they are the necessary result of the limitations of available research, and a lack of agreement within social sciences about how cognitive biases are defined and measured. Further, these limitations are not unique to this study; they apply to all attempts to conduct meta-analysis on confirmation bias and serial position effects. Given these limitations, the results of the meta-analysis can only be an indication of causal relationships between analytical conditions and cognitive biases.

Based on the results of the meta-analysis, I have proposed the following tentative prediction models for confirmation bias and serial position effects. I argue that both serial position effects and confirmation bias share the same origin but are exacerbated by different analytical conditions. Both serial position effects and confirmation bias are the result of a force towards forming a focal hypothesis early on in information processing. The analytical conditions that have a causal impact on serial position effects are those that have a direct impact on the reliance on long-term memory to process information. The analytical conditions that have an impact on the risk of confirmation bias are those that directly influence the point at which a focal hypothesis is formed in the processing of information, increasing the likelihood that it will be formed in initial stages of information processing, as opposed to when all information available has been processed, and preventing the focal hypothesis from being modified appropriately during information processing.

The empirical research presented in this book indicates that, whilst belief acquisition in intelligence is unique in nature, and will, theoretically, be likely to involve a higher degree of epistemic complexity than belief acquisition in some non-intelligence contexts, the level to which belief acquisition in any context will be susceptible to serial position effects or confirmation bias depends on the analytical conditions under which beliefs are acquired. These conditions include the sources of knowledge and epistemic justification from which beliefs derive; however, the impact that this analytical factor has on the risk of occurrence of serial position effects and confirmation bias is not exclusive to epistemological issues. Whilst the higher complexity of establishing the epistemic justification of testimony information exacerbates the risks of serial position effects and confirmation bias, other types of information exacerbate these risks for different reasons. Whilst the research indicates that epistemic complexity increases the risk of serial position effects and confirmation bias, it highlights the importance of developing mitigation approaches to confirmation bias and serial position effects that are based on an understanding of the analytical conditions that exacerbate and reduce the risk that these biases will occur.

Recommendations for Future Research and Best Practice for Intelligence Analysis

There are multiple recommendations that can be made for future research and best practice for intelligence analysis on the results of my research. Some of these are based on the results of the experimental research and meta-analyses presented in this book and are therefore grounded in experimental research. Others are based on my own theoretical stance regarding the efficacy of different approaches to mitigate bias, and the appropriate theoretical foundations for best practice in intelligence analysis.

The first area of recommendations concerns judgements of the epistemic value of information in intelligence analysis. The experimental study and other research indicate that the motivation to lie or the possibility of deception is a significant influencing factor in judging the epistemic justification of information derived through human sources. Intelligence analysis is more likely to consistently contain a higher proportion of false information or deception in information derived from human sources than non-intelligence contexts. As such, it is reasonable to assume that judging the epistemic value of information will be harder in intelligence analysis tasks than in non-intelligence analysis tasks. However, my experimental study also indicated that motivation to lie or the possibility of deception is less likely to be considered for intelligence reports that are consistent with an individual's prior beliefs. As such, it is also reasonable to assume that judgement of epistemic value is a key area of vulnerability to confirmation bias in intelligence analysis: that judgements of the credibility of information will be less rigorous for intelligence that is consistent with an analyst's focal hypothesis. This is therefore an area where intelligence analysis and non-intelligence analysis may legitimately differ from one another in terms of the vulnerability to cognitive bias. This has potential implications for guidance regarding the level of information about human sources that is provided by intelligence collection agencies to intelligence analysts. The experimental study showed that the key influencing factor of judgements of credibility regards the trustworthiness of the source. It is reasonable to infer from the research findings that the level of detail provided about the source of intelligence information has a direct impact on the way that analysts judge how trustworthy (and therefore how credible) the information is. Having more information about potential motivations for the source to provide the information may lead to better-informed judgements of the epistemic value of intelligence information derived from human sources. Most currently available experimental research into confirmation bias in intelligence scenarios was based on the processing of exclusively empirical information. As such, it is unclear whether intelligence analysis that derives exclusively or predominantly from HUMINT and SIGINT is at higher risk of confirmation bias. I recommend that future research into the impact of confirmation bias in intelligence analysis focuses on examining the impact of different types of information and comparing this with non-intelligence scenarios. To be of maximum utility to intelligence analysis, research should be conducted that concentrates on the factors that influence participants' judgements of the epistemic value of information from testimony, as this is arguably the main source of knowledge from which intelligence analysis derives, or at least the source of knowledge from which intelligence derives that provides the greatest complexity for establishing justification for beliefs. More research is also required to identify what impact different serial orders have on judging the epistemic value of information. It is possible that epistemic value judgements may be subject to a discounting effect whereby judgements are different where initial pieces of information in a serial order are internally consistent, compared with a serial order where initial pieces of information are internally inconsistent, or whereby judgements are different where initial pieces of information are consistent with the participant's belief, compared with a serial order in which initial pieces of information are not consistent with the participant's prior belief.

Intelligence analysis cannot rely purely on intuition. It has to involve a conscious rational processing and evaluation of information that can be made available for peer review. Further, support and guidance should be given to analysts to cope with the increased epistemic complexity likely to be involved in forming justified beliefs in an intelligence context. An examination of internal training documents on how to judge the credibility (epistemic value) of information demonstrates that some Western intelligence communities have recommended non-theoretically valid methods for establishing the epistemic value of information to intelligence analysts. I recommend that training for intelligence analysts needs to ensure that guidance on assessing the epistemic value of information, the extent to which specific types of information can legitimately be used as epistemic justification for beliefs and the risk that epistemic value judgements can be made on the basis of non-relevant factors should be based on a professionally qualified understanding of leading theories in epistemology and relevant experimental research. I recommend that guidance on determining the epistemic value of information should be an essential part of training for new intelligence analysts, independently of being taught as part of training in the use of ACH. However, intelligence communities should ensure that this training provided is based on a theoretically valid understanding of leading epistemological theories, and should specifically draw upon the theories of reliabilism, evidentialism and indefeasibilism.

The second area of recommendations concerns the different approaches that can be used to try and reduce the occurrence or mitigate the impact of cognitive biases in analytical tasks, specifically focusing on intelligence analysis. My research indicates that serial position effects and confirmation bias are highly likely to occur during analysis, and there are limits to what can be done to prevent this or reduce the risks of this happening. However, I recommend that drawing on empirical information to identify ways in which effective steps could be taken to mitigate or reduce the risk of bias in intelligence analysis is a more effective way of approaching the issue than a reliance on structured analytical methods that have not been subject to comprehensive experimental validation. Experimental research needs to be conducted into the efficacy of ACH using the scoring systems of consistency of information and subjective Bayesianism, as well as research into the efficacy of ACH using all four of the scoring systems that it has been adapted to include needs to be expanded to additional cognitive biases. Further, ACH, and any other structural analytical method that has been inspired by or adapted from, or that applies legitimate analytical methodologies in mathematics, philosophy and the sciences as a way of mitigating cognitive bias should be subject to comprehensive theoretical and experimental validation before it is adopted in training for intelligence analysis or recommended as best practice for any analytical task. This applies to intelligence analysis and non-intelligence analysis alike. Finally, if it is agreed that the purpose of ACH is not to prevent the occurrence of confirmation bias from affecting analysis, but instead to make the occurrence of cognitive biases clearly visible to external observation, then a consistent design needs to be adopted. A central requirement for being able to identify when biases are impacting the processing of information is to have a system that measures the impact of individual pieces of information on belief adjustment. For this purpose, ACH should be adapted to include a numerical scoring system for recording the degree of belief an analyst has for each of the hypotheses included in the process. This scoring system should measure the changes in degree of belief after processing a single piece of information and should be used in addition to scoring the epistemic value of information. This would theoretically allow the identification of both serial position effects and confirmation bias. Scoring systems for this purpose can easily be adapted from the procedure employed in my experimental study, or the experimental procedures used in other experimental research into serial position effects.

If a hypothesis contains more than one premise, these should be separated out in the ACH process, so that partial and total epistemic justification can be precisely recorded. Some information will have diagnostic relevance for an individual premise, but not for all premises that underpin a single hypothesis: partial justification needs to be able to be reflected. Further, judgements of epistemic credibility should have an impact on the overall scores for the intelligence case for believing each hypothesis to be true. Scoring systems should be set up to take this into account. This can be easily automated through information technology software. Finally, where ACH is recommended as best analytical practice, it must be made clear that ACH cannot predict the likelihood that a given hypothesis is true over others: it can only show the level of epistemic justification for respective hypotheses. This may seem like pedantry but understanding that (1) truth is in no way probable; and (2) being able to demonstrate whether you have sufficient justification for believing a proposition to be true is a crucial part of being able to establish knowledge, are essential for being able to judge the degree of confidence that can be objectively placed on intelligence assessments.

*   *   *

In this book I have examined alternative options for reducing the occurrence of or mitigating the impact of cognitive bias in addition to the reliance on intuition or structured analytical methods. I explored whether there was an empirical basis for the efficacy of controlling the conditions under which analysis is conducted to reduce the likelihood that confirmation bias or serial position effects will occur. The results of the meta-analyses indicate that there is an empirical basis for the impact of specific analytical conditions on the risks of occurrence of serial position effects and confirmation bias. However, attempting to control these factors in an intelligence analysis (or a non-intelligence analysis) scenario has unavoidable practical limitations. You cannot reasonably control most of the factors that are likely to have a causational impact on confirmation bias or serial position effects. You cannot control the volume of information required for processing to fewer than six items without withholding potentially relevant information. Nor can you easily control the diagnostic weighting of initially processed information so that it is neutral between all possible hypotheses. Whilst you could control the information type of raw intelligence reporting that gets disseminated to analysts for information processing, it would be a dangerous precedent to withhold access to information for the purpose of reducing bias. Making explicit references to multiple possible hypotheses prior to beginning each analytical task is likely to be difficult to implement practically. However, there are some factors that can be pragmatically subjected to a degree of control that could aid in reducing the likelihood of serial position effects or confirmation bias occurring. Improvements could be made in reducing analysts' reliance on long-term memory for processing and synthesising information. Information technology systems, intelligence reporting repositories and software that improves the ability to access and retain previously processed information and synthesise it with new information could be developed to reduce the burden on the analyst having to remember key information or rely on long-term memory for synthesising information. This could reduce the risk of serial position effects in intelligence analysis. Further, regularly explicitly instructing analysts to consider multiple hypotheses may aid in reducing cognitive biases. This could easily be introduced as guidance to new and current intelligence analysts or to those who manage intelligence analysts. However, this would need to become a standardised part of each analytical task or applied with sufficient regularity to ensure consistent and sustained utility.

In addition to actively manipulating conditions under which analysis is conducted, knowledge of the analytical conditions that correspond with an increased or decreased risk of cognitive bias can be used to judge the likelihood that serial position effects or confirmation bias occurred in generalised terms. If you can identify whether analytical judgements are more likely than others to have been subject to confirmation bias and which serial position effect analysts are most likely to have been subject to, this can allow more efficient targeting of where challenge analysis may be required.

*   *   *

The weight of empirical evidence lends considerable support to the science side of the art versus science debate in intelligence studies regarding how to reduce cognitive bias in belief acquisition, but not in the way that this debate has previously been framed. The empirical evidence does not support the argument for the use of ACH. The development of ACH pays due homage to the efficiency of eliminative induction in establishing falsity and offers several benefits to improving the quality of analysis over the reliance on intuition alone. However, whilst there are still key research gaps concerning the utility of ACH, the current evidential basis indicates that ACH has no efficacy in mitigating cognitive bias. But imitation is not the only way in which the sciences can be of benefit to reducing cognitive bias in intelligence analysis. Existing experimental research indicates that controlling certain analytical conditions under which analysis is conducted and improving the quality of training provided to new intelligence analysts in establishing epistemic justification for their beliefs may reduce the likelihood of the occurrence of serial position effects and confirmation bias. Giving analysts the best support to cope with epistemic complexity and utilising empirical information to create the optimum environment in which to conduct analysis is likely to be a better way to mitigate intelligence failures that arise through cognitive bias than by the use of ACH in its current forms, or other structured analytical methods that have to date been devised for intelligence analysis.

Note

1. The experimental study faces several limitations. Of these, the most significant limitation is that, due to ethical restrictions regarding the collection of personal information from the participants, the study cannot be used to indicate whether gender, age or prior experience in intelligence analysis has an impact on the susceptibility of participants to serial position effects or confirmation bias. This limitation does not reduce the validity of the results of the study, but it restricts the depth of knowledge that the study can contribute to the wider field of research.

Appendix: Adaptation of Iraq WMD Case Study to Form Intelligence Case for Experimental Study

The intelligence scenario used in the experimental study (Whitesmith 2018) was an adapted version of the intelligence case regarding the development of biological and nuclear weapons by Saddam Hussein's regime in Iraq, prior to 2003. Key elements of intelligence information from the Iraq weapons of mass destruction (WMD) case were used and disguised to create a fictional but realistic scenario using the Pakistan-based Islamist terrorist group Lashkar-e-Tayyiba (LeT) and the development of biological weapons. The key intelligence used from the Iraq WMD case study was taken from the intelligence case for Iraq's biological and nuclear weapons programmes. All information used to inform the intelligence case for the experiment derives from openly available material. Outlined below are the intelligence cases for Iraq's biological and nuclear weapons programmes, and how these cases were adapted to form the experiment scenario.

Intelligence Case for Iraq's Biological Weapons Programme

The collection of intelligence on Iraq's WMD faced significant difficulties. Saddam Hussein's regime had demonstrated a sophisticated capability to conceal its activities from external intelligence services. Much of the relevant information was compartmentalised within the Iraqi regime, and few within the regime would have access to this information. In addition, human intelligence collection was difficult, and largely conducted at a distance. Reliable information about Iraq's biological, chemical and nuclear weapons programme was lacking. As such, the starting point for intelligence analysis on the subject was the past behaviour of the Iraqi regime. The Iraqi regime was known to have acquired biological and chemical weapons in the past, to have successfully concealed its WMD programmes before and after the Gulf War and to have failed to account for previously declared stockpiles. The initial working hypothesis derived from this starting point by the US intelligence community (USIC) was that the Iraq regime was still in possession of biological and chemical weapons and was seeking to develop its capability in both production and delivery of WMD.

In the early 1990s, the USIC judged that Iraq was attempting to develop several biological agents in multiple facilities. The biological agents included anthrax and botulinum toxin. The USIC assessed that these biological agents were intended for use in artillery shells and aerial bombs. However, the USIC knew very little about Iraq's biological weapons programme, and judged at the time that there was insufficient information to gauge testing and deployment of munitions containing biological weapons. Between 1991 and 1995, a small amount of intelligence was received. Some human intelligence indicated that the Iraqi regime had produced a significantly higher quantity of biological agent than the USIC had previously assessed. In 1995, the Iraqi regime admitted to the UN that it had weaponised biological agents. The information provided by the Iraqi regime to the UN showed that the USIC had indeed substantially underestimated the quantity of biological agents that had been produced. Before the first Gulf War, Iraq had weaponised anthrax, botulinum toxin and aflatoxin, and had deployed munitions in Iraq that contained biological agents. In 1997, the USIC assessed that the Iraqi regime retained an active biological weapons programme and was concealing this activity. Further, it was assessed that the Iraqi regime would wait until sanctions had been lifted before resuming production of biological agents. As of 1998, the USIC had no reliable intelligence that indicated a resumption of biological agent production.

By early 2000, a single human source codenamed 'Curveball' provided a substantial volume of new information. Curveball was an Iraqi chemical engineer who had defected from the Iraqi regime and was being run as an intelligence source by the German Federal Intelligence Service, Bundesnachrichtendienst (BND) (Drogin 2008). The BND shared Curveball's reports with the US but did not initially allow the US to have direct access to Curveball. Between January 2000 and September 2001, approximately 100 reports were provided to the USIC from Curveball. These reports claimed that Iraq had several mobile production units for biological weapons, and that one of these units had begun production of biological agents circa 1997. Curveball claimed direct access to this information (Drogin 2008). The lack of access to Curveball made it very difficult to accurately assess the credibility of his reporting. However, elements of his reporting were consistent with information found in open source and with previous knowledge of the Iraqi regime's biological weapons activity. It later transpired that Curveball was an intelligence fabricator, and that some technical elements within his reporting had been derived from internet research (Drogin 2008).

By October 2002, three additional human sources (sources A, B and C) had claimed that Iraq had mobile biological weapons facilities. Additional human source A, who echoed Curveball's claims, was an asylum seeker. The source provided a single report in June 2001 in which he claimed that Iraq had mobile facilities to produce biological weapons. The source also claimed Iraq was fitting warheads with biological weapons at a transport facility near Baghdad. In 2003, the source recanted this claim. His reasons for recanting are unknown. However, the original report was not recalled or corrected. Additional human source B was associated with the Iraqi National Congress. This source provided one report in February 2002 in which he claimed that in 1996 Iraq had decided to establish mobile laboratories to produce biological weapons, to evade detection by inspectors. This source was judged to be unreliable by the CIA and an unspecified foreign liaison service. On the CIA's request, a notice was issued to the USIC stating that the source was deemed to be a fabricator. The source was later confirmed to have been providing false intelligence. Additional source C provided a single report in which it was claimed that Iraq had established mobile fermentation units mounted on trucks and railway cars. No additional information regarding this source was provided.

Investigation by the Iraq Survey Group (ISG) discovered that the USIC's pre-Iraq war assessments regarding the Iraqi regime's biological weapons capability were almost completely wrong. The ISG reported that Iraq appeared to have destroyed its undeclared stocks of biological weapons and had probably destroyed its remaining holdings of bulk biological agent shortly after the first Gulf War. The Iraqi regime retained the intellectual capability to produce biological weapons and a facility suitable for this purpose. However, this plant was destroyed in 1996. This ended Iraq's ambitions for large-scale production of biological weapons. However, the ISG assessed that the Iraqi regime retained the intellectual capability for biological weapons production and dual-use facilities that could be converted for use in small-scale biological agent production. However, the ISG found no direct evidence after 1996 that the Iraqi regime was conducting work in biological weapons or had the intent to do so (Duelfer 2004a). The ISG also found no evidence that the Iraqi regime had or was developing production systems on trucks or railway wagons.

Intelligence Case for Iraq's Nuclear Weapons Programme

Like the USIC's assessment regarding the Iraqi regime's biological weapons programme, assessments regarding the regime's nuclear weapons programme were informed by analysis of Iraq's capabilities over the ten years following the first Gulf War. Following the first Gulf War, multiple intelligence reports indicated that Iraq's nuclear programme had been underestimated by the USIC, and that the regime had a wide-ranging nuclear programme, which included the pursuit of uranium enrichment. Further, the regime had successfully hidden its activities from external intelligence agencies. The regime made further attempts to evade international inspectors between 1990 and 1994. However, the USIC continued during the 1990s to assess that Iraq had not reconstituted its nuclear programme, but that attempts would be likely to accelerate following the lifting of sanctions. In 1997, the USIC had obtained no firm evidence that this reconstitution had begun. In 1998, it reported that the limited intelligence on the subject was contradictory: some human sources reported that the regime had halted all its nuclear activity, whilst another source claimed that the regime was engaging in low-level theoretical research regarding a weapons programme.

In March 2001, intelligence was received that indicated the Iraqi regime was seeking high-strength aluminium alloy tubes. The USIC obtained a sample of these tubes through the seizure of a shipment bound for Iraq. The CIA assessed that the tubes were most likely intended for use in gas centrifuges for the enrichment of uranium. However, the CIA subsequently identified plausible non-nuclear-related uses for the tubes: for use in conventional rockets. The US Army's National Ground Intelligence Centre (NGIC) assessed that the tubes would be a poor choice for use in conventional rockets, and that although it was possible, the probability that the tubes were intended for use in rockets was very low. This report increased the confidence of CIA analysts that the tubes were intended for use in uranium enrichment. The US Department of Energy (DoE) assessed that whilst the tubes could possibly be used to manufacture centrifuge rotors, they were not well suited for use in centrifuges. Further, the DoE assessed that the tubes were more likely to be used in Iraq's Nasser 81 mm Multiple Rocket Launcher system. This assessment was seconded by the US International Atomic Energy Agency (IAEA). These assessments did not materially influence the CIA's assessment, although these assessments were cited in CIA briefings to senior US policymakers. The CIA later assessed that the plausible alternative use of the aluminium alloy tubes in conventional rockets was a cover story by the Iraqi regime.

Subsequent intelligence reporting indicated that Iraq was attempting to procure additional dual-use material that could feasibly be used in a nuclear weapons programme, including high-speed balancing machines. However, these reports did not directly indicate that this material was for use in a nuclear weapons programme. Intelligence also indicated that the Iraqi regime had reassigned some scientists to the Iraqi Atomic Agency Commission (IAAC), and that some scientists involved in Iraq's previous nuclear weapons programme had been reassembled. Two human sources indicated that the Iraqi regime was attempting to obtain a magnet production line between 1999 and 2001. However, both sources indicated that this activity was likely to be linked to Iraq's missile programme. A foreign government intelligence source claimed that Iraq was trying to obtain uranium ore and yellowcake from Niger, and that Niger planned to send 500 tonnes of yellowcake to Iraq. This report was later judged to be based on forged documents and was subsequently recalled.

The investigation by the ISG concluded that the Iraqi regime's efforts to enrich uranium had ended after 1991. Between 1980 and 1990, the Iraqi regime had built two magnetic bearing centrifuges. However, nearly all the nuclear facilities in Iraq were destroyed during the first Gulf War. After the first Gulf War, the regime was reluctant to disclose details of its nuclear programme and sought to conceal evidence of its existence. The ISG found no evidence that the regime had attempted to reconstitute this work. Whilst the ISG found evidence that Saddam Hussein remained interested in developing nuclear capability after 1991, the regime's capability was unable to match this intent. The ISG further concluded that Iraq's interest in the aluminium alloy tubes was for production of 81 mm rockets, rather than on any effort related to re-establishing a nuclear programme.

Adapting the Iraq WMD Case Study for a Fictional Scenario

Multiple elements from the intelligence case behind the USIC's assessment of the Iraqi regime's biological weapons development were combined with one element of the intelligence case behind the USIC's assessment of Iraq's nuclear weapons programme to form an ecologically valid intelligence analysis scenario. These details were transposed into a fictional scenario concerning the possible development or acquisition of biological weapons by the terrorist group LeT. The scenario was set in 2016, and provided intelligence dating back to the late 2000s. The documents used to provide the intelligence case for this scenario, and the elements on which they are based regarding Iraqi WMD, are outlined below.

Background Information

A background report was produced that contained the following information on LeT: history; ideology; areas of operation; senior leadership; external relations (including relationships with al-Qaeda, and the level of command and control exercised over the group by the Pakistani Inter-Services Intelligence agency (ISI)); significant attacks; historical biological weapons activity; the threat that LeT posed to the West; and intelligence coverage of the group. No information in this document covered beyond 2009. Most the information was referenced as having come from openly available information. In addition, an open source summary of a study by the University of Virginia conducted in 2012 regarding conditions in which anthrax spores could be reproduced was provided to give technical context for anthrax production. This body of information was designed to mirror the following aspects from the Iraq case study: the section on biological weapons activity revealed a previous history of LeT having attempted to develop an anthrax capability. This information provided a mirroring situation between the scenario and the Iraq case studies, whereby analysts were aware that the group in question had some historic precedent for the subject of the assessment. The intelligence coverage of LeT was described as challenging, with minimal collection capability in country and very little access to key information. Further, it was stated that little was known regarding LeT's current intent and capability, or the degree of control exercised over the group by the ISI. This mirrored the precedent of the Iraqi regime's sophisticated ability to conceal its activities from external intelligence agencies, and the difficulties faced by the USIC regarding intelligence collection on the Iraqi regime. The inclusion of open source information on anthrax production provided the participants with a way of examining whether such information could have been gleaned from open source research.

Intelligence Report I

An intelligence report was provided by an unidentified liaison service described as 'friendly'. The friendly international liaison service claimed that the source of the information was a defector from LeT who left the group in late January 2016 and was a member of LeT's research and development team. No further details regarding the source were provided. This human source provided an initial report in which he claimed that, as of early January 2016, LeT was attempting to produce a large amount of anthrax to use in a terrorist attack targeting significant tourist sites in New Delhi, India.

The source claimed that LeT had established a laboratory in a storage container inside a LeT training camp in Muzaffarabad,

Pakistan. The laboratory had previously been located in a LeT training camp in Manshera, Pakistan; however, it was moved to avoid being discovered by members of the ISI who were due to visit the Manshera camp. Details of the size and colour of the storage container and its location in the camp in Muzaffarabad were also provided. The source claimed that the use of anthrax had been approved by a senior leader within LeT, and that LeT had recruited a microbiologist from the University of the Punjab who had the relevant expertise to produce anthrax. The microbiologist had stolen anthrax spores from the University of the Punjab that were originally taken as a sample from a lion in Hyderabad that died of anthrax in 2010. The research and development team were informed that the anthrax was intended to be used in a forthcoming attack targeting tourist sites in New Delhi, and that LeT intended to place anthrax spores into explosive devices built using pressure cookers. A report issuer comment was included at the end of the report in which it was stated:

> The University of Punjab was confirmed to have a Microbiology department; media reporting confirmed that a lion died of anthrax in Hyderabad in 2010; and it is possible for anthrax to be weaponised in improvised explosive devices. However, there is insufficient information provided regarding the production process reported to assess whether the method of production is viable.

This report was designed to mirror the following aspect from the Iraq case study: the human source was designed to be a close approximation of Curveball, a defector from the group in question who claimed to have some degree of legitimate first-hand access to the information he was providing and who was being run by an allied intelligence service. The information provided contained details that were corroborated in openly available information. This information was provided to the participants in the background report. Further, the information was plausible considering what was known about LeT's historic activities in attempting to acquire anthrax and in conducting terrorist attacks in India. In the scenario, like Curveball, this human source was an intelligence fabricator. However, this aspect was not revealed to the participants during the study.

Intelligence Report 2

An intelligence report was provided by an unidentified liaison service, with an identical source description as intelligence report 1. This report provided details about LeT's mobile laboratory located in a training camp in Muzaffarabad that was being used to produce anthrax spores. The report contained information about the same microbiologist named in intelligence report 1 as well as about his team's efforts to produce large amounts of anthrax spores. The report claimed that the anthrax would be placed in improvised explosive devices made from pressure cookers. It was also claimed that LeT had previously tried and failed to obtain anthrax from the terrorist group al-Qaeda. The report provided a description of the laboratory and claimed that it could be moved to evade detection by the ISI, and that LeT was attempting to produce anthrax without the ISI's knowledge. The source claimed that the microbiologist leading the cell was attempting to produce anthrax spores by germinating it in a type of amoeba common in soils and pools of standing water. The amoeba could increase the number of anthrax spores by fifty times in the space of three days. The microbiologist was using a stolen sample of *Bacillus anthracis* spores. Anthrax spores were generated in plastic containers containing agar. The amoeba was grown in tissue culture flasks in a solution containing yeast. The flasks were kept at a constant temperature using heat lamps. Every three or four days the amoeba growth was harvested. The amoeba was then added to water collected from a local stream. The anthrax spores were added to the amoeba and stream water and then incubated using heat lamps. Using a microscope and a blue staining liquid called trypan the microbiologist could identify the new anthrax growth. The source claimed that by using this method, the microbiologist could increase anthrax spore growth by nearly a hundredfold in three days. This intelligence report did not contain a report issuer comment. The report was provided by the same source as intelligence report 1; however, this was not made clear to the participants during the study.

This report was designed to mirror the following aspect from the Iraq case study: a human source with some degree of legitimate access to the information he was providing, who provided a good degree of detail, including technical information. Like Curveball, there were several inconsistencies in aspects of the source's report with what he had previously claimed. In the fictional scenario, these details included the location of the laboratory in the LeT training camp in Muzaffarabad (this changed from the centre of the camp to the outskirts); the colour of the storage container (this changed from blue to grey); and the description of how the storage container was moved (this changed from being mounted on wheels and capable of being moved by a truck if necessary, to being mounted on the back of a truck). These inconsistencies, taken as a whole, were reasonable enough to call the credibility of the source's reporting into question. However, when considered in isolation, some of the inconsistencies, such as the colour, could be explained away without detracting from the overall credibility of the information. In addition, similarities between the description of the anthrax production methodology and the rate of anthrax spore production were very similar to the information provided in the summary of the University of Virginia 2012 study into anthrax spore production. This mirrored the fact that Curveball sourced much of the technical detail regarding the alleged mobile laboratory units from open source information. However, unlike the Iraq case study, the participants did not know that this information came from the same source as intelligence report 1. This could be reasonably inferred through the identical source description, agent runner agency description, and the consistency in several details of the report with that of intelligence report 1. However, there remained the possibility that the reports could be from separate human sources.

Intelligence Report 3

An intelligence report was provided by the Danish Security and Intelligence Service (PET). The report was from a human source being run by PET. The source was described as a former member of the ISI who claimed access to the information from ISI records. It was stated that it was unknown how the ISI originally obtained this information. The source claimed that, as of early May 2016, LeT was making bombs using unspecified chemicals in Jammu and Kashmir province in Pakistan. LeT had built bomb-making factories in the backs of trucks to evade detection by foreign intelligence agencies. The report had a notice on it stating that it was a revised copy of a previous original report. The reason for revision was to include a report issuer comment regarding the source of the information provided by PET. In the report issuer comment, PET stated that the source was currently applying for asylum in Denmark. Further, the source had provided several reports which PET had been unable to verify, and PET was concerned that the source was an intelligence fabricator.

This report was designed to mirror the following aspect from the Iraq case study: the human source associated with the Iraqi National Congress who claimed that the regime was fitting warheads with biological weapons at a transport facility near Baghdad. The source was later deemed to have fabricated this information. However, unlike the Iraq case scenario, the PET source was not described as having recanted his claim; it was only stated that it had not been validated and PET suspected he was lying.

Intelligence Report 4

An intelligence report showed satellite imagery of a LeT training camp in Muzaffarabad, taken in mid-January 2016. The report did not state which intelligence collection agency provided the image; however the report was classified as 'Top Secret UK Eyes Only'. The imagery was stated as having captured the entirety of the training camp, and that twenty-nine buildings were identified that together comprised the training facility.

This report was designed to mirror the following aspect from the Iraq case study: satellite imagery was obtained of the site where Curveball claimed that the Iraqi regime had a mobile biological weapons laboratory. Like the Iraq case study, it could be legitimately argued that the lack of corroboration provided by this image was the result of concealment activity by LeT: that the storage container could have been moved by the group to avoid detection by the ISI. In addition, even if the imagery was taken to be confirmation of the part of the human source's claim describing a storage container, the imagery alone was not enough to corroborate the claim that the container was being used as an anthrax laboratory. However, unlike the Iraq case study, the imagery provided in the LeT case study is not directly inconsistent with the account provided by the human source. The level of detail seen by the naked eye is insufficient to identify with confidence whether a storage container matching either of the descriptions given by the Curveball equivalent human source was corroborated in the imagery.

Intelligence Report 5

A SIGINT report was provided with details of a conversation between a LeT liaison representative to the ISI and his ISI liaison counterpart, that took place in mid-January 2016. LeT representative and Pakistani national Adeel Khan (henceforth Khan) provided the ISI representative, Hasan Ajwa (henceforth Ajwa), with an account of LeT's operational intentions on 17 January 2016. Khan confirmed that LeT had received the transfer of 750,000 Pakistani rupees from the ISI (approximately equivalent to £50,000), as of late December 2015. Khan explained that the delay in confirming receipt of the funds was due to LeT replacing its ISI accounts manager, Nabeel Lahkani. Lakhani had been caught stealing money from LeT funds. Ajwa requested an update on LeT's operational activity since November 2015. Khan claimed that the group had been concentrating its activity on political lobbying, charitable work, fundraising and expanding its educational programme in Punjab and Jammu. Khan claimed that LeT had conducted two successful small-scale attacks targeting Indian armed forces in Kashmir. One was a roadside improvised explosive device (IED) attack that killed eight Indian soldiers and wounded many others. The IED attack had been blamed on local insurgents. The second attack was a rocket-propelled grenade attack against an old school building that was being used as a temporary camp by Indian Forces. LeT had been unable to confirm the casualties for this attack. Ajwa referred Khan to a recent article in the *New York Times* regarding the conviction of al-Qaeda member Nazmut Tariq (henceforth Tariq). Ajwa requested assurance from Khan that LeT was abiding with its agreement with ISI and had not restarted its research and development activity into biological weapons. Khan assured Ajwa that LeT's attempts to acquire biological agents were limited to its communications with Tariq, and that it had been unsuccessful in acquiring anthrax. Khan claimed that LeT had not attempted to acquire or develop anthrax since Tariq's arrest, and would abide by its agreement with ISI not to do so. Khan claimed that LeT did not have the intellectual capability within the group to use biological agents for attacks against India. The report also contained a report issuer comment, which provided the following information

Khan has been LeT's main interlocutor with ISI since 2009. Khan meets approximately every three months with an ISI representative to provide an account of LeT activities. Ajwa was assigned to the role of liaison officer with LeT as of May 2014.

This report was designed to mirror the following aspect from the Iraq case study: in 1996, the Iraq regime told international inspectors that the aluminium alloy tubes seized on their way to Iraq were for use in the making of rockets and not for the enrichment of uranium. The SIGINT report provides a direct refutation of biological weapons activity from an official LeT representative. Further, the organisation that the denial was provided to had ordered LeT to cease biological activity and gained its agreement that it would do so. However, unlike the Iraq case study, this information was collected in a covert manner.

Intelligence Report 6

An intelligence report was provided from the Indian armed forces, dated mid-April 2016. The report claimed that on 10 April 2016, the Indian armed forces disarmed six IEDs in Kashmir. The IEDs had been built using high charge explosives contained in pressure cooker pots. They had been planted alongside a road leading to an army barracks being used by the Indian armed forces. The Indian armed forces IED unit assessed that the devices had been built by LeT, due to the significant similarities in design of the devices and IEDs used in several previous attacks in India that had been claimed by LeT.

This report was designed to mirror the following aspect from the Iraq case study: material described by previous human sources as being linked to biological weapons activity had a dual use in LeT attacks. This mirrors the aluminium tubes seized on their way to Iraq, and their potential dual use in centrifuges and in conventional rockets. Further, information regarding LeT's prior use of IEDs using pressure cooker pots was contained in the background report on LeT, in the section regarding the group's significant attacks. However, unlike the Iraq case study, the LeT scenario had intelligence that highlighted the dual use of equipment linked to alleged WMD activity by prior human sources, whereas in the Iraq case, analysts did not have intelligence indicating the current use of such tubes by the Iraq regime in conventional attacks as opposed to WMD-related activity.

Table A.1 Experimental study results: rationales for degree of belief scores.

Rationale	Epistemic Relevance
Whether LeT had the funding that would allow an anthrax development programme	No
The level of control ISI has over LeT behaviour	No
Whether LeT would consider biological warfare as an attractive/viable methodology for terrorist attacks	No
Whether anthrax spores could grow in Pakistan	No
Whether LeT was assessed to have previously attempted to gain access to anthrax	No
Access to individuals who have the appropriate skills to manufacture or weaponise anthrax	No
Indication of active attack planning	No
Whether LeT is continuing to avoid terrorism (as stated in 2009) and pursuing political avenues instead of terrorism or insurgency	No
Whether an intent to compete with ISIL will spur LeT towards considering mass casualty terrorist attack methodologies	No
Whether there is an internal fraction/division between Jamaat ud-Dawa (JuD) and LeT that constrains LeT's capabilities to acquire/develop anthrax	No
Whether LeT has ever been a terrorist group/engaged in terrorism over being an insurgent movement	No
Whether LeT has access to the necessary equipment to develop or store anthrax properly/safely	No
How easy it is to cultivate/develop anthrax	No
Whether the information required to develop anthrax is readily available	No
Whether LeT is currently capable of carrying out a terrorist attack using BW	No
Whether LeT has previously expressed an interest in BW	No
Influence of external actors on intent (ISI, al-Qaeda or the Liberation Tigers of Tamil Eelam)	No
The reliability of evidence that has direct diagnostic value to the exam question	Yes
Whether LeT is interested in acquiring/developing BW to use as a threat, but not to actually use in terrorist attacks	No
The volume of available evidence	No
Whether LeT would have the intent to conduct a terrorist attack against/that would risk UK interests	No
Whether LeT would have the capability to conduct a terrorist attack against/that would risk UK interests	No
Whether LeT intends to acquire BW or develop BW	No
Comparison of LeT's capability to other regional actors or historical terrorist activity	No

Whether LeT's rhetoric is consistent with the intent to conduct mass casualty attacks against perceived enemies of Islam	No
Whether LeT would consider BW as a favourable attack methodology	No
Whether LeT has previously threatened to conduct or conducted a terrorist attack using BW	No
Whether the available evidence basis is current or not	Yes
Whether it would be a risk to undervalue the possibility that LeT is/is not attempting to develop or acquire BW for use in terrorist attacks	No
Consistency of information provided	No
The perception of the existence of corroborating information	Yes
The level of detail provided in human source reports	No
Diagnostic value/relevance/specificity of available information on LeT	Yes
The possibility that evidence has been misinterpreted within the reporting chain/doesn't accurately reflect the original source of information.	Yes
Level of support provided by available information to the exam question	Yes
The plausibility of information provided by human sources	Yes
Whether senior LeT leaders approve the acquisition or development of anthrax by the group	No
Whether a human ultimate sub-source providing information has any motivation for providing false information	Yes
Whether the use of BW would be ideologically permissible (including considerations of the risks to killing individuals not classed as enemies by LeT)	No
Whether a human ultimate sub-source has genuine/unique access to the information he or she is providing	Yes
Whether the providers of available information are believed to have no motivation for providing false information	Yes
Whether the providers of available information are believed to apply rigorous/sufficient validation processes, appropriate collection methods and/or appropriate ethical approaches towards either	Yes
Whether available information is consistent with LeT's prior behaviour or declared/demonstrated intentions	No
Whether using BW in terrorist attacks would be a significant change in previous assessed/demonstrated intent	No
Consistency of available information with previous knowledge of LeT	No
Whether information provided is internally consistent	Yes
Whether new information is judged to be of sufficient quality to challenge prior, contradictory evidence	No
Whether new information is judged to be of sufficient quality to challenge the beliefs of the assessor	No
Whether information indicates LeT is trying to aerosolise BW that it has in its possession	No
Whether there are any credible claims/evidence that LeT is attempting to acquire/develop BW	Yes

243

Table A.2 Experimental study results: rationales for assessments of credibility.

Rationale	Proportion of participants citing rationale: intelligence report 1	Proportion of participants citing rationale: intelligence report 2	Proportion of participants citing rationale: intelligence report 3	Proportion of participants citing rationale: intelligence report 4	Proportion of participants citing rationale: intelligence report 5	Proportion of participants citing rationale: intelligence report 6
Ability to verify the information	5.13%	2.56%	0.00%	0.00%	0.00%	7.69%
Classification of intelligence report	0.00%	0.00%	2.56%	0.00%	0.00%	0.00%
Collection method/Sourcing chain	5.13%	10.26%	20.51%	43.59%	15.39%	2.64%
Concerns over source validation	5.13%	5.13%	28.21%	0.00%	0.00%	0.00%
Consistency of information with analysts' beliefs	0.00%	53.84%	20.51%	5.13%	28.21%	28.21%
Consistency of information with prior reporting	30.76%	25.64%	0.00%	7.69%	23.08%	7.69%
Diagnostic value of information	0.00%	0.00%	0.00%	40.03%	5.13%	15.39%
Epistemological status or quality of information	0.00%	0.00%	0.00%	5.13%	0.00%	12.81%
Information out of date	2.56%	5.13%	0.00%	0.00%	2.56%	0.00%
Intelligence provider agency unidentified	10.25%	2.56%	0.00%	2.56%	0.00%	0.00%
Internal consistency of the claim	0.00%	2.56%	0.00%	0.00%	0.00%	0.00%
Lack of independent corroboration	7.69%	0.00%	5.13%	0.00%	0.00%	0.00%
Level of source's access to the information	5.13%	5.13%	0.00%	0.00%	2.56%	7.69%
Level of detail provided	35.89%	30.78%	20.51%	12.82%	0.00%	2.64%
Level of trust agent runners have in source	0.00%	0.00%	38.46%	0.00%	0.00%	0.00%
Level of trust in intelligence provider	7.69%	5.13%	2.56%	10.26%	5.13%	17.95%
Motivations/Possibility of deception	30.76%	46.15%	51.28%	23.08%	74.36%	35.89%
Plausibility of information	7.69%	5.13%	0.00%	0.00%	0.00%	0.00%
Relationship between sub-sources	0.00%	0.00%	0.00%	0.00%	25.64%	0.00%
Reliability of source(s) in sourcing chain	2.56%	2.56%	0.00%	0.00%	2.56%	56.41%
Requires subject matter expertise to interpret claim	0.00%	0.00%	0.00%	7.69%	0.00%	0.00%
Whether the ultimate source is identified/known	15.38%	7.69%	0.00%	0.00%	2.56%	0.00%

Bibliography

Abelson, R. P. (1959), 'Modes of Resolution of Belief Dilemmas', *Conflict Resolution*, 3, pp. 343–52.

Ackerman, G. (2008), 'WMD Terrorism and the Perils of Prediction', in Chesser, N. (ed.), *Anticipating Rare Events: Can Acts of Terror, Use of Weapons of Mass Destruction or Other High-Profile Acts Be Anticipated? Scientific Perspective on Problems, Pitfalls and Prospective Solutions*, United States Department of Defense, <https://www.hsdl.org/?abstract&did=233523>, pp. 11–16.

Adamson, R. (1911), 'Roger Bacon', in Chisholm, H. (ed.), *Encyclopædia Britannica*, 11th edn, Cambridge: Cambridge University Press.

Adelman, L. and Bresnick, T. A. (1992), 'Examining the Effect of Information Sequence on Expert Judgment: An Experiment with Patriot Air Defense Officers using the Patriot Air Defense Simulator', *Organizational Behavior and Human Decision Processes*, 53, pp. 204–28.

Adelman, L., Bresnick, T.A., Black, P. K., Marvin, F. F. and Sak, S. G. (1996), 'Research with Patriot Air Defence Officers: Examining Information Order Effects', *Human Factors*, 38(2), pp. 250–61.

Adelman, L., Bresnick, T. A., Christian, M., Gualtieri, J. and Minionis, D. (1997), 'Demonstrating the Effect of Context on Order Effects for an Army Air Defense Task using the Patriot Simulator', *Journal of Behavioral Decision Making*, 10, pp. 327–42.

Adelman, L., Tolcott, M. A. and Bresnick, T. A. (1993), 'Examining the Effect of Information Order on Expert Judgment', *Organizational Behavior and Human Decision Processes*, 56, pp. 348–69.

Agrell, W. (2012), *Essence of Assessment: Methods and Problems of Intelligence Analysis*, trans. S. Moores, Mölnlycke: Gleerups Utbildning AB.

Allen, V. L. and Feldman, R. S. (1974), 'Tutor Attributions and Attitude as a Function of Tutee Performance', *Journal of Applied Social Psychology*, 4(4), pp. 311–20.

Anderson, N. H. (1959), 'Test of a Model for Opinion Change', *Journal of Abnormal and Social Psychology*, 59, pp. 371–81.

Anderson, N. H. (1964a), 'Note on Weighted Sum and Linear Operator Models', *Psychonomic Science*, 1, pp. 189–90.

Anderson, N. H. (1964b), 'Test of a Model for Number Averaging Behaviour': *Psychonomic Science*, 1, pp. 191–2.

Anderson, N. H. (1965a), 'Averaging versus Adding as a Stimulus-Combination Rule in Impression Formation', *Journal of Experimental Psychology*, 70, pp. 394–400.

Anderson, N. H. (1965b), 'Primacy Effects in Personality Impression Formation Using a Generalized Order Effect Paradigm', *Journal of Personality and Social Psychology*, 2(1), pp. 1–9.

Anderson, N. H. (1966), 'Component Ratings in Impression Formation', *Psychonomic Science*, 6, pp. 279–80.

Anderson, N. H. (1967a), 'Application of a Weighted Average Model to a Psychological Averaging Task', *Psychonomic Science*, 8(6), pp. 227–8.

Anderson, N. H. (1967b), 'Averaging Model Analysis of Set Size Effect in Impression Formation', *Journal of Experimental Psychology*, 75, pp. 158–65.

Anderson, N. H. (1968a), 'A Simple Model for Information Integration', in Abelson, R. P., Aronson, E., McGuire, W. J., Newcomb, T. M., Rosenberg, M. J. and Tannenbaum, P. H. (eds), *Theories of Cognitive Consistency: A Sourcebook*, Chicago: Rand McNally, pp. 731–43.

Anderson, N. H. (1968b), 'Likableness Ratings of 555 Personality-Trait Words', *Journal of Personality and Social Psychology*, 9, pp. 272–9.

Anderson, N. H. (1968c), 'Application of a Linear-Serial Model to a Personality-Impression Task Using Serial Presentation', *Journal of Personality and Social Psychology*, 10(4), pp. 354–62.

Anderson, N. H. (1971), 'Two More Tests against Change of Meaning in Adjective Combinations', *Journal of Verbal Learning and Verbal Behavior*, 10, pp. 75–85.

Anderson, N. H. (1972), *Information Integration Theory: A Brief Survey*, La Jolla, CA: University of California San Diego.

Anderson, N. H. (1973a), 'Information Integration Theory Applied to Attitudes about US Presidents', *Journal of Educational Psychology*, 84(1), pp. 1–8.

Anderson, N. H. (1973b), 'Serial Position Curves in Impression Formation', *Journal of Experimental Psychology*, 97(1), pp. 8–12.

Anderson, N. H. and Alexander, G. R. (1971), 'Choice Test of the Averaging Hypothesis for Information Integration', *Cognitive Psychology*, 2, pp. 313–24.

Anderson, N. H. and Barrios, A. A. (1961), 'Primacy Effects in Personality Impression Formation', *Journal of Abnormal and Social Psychology*, 63(2), pp. 346–60 .

Anderson, N. H. and Farkas, A. J. (1973), 'New Light on Order Effects in Attitude Change', *Journal of Personality and Social Psychology*, 28(1), pp. 88–93.

Anderson, N. H. and Hovland, C. I. (1957), 'The Representation of Order Effects in Communication Research', in Hovland, C. I. (ed.), *The Order of Presentation in Persuasion*, New Haven, CT: Yale University Press, pp. 158–69.

Anderson, N. H. and Hubert, S. (1963), 'Effects of Concomitant Verbal Recall on Order Effects in Personality Impression Formation', *Journal of Verbal Learning and Verbal Behavior*, 2, pp. 379–91.

Anderson, N. H. and Jacobson, A. (1965), 'Effects of Stimulus Inconsistency and Discounting Instructions in Personality Impression Formation', *Journal of Personality and Social Psychology*, 2, pp. 531–9.

Anderson, N. H. and Jacobson, A. (1968), 'Further Data on a Weighted Average Model for Judgment in a Lifted Weight Task', *Perception & Psychophysics*, 4, pp. 81–4.

Anderson, N. H. and Norman, A. (1964), 'Order Effects in Impression Formation in Four Classes of Stimuli', *Journal of Abnormal and Social Psychology*, 69(5), pp. 467–71.

Aquinas, T. ([1265–74] 1917), Summa Theologica, New York: Benziger Brothers.

Arkes, H. R. and Harkness, A. R. (1983), 'Estimates of Contingency between Two Dichotomous Variables', *Journal of Experimental Psychology: General*, 112, pp. 117–35.

Armstrong, D. M. (1973), *Belief, Truth and Knowledge*, Cambridge: Cambridge University Press.

Arnold, V., Collier, P. A., Leech, S. A. and Gurron, S. G. (2000), 'The Effect of Experience and Complexity on Order and Recency Bias in Decision-Making by Professional Accountants', *Accounting and Finance*, 40, pp. 109–34.

Aristotle (1998), *The Metaphysics*, London: Penguin Books Ltd.

Asare, S. (1992), 'The Auditor's Going Concern Decision: Interaction of Task Variables and the Sequential Processing of Evidence', *The Accounting Review*, 67(2), pp. 379–93.

Asch, S. E. (1946), 'Forming Impressions of Personality', *Journal of Abnormal and Social Psychology*, 41, pp. 258–90.

Ashton, A. H. and Ashton, R. H. (1988), 'Sequential Belief Revision in Auditing', *The Accounting Review*, 63, pp. 623–41.

247

Astorino-Courtois, A. and Vona, D. (2008), 'Bounding a Known Unknown: The Role of Decision Theory in Rare Events Analysis', in Chesser, N. (ed.), *Anticipating Rare Events: Can Acts of Terror, Use of Weapons of Mass Destruction or Other High-Profile Acts Be Anticipated?*, United States Department of Defense, <https://www.hsdl.org/?abstract&did=233523>, pp. 105–9.

Atkinson, R. C. (1963), 'A Variable Sensitivity Theory of Signal Detection', *Psychological Review*, 70, pp. 91–106.

Audi, R. (2002), 'The Sources of Knowledge', in Moser, P. K. (ed.), *The Oxford Handbook of Epistemology*, Oxford: Oxford University Press, pp. 71–94.

Ayer, A. J. (1956), *The Problem of Knowledge*, London: Penguin Books Ltd.

Ayer, A. J. (1976), *The Central Problems of Philosophy*, London: Pelican Books Ltd.

Bacon, F. ([1620] 2009), *Novum Organum*, Ann Arbor, MI: University of Michigan Library.

Bakker, E. (2012), 'Forecasting Terrorism: The Need for a More Systematic Approach', *Journal of Strategic Security*, 5(4), pp. 69–84.

Bargh, J. A., Chen, M. and Burrow, L. (1996), 'Automaticity of Social Behaviour: Direct Effects of Trait Construct and Stereotype Activation on Action', *Journal of Personality and Social Psychology*, 71, pp. 230–44.

Bar-Hillel, M. (1980), 'The Base-Rate Fallacy in Probability Judgements', *Acta Psychologica*, 44, pp. 211–33.

Bar-Joseph, U. and Kruglanski, A. W. (2003), 'Intelligence Failure and the Need for Cognitive Closure: On the Psychology of the Yom Kippur Surprise', *Political Psychology*, 24(1), pp. 75–99.

Bar-Joseph, U. and McDermott, R. (2010), 'The Intelligence Analysis Crisis', in Johnson, L. K. (ed.), *The Oxford Handbook of National Security Intelligence*, Oxford: Oxford University Press, <DOI:10.1093/oxfordhb/9780195375886.003.0022>.

Barnes, G. (2002), 'Conceivability, Explanation, and Defeat', *Philosophical Studies*, 108, pp. 327–38.

Barnes, G. (2006), 'Necessity and A Priority', *Philosophical Studies*, 132(3), pp. 495–523.

Barrows, H. S., Norman, G. R., Neufeld, V. R. and Feightner, J. W. (1982), 'The Clinical Reasoning of Randomly Selected Physicians in General Medicine Practice', Clinical and Investigative Medicine, 5, pp. 49–55.

Bayes, T. (1764), 'An Essay Toward Solving a Problem in the Doctrine of Chances', Philosophical Transactions of the Royal Society of London, 53, pp. 370–418.

Bealer, G. (1987), 'Philosophical Limits of Scientific Essentialism', *Philosophical Perspectives*, 1 (Metaphysics), pp. 289–365.

Bealer, G. (2002), 'Modal Epistemology and the Rationalist Renaissance', in Gendler, T. and Hawthorne, J. (eds), *Conceivability and Possibility*, Oxford: Oxford University Press, pp. 71–125.

Bealer, G. (2006), 'A Definition of Necessity', *Philosophical Perspectives*, 20, pp. 17–39.

Beattie, J. and Baron, J. (1988), 'Confirmation and Matching Biases in Hypothesis Testing', *Quarterly Journal of Experimental Psychology*, 40A(2), pp. 269–97.

Beebe, S. and Pherson, R. (2008), 'Cognitive Pitfalls', in Chesser, N. (ed.), *Anticipating Rare Events: Can Acts of Terror, Use of Weapons of Mass Destruction or Other High-Profile Acts Be Anticipated?*, United States Department of Defense, <https://www.hsdl.org/?abstract&did=233523>, pp. 50–4.

Benaceraff, P. (1973), 'Mathematical Truth', *Journal of Philosophy*, 70, pp. 661–79.

Benassi, M. A. (1982), 'Effects of Order Presentation, Primacy, and Physical Attractiveness on Attributions of Ability', *Journal of Personality and Social Psychology*, 43(1), pp. 48–58.

Ben-Israel, B. (1989), 'Philosophy and Methodology of Intelligence: The Logic of the Estimate Process', *Intelligence and National Security*, 4(4), pp. 660–718.

Ben-Israel, I. (2001), 'Philosophy and Methodology of Military Intelligence – Correspondence with Paul Feyerabend', *Philosophia*, 28(1–4), pp. 71–102.

Berkeley, G. ([1710] 2016), *A Treatise Concerning the Principles of Human Knowledge*, Scotts Valley, CA: CreateSpace Independent Publishing Platform.

Berkowitz, B. D. and Goodman, A. E. (2000), *Best Truth: Intelligence in the Information Age*, New Haven, CT: Yale University Press.

Bernardo, J. M. (1994), 'Bayesian Statistics', in Viertl, R. (ed.), *Probability and Statistics Volume II: Probabilistic Models and Methods, Foundations of Statistics*, Oxford: Eolss Publishers Ltd.

Bernardo, J. M. and Smith, A. F. M. (1994), *Bayesian Theory*, Chichester: Wiley.

Betts, R. K. (1979), *Analysis, War and Decision: Why Intelligence Failures are Inevitable*, Washington DC: Central Intelligence Agency.

Betts, R. K. and Mahnken, T. G. (eds), *Paradoxes of Strategic Intelligence*, London: Frank Cass, pp. 80–100.

Bienenstock, E. and Toman, P. (2008), 'Social Network Analysis for Detecting the Web of Rare Event Planning and Preparation', in

Chesser, N. (ed.), *Anticipating Rare Events: Can Acts of Terror, Use of Weapons of Mass Destruction or Other High-Profile Acts Be Anticipated?* United States Department of Defense, <https://www.hsdl.org/?abstract&did=233523>, pp. 110–15.

Bigelow, J. (1988), The Reality of Numbers: A Physicalist's Philosophy of Mathematics, Oxford: Oxford University Press.

Bisanz, J., Bisanz, G. L. and Corpan, C. A. (1994), 'Inductive Reasoning', in Sternberg, R. J. (ed.), *Thinking and Problem Solving: Handbook of Perception and Cognition*, 2nd edn, New Haven, CT: Yale University Press.

Bjork, R. A. and Whitten, W. B. (1974), 'Recency-Sensitive Retrieval Processes in Long-Term Free Recall', *Cognitive Psychology*, 6, pp. 173–89.

Block, R. A. and Harper, D. R. (1991), 'Overconfidence in Estimation: Testing the Anchoring-and-Adjustment Hypotheses', *Organizational Behaviour and Human Decision-Making Processes*, 49, pp. 188–207.

Bodnar, J. W. (2003), 'Warning Analysis for the Information Age: Rethinking the Intelligence Process', Washington DC: Joint Military Intelligence College.

BonJour, L. (1985), *The Structure of Empirical Knowledge*, Cambridge, MA and London: Harvard University Press.

Boole, G. (1894), *An Investigation into The Laws of Thought*, London: Walton & Mamberly.

Bossart, P. and Di Vesta, F. J. (1966), 'Effects of Context, Frequency, and Order of Presentation of Evaluative Assertions on Impression Formation', *Journal of Personality and Social Psychology*, 4(5), pp. 538–44.

Bowell, T. and Kemp, G. (2002), *Critical Thinking: A Concise Guide*, 2nd edn, London: Routledge.

Bower, G. H. (1971), 'Adaptation-Level Coding of Stimuli and Serial Position Effects', in Appley, M. H. (ed.), *Adaptation-Level Theory*, New York: Academic Press, pp. 175–201.

Boyd, R. (1981), 'Scientific Realism and Naturalistic Epistemology', in Asquith, P. and Giere, R. (eds), *PSA 1980*, vol. 2, East Lansing, MI: Philosophy of Science Association.

Boyd, R. (1984), 'The Current Status of Scientific Realism', in Lepin, J. (ed.), *Scientific Realism*, Berkeley, CA: University of California Press.

Bradley, F. H. (1914), Essays on Truth and Reality, Oxford: Clarendon Press.

Brandwein, D. S. (1995), 'Telemetry Analysis', Central Intelligence Agency, <https://www.cia.gov/library/center-for-the-study-of-intelligence/kent-csi/vol8no4/html/v08i4a03p_0001.htm>.

Brennan, A. (2011), 'Necessary and Sufficient Conditions', in Zalta, E. N. (ed.), *The Stanford Encyclopedia of Philosophy*, <http://plato. stanford.edu/entries/necessary-sufficient/>.

Broomberger, S. (1966), 'Why-Questions', in Colodny, R. (ed.), *Mind and Cosmos: Essays in Contemporary Science and Philosophy*, Pittsburgh, PA: University of Pittsburgh Press, pp. 68–111.

Bruce, J. B. (2008), 'Making Analysis More Reliable: Why Epistemology Matters to Intelligence', in George, R. Z. and Bruce, J. B. (eds), *Analyzing Intelligence: Origins, Obstacles, and Innovations*, Washington DC: Georgetown University Press, pp. 171–90.

Bruce, J. B. and George, R. Z. (eds) (2008), *Analysing Intelligence: Origins, Obstacles and Innovations*, Washington DC: Georgetown University Press.

Bruner, J. S. and Postman, L. (1949), 'On the Perception of Incongruity: A Paradigm', in Bruner, J. S. and Kraut, D. (eds), *Perception and Personality: A Symposium*, New York: Greenwood Press.

Bruner, J. S. and Potter, M. C. (1964), 'Interference in Visual Recognition', *Science*, 144, pp. 424–5.

Butt, J. L. and Campbell, T. L. (1989), 'The Effects of Information Order and Hypothesis Testing Strategies on Auditors' Judgments', *Accounting, Organizations and Society*, 14, pp. 471–9.

Butterfield, A. P. (1993), 'The Accuracy of Intelligence: Bias, Perception and Judgement in Analysis and Decision', paper submitted for Advanced Research Project at Center for Naval Warfare Studies, Newport, RI: Naval War College.

Cabinet Office (2004), *Review of Intelligence on Weapons of Mass Destruction (Butler Review)*, London: Cabinet Office.

Cabinet Office (2015), *Quick Wins for Busy Analysts*, Professional Heads of Intelligence Analysis, London: Cabinet Office.

Capitani, E., Della Salla, S., Logie, R. H. and Spinnler, H. (1992), 'Recency, Primary and Memory: Reappraising and Standardising the Serial Position Curve', *Cortex*, 28(3), pp. 315–42.

Card, S., Hutchins, S. G. and Pirolli, P. (2003), 'Use of Critical Analysis Method to Conduct a Cognitive Task Analysis of Intelligence Analysts', *Proceedings of the Human Factors and Ergonomics Society 47th Annual Meeting, Denver, Colorado, October 13–17, 2003*, Santa Monica, CA: Human Factors and Ergonomics Society.

Carlson, K. A. and Russo, J. E. (2001), 'The Effects of Information Order and Hypothesis Testing Strategies on Auditors' Judgments', *Journal of Applied Experimental Psychology*, 7(2), pp. 91–103.

Carlson, R. A. and Dulany, D. E. (1988), 'Diagnostic Reasoning with Circumstantial Evidence', *Cognitive Psychology*, 20, pp. 463–92.

Carnap, R. (1950), *Logical Foundations of Probability*, Chicago: University of Chicago Press.

Central Intelligence Agency (1975), *Handbook of Bayesian Analysis for Intelligence*, Washington DC: Central Intelligence Agency.

Central Intelligence Agency (1997), 'A Compendium of Analytic Tradecraft Notes', Directorate of Intelligence, Washington DC: Central Intelligence Agency.

Central Intelligence Agency (2009), *A Tradecraft Primer: Structured Analytical Methods for Improving Intelligence Analysis*, Washington DC: Central Intelligence Agency.

Chalmers, D. (1999), 'Materialism and the Metaphysics of Modality', *Philosophy and Phenomenological Research*, 59, pp. 473–96.

Chalmers, D. (2002), 'Does Conceivability Entail Possibility?', in Gendler, T. and Hawthorne, J. (eds), *Conceivability and Possibility*, Oxford: Oxford University Press.

Chalmers, D. (2004), 'Epistemic Two-Dimensional Semantics', *Philosophical Studies*, 118, pp. 153–226.

Chalmers, D. (2009), 'Ontological Anti-Realism', in Chalmers, D., Manley, D. and Wasserman, R. (eds), *Metaphysics: New Essays on the Foundation of Ontology*, Oxford: Oxford University Press.

Chalmers, D., Manley, D. and Wasserman, R. (2009), *Metaphysics: New Essays on the Foundation of Ontology*, Oxford: Oxford University Press.

Chalmers, D. K. (1971), 'Repetition and Order Effects in Attitude Formation', *Journal of Personality and Social Psychology*, 17, pp. 219–28.

Chalmers, D. K. (1979), 'Meanings, Impressions, and Attitudes: A Model of the Evaluation Process', *Psychological Review*, 76, pp. 450–60.

Chamberlain, T. C. ([1890] 1931), 'Method of Multiple Working Hypotheses', *Journal of Geology*, 5, 837–48,

Chang, W., Berdinj, E., Mandel, D. M. and Tetlock, P. E. (2017), 'Restructuring Structured Analytical Methods in Intelligence', *Intelligence and National Security*, DOI: 10.1080/02684527.2017.1400230.

Chapman, L. and Chapman, J. (1967), 'Genesis of Popular but Erroneous Diagnostic Observations', *Journal of Abnormal Psychology*, 72, pp. 193–204.

Charters, D. A., Farson, S. and Hastedt, G. P. (eds) (2004), *Intelligence Analysis and Assessment*, Oxford: Frank Cass & Co Ltd.

Cheikes, B. A., Brown, M. J., Lehner, P. E. and Adelman, L. (2004), 'Confirmation Bias in Complex Analyses', MITRE technical report MTR 04B0000017, Bedford, MA: MITRE, Centre for Integrated Intelligence Systems.

Chen, S., Schechter, D. and Chaiken, S. (1996), 'Getting at the Truth or Getting Along: Accuracy- versus Impression-Motivated Heuristic and Systematic Processing', *Journal of Personality and Social Psychology*, 71, pp. 262–75.

Chisholm, R. M. (1966), *Theory of Knowledge*, Englewood Cliffs, NJ: Prentice-Hall.

Churchill, R. P. (1990), *Logic: An Introduction*, 2nd edn, New York: St. Martin's Press.

Clauser, J. K. and Weir, S. M. (1975), Intelligence Research Methodology, An Introduction to Techniques and Procedures for Conducting Research in Defense Intelligence, Washington DC: Defense Intelligence School.

Cooper, J. (2005), 'Curing Analytic Pathologies: Pathways to Improved Intelligence Analysis', Washington DC: Center for the Study of Intelligence Analysis.

Commission on the Intelligence Capabilities of the United States Regarding Weapons of Mass Destruction (2005), *Report of the Commission on the Intelligence Capabilities of the United States Regarding Weapons of Mass Destruction*, Washington DC: United States Government.

Conrad, R. (1960), 'Serial Order Intrusions in Immediate Memory', *British Journal of Psychology*, 51, pp. 45–8.

Conrad, R. (1965), 'Order Error in Immediate Recall of Sequences', *Journal of Verbal Learning and Verbal Behavior*, 4, pp. 161–9.

Corballis, M. (1967), 'Serial Order in Recognition and Recall', *Journal of Experimental Psychology*, 74, pp. 99–105.

Covey, J. A. and Lovie, A. D. (1998), 'Information Selection and Utilization in Hypotheses Testing: A Comparison of Process-Tracing and Structural Analysis Techniques', *Organizational Behaviour and Human Decision Processes*, 75(1), pp. 56–74.

Cowan, N. (2001), 'The Magical Number 4 in Short-Term Memory: A Reconsideration of Mental Storage Capacity', Behavioural and Brain Sciences, 24, pp. 87–185.

Cox, J. R. and Griggs, R. A. (1982), 'The Effect of Experience on Learning in Wason's Selection Task', *Memory and Cognition*, 10(5), pp. 496–502.

Crano, W. D. (1977), 'Primacy versus Recency in Retention of Information and Opinion Change', *Journal of Social Psychology*, 101, pp. 87–96.

Criminal Intelligence Service Canada (2007), *Strategic Early Warning for Criminal Intelligence: Theoretical Framework and Sentinel Methodology*, Ottowa: Criminal Intelligence Service.

Crocker, J. (1981), 'Judgement of Covariation by Social Perceivers', *Personality and Social Psychology Bulletin*, 90, pp. 272–92.

Crombie, A. C. (1971), *Robert Grosseteste and the Origins of Experimental Science 1100–1700*, Oxford: Clarendon Press.

Cromwell, H. (1950), 'The Relative Effect on Audience Attitude of the First versus the Second Argumentative Speech of a Series', *Speech Monogram*, 17, pp. 105–22.

Croskerry, P. (2009), 'A Universal Model of Diagnostic Reasoning', *Academic Medicine*, 84(8), pp. 1022–8.

Crosston, M. (2013), 'Occam's Follies: Real and Imagined Biases Facing Intelligence Studies', *Journal of Strategic Security*, 6(3), pp. 40–53.

Crowder, R. G. (1979), 'Similarity and Order in Memory', in Bower, G. H. (ed.), *The Psychology of Learning and Motivation*, vol. 13, New York: Academic Press, pp. 319–53.

Curley, S. P., Young, M. J., Kingry, M. J. and Yates, J. F. (1988), 'Primacy Effects in Clinical Judgments of Contingency', *Medical Decision Making*, 8, pp. 216–22.

Dale, H. C. A. (1968), 'Weighing Evidence: An Attempt to Assess the Efficiency of the Human Operator', *Ergonomics*, 11, pp. 215–30.

Darley, J. M. and Gross, P. H. (1983), 'A Hypothesis Confirming Bias in Labelling Effects', *Journal of Personality and Social Psychology*, 44, pp. 20–33.

David, M. (2013), 'The Correspondence Theory of Truth', in Zalta, N. E. (ed.), The Stanford Encyclopedia of Philosophy, <http://plato.stanford.edu/archives/fall2013/entries/truth-correspondence/>.

Davis, E. G. (1969), 'A Watchman for All Seasons: Intelligence Evaluation for Warning', *Studies in Intelligence*, 13(2), p. 68.

Davis, J. (2007), 'Strategic Warning: Intelligence Support in a World of Uncertainty and Surprise', in Johnson, L. K. (ed.), *Handbook of Intelligence Studies*, London: Routledge, pp. 173–88.

Davis, J. (2008), 'Why Bad Things Happen to Good Analysts', in Bruce, J. B. and George, R. Z. (eds), *Analysing Intelligence: Origins, Obstacles and Innovations*, Washington DC: Georgetown University Press.

Descartes, R. ([1673] 2017), *Discourses on the Method of Rightly Conducting One's Reason and Seeking Truth in the Sciences*, Scott's Valley, CA: CreateSpace Independent Publishing Platform.

Descartes, R. ([1641] 2010), *Meditations*, London: Penguin Classics.

Deshmukh, H., Lee, J. and Wheaton, K. J. (2009), 'Teaching Bayesian Statistics to Intelligence Analysts: Lessons Learned', *Journal of Strategic Studies*, 3(1), pp. 39–58.

De Wit, H., Hogarth, R. M., Koehler, J. J. and Luchins, D. J. (1989), 'Effects of Diazepam on a Belief-Updating Task', *Psychological Reports*, 64, pp. 219–26.

Devine, P. G., Hirt, E. R. and Gehrke, E. M. (1990), 'Diagnostic and Confirmation Strategies in Trait Hypothesis Testing', *Journal of Personality and Social Psychology*, 58, pp. 952–63.

Dijksterhuis, A., Spears, R., Postmes, T., Stapel, D. A., Koomen, W., Van Knippenberg, A. and Scheepers, D. (1998), 'Seeing One Thing and Doing Another: Contrast Effect in Automatic Behavior', *Journal of Personality and Social Psychology*, 75, pp. 862–71.

Dillard, J. F., Kauffman, N. L. and Spires, E. E. (1991), 'Evidence Order and Belief Revision in Management Accounting Decisions', *Accounting, Organizations and Society*, 16(7), pp. 619–33.

Doherty, M. E., Chadwick, R., Garayan, H., Barr, D. and Mynatt, C. R. (1996), 'On People's Understanding of the Diagnostic Implications of Probabilistic Data', *Memory and Cognition*, 24, pp. 644–54.

Doherty, M. E., Mynatt, C. R., Tweney, R. D. and Schiavo, M. D. (1979), 'Pseudodiagnosticity', *Acta Psychologica*, 43, pp. 11–21.

Donnel, M. L. and DuCharme, W. M. (1965), 'The Effect of Bayesian Feedback on Learning in an Odds Estimation Task', *Organization Behaviour and Human Performance*, 14, pp. 305–13.

Dougherty, M. R. P., Gettys, C. F. and Thomas, R. P. (1997), 'The Role of Mental Simulation in Judgments of Likelihood', Organizational Behavior and Human Decision Processes, 70, pp. 135–48.

Dougherty, R. P. and Hunter, J. E. (2003), 'Hypothesis Generation, Probability Judgment, and Individual Differences in Working Memory Capacity', Acta Psychologica, 113, pp. 263–82.

Douven, I. (2011), 'Abduction', in Zalta, E. N. (ed.), *The Stanford Encyclopedia of Philosophy*, <http://plato.stanford.edu/archives/spr2011/entries/abduction/>.

Dreben, E. K., Fiske, S. T. and Hastie, R. (1979), 'The Independence of Evaluative and Item Information: Impression and Recall Order Effects in Behaviour-Based Impression Formation', *Journal of Personality and Social Psychology*, 37(10), pp. 1758–68.

Dretske, F. I. (1971), 'Perception from an Epistemological Point of View', *Journal of Philosophy*, 68(19), pp. 584–91.

Drogin, R. (2008), *Curveball: Spies, Lies and the Man Behind Them: The Real Reason America Went to War in Iraq*, London: Ebury Press.

Duelfer. C. (2004a), *Comprehensive Report of the Special Advisor to the DCI on Iraqi WMD*, vol. II, Washington DC: Central Intelligence Agency.

Duelfer, C. (2004b), *Comprehensive Report of the Special Advisor to the DCI on Iraqi WMD*, vol. III, Washington DC: Central Intelligence Agency.

Dummett, M. (1978), *Truth and Other Enigmas*, London: Duckworth.

Dummett, M. (2005), 'The Justificationist's Response to a Realist', *Mind*, 114(445), pp. 671–88.

Duncan, K. A. and Wilson, J. L. (2009), 'A Multinomial-Dirichlet Model for Analysis of Competing Hypotheses', *Risk Analysis*, 28(6), pp. 1609–709.

Duvenage, M. A. (2010), *Intelligence Analysis in the Information Age: An Analysis of the Challenges Facing the Practice of Intelligence Analysis*, Stellenbosch: University of Stellenbosch.

Larson, E. V., Eaton, D., Nichiporuk, B. and Szayna, T. S. (2008), *Assessing Irregular Warfare: A Framework for Intelligence Analysis*, Arlington, VA: RAND Corporation.

Edwards, W. and Phillips, L. D. (1964), 'Man as Transducer for Probabilities in Bayesian Command and Control Systems', in Shelly, M. W. and Bryan, G. L. (eds), *Human Judgements and Optimality*, New York: Wiley.

Einhorn, H. J. (1980), 'Learning from Experience and Suboptimal Rules in Decision-Making', in Wallsten, T. S. (ed.), Cognitive Processes in Choice and Decision Behaviour, Hillsdale, NJ: Lawrence Erlbaum Associates Inc.

Einhorn, H. J. and Hogarth, R. M. (1978), 'Confidence in Judgement: Persistence in the Illusion of Validity', *Psychological Review*, 85, pp. 396–416.

Einhorn, H. J. and Hogarth, R. M. (1981), 'Behavioural Decision Theory: Processes of Judgement and Choice', *Annual Review of Psychology*, 32, pp. 53–88.

Einhorn, H. J. and Hogarth, R. M. (1986), 'Judging Probable Cause', *Psychological Bulletin*, 99, pp. 3–19.

Einhorn, H. J. and Hogarth, R. M. (1987), *Adaptation and Inertia in Belief Updating: The Contrast-Inertia Model*, Chicago: University of Chicago.

Elliot, L. P. and Brook, B. W. (2007), 'Revisiting Chamberlain: Multiple Working Hypotheses for the 21st Century', *BioScience*, 57(7), pp. 608–14.

Engle, R. W., Kane, M. J. and Tuholski, S. W. (1999), 'Individual Differences in Working Memory Capacity and What They Tell Us about Controlled Attention, General Fluid Intelligence, and Functions of the Prefrontal Cortex', in Miyake, A. and Shah, P. (eds), Models of Working Memory: Mechanisms of Active Maintenance and Executive Control, New York: Cambridge University Press, pp. 102–34 .

Engle, R. W., Tuholsk, S. W., Laughlin, J. E. and Conway, A. R. A. (1999), 'Working Memory, Short-Term Memory, and General Fluid Intelligence: A Latent-Variable Approach', Journal of Experimental Psychology: General, 128, pp. 309–31.

Entin, E. E., James, R. M., Serfaty, D. and Forester, J. (1987), 'The Effects of Cognitive Style and Prior Information on Multi-Stage Decision-Making', Technical Report TR-277-1, Burlington, MA: ALPHATECH Inc.

Entin, E. E., Serfaty, D. and Forester, J. (1989), 'Sequential Processing of Information from Multiple Sources', in *Proceedings of the System, Man, and Cybernetics Society, November 14–17, 1989, Cambridge, Massachusetts*, New York: Institute of Electrical and Electronics Engineers (IEEE) Press, pp. 91–100.

Entin, E., Serfaty, D. and Forester, J. (1997), 'Sequential Revision of Belief: An Application to Complex Decision-Making Situations', *Institute of Electrical and Electronics Engineers (IEEE) Transactions on Systems, Man, and Cybernetics. Part A: Systems and Humans*, 27(3), pp. 289–301.

Evans, J. St. B. T. (1984), 'Heuristic and Analytic Processes in Reasoning', *British Journal of Psychology*, 75, pp. 451–68.

Evans, J. St. B. T. (1989), *Bias in Human Reasoning: Causes and Consequences*, Mahwah, NJ: Laurence Erlbaum Associates, Inc.

Evans, J. St. B. T. (2016), 'Reasoning, Bias and Dual Processes: The Lasting Impact of Wason (1960)', *Quarterly Journal of Experimental Psychology*, 69(10), pp. 2076–92.

Evans, J. St. B. T., Handley, S. J., Harper, C. and Johnson-Laird, P. N. (1999), 'Reasoning about Necessity and Possibility: A Test of the Mental Model Theory of Deduction', *Journal of Experimental Psychology: Learning, Memory and Cognition*, 25, pp. 1495–513.

Evans, J. St. B. T. and Lynch, J. S. (1973), 'Matching Bias in the Selection Task', *British Journal of Psychology*, 64, pp. 391–7.

Evans, J. St. B., Venn, S. and Feeney, A. (2002), 'Implicit and Explicit Processes in a Hypothesis Testing Task', *British Journal of Psychology*, 93(1), pp. 31–46.

Everitt, N. and Fisher, A. (1995), *Modern Epistemology: A New Introduction*, New York: McGraw-Hill, Inc.

Feeney, A., Evans, J. St. B. T. and Venn, S. (2000), 'Background Beliefs and Evidence Interpretation', *Thinking and Reasoning*, 6, pp. 97–124.

Feldman, R. S. and Bernstein, A. G. (1977), 'Degree and Sequence of Success as Determinants of Self-Attribution of Ability', *Journal of Social Psychology*, 102, pp. 223–31.

Feldman, R. S. and Bernstein, A. G. (1978), 'Primacy Effects in Self-Attribution of Ability', *Journal of Personality*, 46, pp. 732–42.

Feng, J. and Hu, W. (2005), 'Data Information Quality: An Information-Theoretic Perspective', *Computing and Information Systems*, 9(3), pp. 32–47.

Field. H. ([1989] 1991), *Realism, Mathematics and Modality*, Oxford: Blackwell Publishing.

Fingar, T. (2011), *Reducing Uncertainty: Intelligence and National Security*, Palo Alto, CA: Stanford University Press.

Fischoff, B. (1975), 'Hindsight Does Not Equal Foresight: The Effect of Outcome Knowledge on Judgement Under Uncertainty', *Journal of Experimental Psychology: Human Perception and Performance*, 1(3), pp. 288–99.

Fischoff, B. (1976), 'The Perceived Informativeness of Factual Information', Technical Report DDI-I, Eugene, OR: Oregon Research Institute.

Fischoff, B. and Beyth-Marom, R. (1983), 'Hypothesis Evaluation from a Bayesian Perspective', *Psychological Review*, 90, pp. 239–60.

Fischoff, B. and MacGregor, D. (1982), 'Subjective Confidence in Forecasts', *Journal of Forecasting*, 1, pp. 155–72.

Fishbein, W. (2004), 'Rethinking "Alternative Analysis" to Address Transnational Threats', The Sherman Kent Center for Intelligence Analysis, Occasional Papers, 3(4).

Fisher, R. and Johnston, R. (2008), 'Is Intelligence Analysis a Discipline?', in Bruce, J. B. and George, R. Z. (eds), *Analyzing Intelligence: Origins, Obstacles, and Innovations*, Washington DC: Georgetown University Press.

Fisher, S. D., Gettys, C. F., Manning, C., Mehle, T. and Baca, S. (1983), 'Consistency Checking in Hypothesis Generation', Organizational Behavior and Human Performance, 31, pp. 233–54.

Fisk, C. E. (1972), 'The Sino-Soviet Border Dispute: A Comparison of the Conventional and Bayesian Methods for Intelligence Warning', *Studies in Intelligence*, 16(2), pp. 53–62.

Fitting, M. (2012), 'Intensional Logic', in Zalta, E. N. (ed.), *The Stanford Encyclopedia of Philosophy*, <http://plato.stanford.edu/archives/win2012/entries/logic-intensional/>.

Foley, R. (2002), 'Conceptual Diversity in Epistemology', in Moser, P. K. (ed.), *The Oxford Handbook of Epistemology*, Oxford: Oxford University Press.

Folker, R. D. (2000), 'Intelligence Analysis in Theater Joint Intelligence Centers: An Experiment in Applying Structured Methods', Occasional Paper Number Seven, Washington DC: Joint Military Intelligence College.

Foster, G., Schmidt, C. and Sabatino, D. (1976), 'Teacher Expectancies and the Label "Learning Disabilities"', *Journal of Learning Disabilities*, 9, pp. 111–14.

Fox, J. F. (1980), 'Making Decisions Under the Influence of Memory', *Psychological Review*, 87, pp. 190–211.

Fox, J. F. (1987), 'Truth-Maker', Australasian Journal of Philosophy, 65, pp. 188–207.

Frege, G. (1879), *Begriffsschrift: eine der arithmetischen nachgebildete, Formelsprache des reinen Denkens*, Halle a. S.: Louis Nebert.

Frege, G. (1892), 'On Sense and Reference (*Begriffsschrif*)', *The Philosophical Review*, 57(3), pp. 209–30.

Frewer, L. J., Howard, C., Hedderley, D. and Shepherd, R. (1996), 'What Determines Trust in Information about Food-Related Risks? Underlying Psychological Constructs', *Risk Analysis*, 16(4), pp. 343–53.

Friedman, J. A. and Zeckhauser, R. (2012), 'Assessing Uncertainty in Intelligence', *Intelligence and National Security*, 27(6), pp. 824–47.

Friedman, U. (2012), 'The Ten Biggest American Intelligence Failures', *Foreign Policy*, 3 January, <https://foreignpolicy.com/2012/01/03/the-ten-biggest-american-intelligence-failures/>.

Fuchs, A. H. (1969), 'Recall for Order and Content of Serial Word Lists in Short-Term Memory', *Journal of Experimental Psychology*, 82, pp. 14–21.

Fumerton, R. and Hasan, A. (2010), 'Foundationalist Theories of Epistemic Justification', in Zalta, E. N. (ed.), *The Stanford Encyclopedia of Philosophy*, <http://plato.stanford.edu/archives/sum2010/entries/justep-foundational/>.

Furnham, A. (1986), 'The Robustness of the Recency Effect: Studies Using Legal Evidence', *Journal of General Psychology*, 113, 351–7.

Gabbard, B. D. and Treverton, G. F. (2008), 'Assessing the Tradecraft of Intelligence Analysis: Technical Report', Arlingon, VA: RAND Corporation.

Galinsky, A. D. (1999), 'Perspective-Taking: Debiasing Social Thought', unpublished PhD dissertation, Princeton University.

Galinsky, A. D. and Moskowitz, G. B. (2000), 'Counterfactuals as Behavioural Primes: Priming the Simulation Heuristic and Consideration of Alternatives', *Journal of Experimental Social Psychology*, 36, 384–409.

Galinsky, A. D., Moskowitz, G. B. and Sturnik, W. (2000), 'Counterfactuals as Self-Generated Primes: The Role of Prior Counterfactual Activation on Person Perception Judgements', *Social Cognition*, 18(3), pp. 252–80.

Gantner, B. and Wille, R. (2008), *Formal Concept Analysis*, Dresden: Institut fur Algebra, Dresden University.

Garst, R. (1989), 'Fundamentals of Intelligence Analysis', in Garst, R. (ed.), A Handbook of Intelligence Analysis, 2nd edn, Washington DC: Defense Intelligence College.

Geiselman, R. E. and Thompson, J. R. (1984), 'The Cognitive Bases for Intelligence Analysis', Research Report 1362, US Army Institute for Behavioral and Social Sciences.

Gendler, T. and Hawthorne, J. (eds) (2002), *Conceivability and Possibility*, Oxford: Oxford University Press.

George, R. Z. (2004), 'Fixing the Problem of Analytical Mind-Sets: Alternative Analysis', *International Journal of Intelligence and Counterintelligence*, 38(5), pp. 399–400.

Gettier, E. ([1963] 1996), 'Is Justified True Belief Knowledge?', *Analysis*, 23(6), pp. 121–3.

Gettys, C. F. and Fisher, S. D. (1979), 'Hypothesis Plausibility and Hypothesis Generation', Organizational Behaviour and Human Performance, 24, 93–110.

Gettys, C., Fisher, S., Manning, C. and Mehle, T. (1980), 'Hypothesis Generation: A Final Report on Three Years of Research', Technical Report 15-10-80, Normal, OK: University of Oklahoma, Decision Process Laboratory.

Gettys, C. F., Pliske, R. M., Manning, C. and Casey, J. T. (1987), 'An Evaluation of Human Act Generation Performance', Organizational Behavior and Human Decision Processes, 39, pp. 23–51.

Gill, P. (2010), 'Theories of Intelligence', in Johnson, L. K. (ed.), *The Oxford Handbook of National Security Intelligence*, Oxford: Oxford University Press, pp. 43–59.

Gill, P., Marrin, S. and Pythian, M. (eds) (2009), *Intelligence Theory: Key Questions and Debates*, London: Routledge, Taylor & Francis Ltd.

Gilovich, T. (1991), *How We Know What Isn't So: The Fallibility of Human Reason in Everyday Life*, New York: The Free Press.

Glanzberg, M. (2009), 'Truth', in Zalta, E. N. (ed.), *The Stanford Encyclopedia of Philosophy*, <http://plato.stanford.edu/archives/spr2009/entries/truth/>.

Glenberg, A. M. (1990), 'Common Processes Underlie Enhanced Recency Effects for Auditory and Changing State Stimuli', *Memory and Cognition*, 18, pp. 638–50.

Glenberg, A. M. and Swanson, N. G. (1986), 'A Temporal Distinctiveness Theory of Recency and Modality Effects', *Journal of Experimental Psychology: Learning, Memory and Cognition*, 12, pp. 3–15.

Goldman, A. I. (1976), 'Discrimination and Perceptual Knowledge', *Journal of Philosophy*, 73, pp. 771–91.

Goldstein, W. M. and Einhorn, H. J. (1987), 'Expression Theory and the Preference Reversal Phenomena', *Psychological Review*, 94(2), pp. 236–54.

Gollwitzer, P. M., Heckhausen, H. and Steller, B. (1990), 'Deliberative vs. Implemental Mind-Sets: Cognitive Turning Toward Congruous Thoughts and Information', *Journal of Personality and Social Psychology*, 59, pp. 1119–27.

Gomez-Torrente, M. (2011), 'Logical Truth', in Zalta, E. N. (ed.), *The Stanford Encyclopedia of Philosophy*, <http://plato.stanford.edu/archives/sum2011/entries/logical-truth/>.

Goodman, M. S. (2007), 'The Dog that Didn't Bark: The JIC and the Warning of Aggression', *Cold War History*, 7(4), pp. 529–51.

Goodman, M. S. (2014), *The Official History of the Joint Intelligence Committee: Volume I: From the Approach of the Second World War to the Suez Crisis*, London: Routledge.

Goodman, N. (1961), 'About', Mind, 70, pp. 1–24.

Gorman, M. E. and Gorman, M. E. (1984), 'A Comparison of Disconfirmatory, Confirmatory, and a Control Strategy on Wason's 2-4-6 Task', *Quarterly Journal of Experimental Psychology*, 36(A), pp. 629–48.

Grabo, C. M. (2002a), 'Strategic Warning: The Problem of Timing; On Assessing Timing', in *A Handbook of Warning Intelligence: Assessing the Threat to National Security*, Washington DC: Central Intelligence Agency.

Grabo, C. M. (2002b), 'Anticipating Surprise: Analysis for Strategic Warning', Washington DC: Center for Strategic Intelligence Research, Joint Military Intelligence College.

Grabo, C. (2010), *A Handbook of Warning Intelligence: Assessing the Threat to National Security*, Lanham, MD: The Scarecrow Press Inc.

Greco, J. and Sosa, E. (eds) (1999), *The Blackwell Guide to Epistemology*, Oxford: Blackwell Publishers Ltd.

Greene, R. L. (1986), 'Sources of Recency Effects in Free Recall', *Psychological Bulletin*, 99, pp. 221–8.

Greitzer, F. L. (2005), 'Methodology, Metrics and Measures for the Evaluation of Intelligence Analysis Tools', PNWD-3550, Richland, WA: Battelle-Pacific Northwest Division.

Griffiths, T. L. and Tenenbaum, J. B. (2001), 'Randomness and Coincidences: Reconciling Intuition and Probability Theory', Stanford, CA: Stanford University Press.

Griffiths, T. L. and Tenenbaum, J. B. (2007), 'From Mere Coincidences to Meaningful Discoveries', *Cognition*, 103, pp. 180–226.

Griggs, R. A. and Cox, J. R. (1983), 'The Effect of Problem Content on Strategies in Wason's Selection Task', *Quarterly Journal of Experimental Psychology*, 35, pp. 519–33.

Gunzler, H. and Williams, A. (eds) (2002), *Handbook of Analytical Techniques*, Weinheim: Wiley-VCH.

Gustafson, K. (2010), 'Strategic Horizons: Futures Forecasting and the British Intelligence Community', *Intelligence and National Security*, 25(5), pp. 589–610.

Hacking, I. (2006), *The Emergence of Probability*, Cambridge: Cambridge University Press.

Hájek, A. (2012), 'Interpretations of Probability', in Zalta, E. N. (ed.), The Stanford Encyclopedia of Philosophy, <http://plato.stanford.edu/archives/win2012/entries/probability-interpret/>.

Hale, B. (2003), 'Knowledge of Possibility and of Necessity', *Proceedings of the Aristotelian Society*, 103, pp. 1–20.

Handel, M. I. (1984), 'Intelligence and the Problem of Strategic Surprise', *Journal of Strategic Studies*, 7(3), pp. 229–81.

Hardin, C. L. (1980), 'Rationality and Disconfirmation', *Social Studies of Science*, 10, pp. 509–14.

Harré, R. (1986), *Varieties of Realism*, Oxford: Blackwell.

Harré, R. (1988), 'Realism and Ontology', *Philosophia Naturalis*, 25, pp. 386–98.

Hart, D. and Simon, S. (2006), 'Thinking Straight and Talking Straight: Problems of Intelligence Analysis', *Survival*, 48(1), pp. 35–60.

Hasan, A. and Fumerton, R. (2016), 'Foundationalist Theories of Epistemic Justification', in Zalta, E. N. (ed.), *The Stanford Encyclopedia of Philosophy*, <https://plato.stanford.edu/archives/win2016/entries/justep-foundational/>.

Hasher, L. and Zacks, R. T. (1988), 'Working Memory, Comprehension, and Aging: A Review and a New View', in Bower, G. H. (ed.), The Psychology of Learning and Motivation: Advances in Research and Theory: Volume 22, San Diego, CA: Academic Press, pp. 193–225.

Hawthorne, J. (2014), 'Inductive Logic', in Zalta, E. N. (ed.), *The Stanford Encyclopedia of Philosophy*, <http://plato.stanford.edu/archives/win2014/entries/logic-inductive/>.

Hayden, T. and Mischel, D. (1976), 'Maintaining Trait Consistency in the Resolution of Behavioral Inconsistency: The Wolf in Sheep's Clothing?', *Journal of Personality*, 44, pp. 109–32.

Healy, A. F. (1982), 'Short-Term Memory for Order Information', in Bower, G. H. (ed.), *The Psychology of Learning and Motivation, vol. 16*, New York: Academic Press, pp. 191–238.

Healy, A. F., Fendrich, D. W., Cunningham, T. F. and Till, R. E. (1987), 'Effects of Cuing on Short-Term Retention of Order Information', *Journal of Experimental Psychology: Learning, Memory and Cognition*, 13, pp. 413–25.

Hedley, J. H. (2007), 'Analysis for Strategic Intelligence', in Johnson, L. K. (ed.), *Handbook of Intelligence Studies*, London: Routledge, pp. 221–8.

Heinderich, J. G. (2007), 'The State of Strategic Intelligence: The Intelligence Community's Neglect of Strategic Intelligence', Studies in Intelligence, 51(2).

Hempel, C. (1935), 'On the Logical Positivist's Theory of Truth', *Analysis*, 2, pp. 49–59.

Hempel, C. (1965a), *Aspects of Scientific Explanation and Other Essays in the Philosophy of Science*, New York: The Free Press.

Hempel, C. and Oppenheim, P. (1948), 'Studies in the Logic of Explanation', *Philosophy of Science*, 15(2), pp. 135–75.

Hendrick, C. (1972), 'Effects of Salience of Stimulus Inconsistency on Impression Formation', *Journal of Personality and Social Psychology*, 22, pp. 219–22.

Hendrick, C. and Costantini, A. F. (1970a), 'Effects of Varying Trait Inconsistency and Response Requirements on the Primacy Effect in Impression Formation', *Journal of Personality and Social Psychology*, 15, pp. 158–64.

Hendrick, C. and Costantini, A. F. (1970b), 'Number Averaging Behaviour: A Primacy Effect': *Psychonomic Science*, 19(2), pp. 121–2.

Hendrick, C., Costantini, A. F., McGarry, J. and McBride, K. (1973), 'Attention Decrement, Temporal Variation, and the Primacy Effect in Impression Formation', *Memory and Cognition*, 1, 193–5.

Hendricks, V. and Symons, J. (2009), 'Epistemic Logic', in Zalta, A. N. (ed.), *The Stanford Encyclopedia of Philosophy,* <http://plato.stanford.edu/archives/spr2009/entries/logic-epistemic/>.

Hendrickson, N. (2008), 'Critical Thinking in Intelligence Analysis', *International Journal of Intelligence and Counterintelligence*, 21, pp. 679–91.

Henson, R. N. A. (1998), 'Short-Term Memory for Serial Order: The Start-End Model', *Cognitive Psychology*, 36(2), pp. 73–137.

Herbert, M. (2006), 'The Intelligence Analyst as Epistemologist', *International Journal of Intelligence and Counterintelligence*, 19(4), pp. 666–84.

Herman, M. (1995), 'Assessment Machinery: British and American Models', *Intelligence and National Security*, 10(4), pp. 13–33.

Herman, M. (1996), Intelligence Power in Peace and War, Cambridge: Cambridge University Press.

Herman, M. (2001), Intelligence Services in the Information Age: Theories and Practice, London: Routledge.

Heuer, R. J. Jr. (1999), *The Psychology of Intelligence Analysis*, Washington DC: Central Intelligence Agency.

Heuer, R. J. Jr. (2005a), 'Tradecraft Review', in *A Tradecraft Primer: Structured Analytical Techniques for Improving Intelligence Analysis*, Washington DC: Center for the Study of Intelligence Analysis, Central Intelligence Agency.

Heuer, R. J. Jr. (2005b), 'Improving Intelligence Analysis with ACH', Washington DC: Center for the Study of Intelligence Analysis, Central Intelligence Agency.

Heuer, R. J. Jr. (2005c), 'The Limits of Intelligence Analysis', Washington DC: Center for the Study of Intelligence Analysis, Central Intelligence Agency.

Heuer, R. J. Jr. (2005d), 'How Does Analysis of Competing Hypotheses (ACH) Improve Intelligence Analysis?', <http://www.pherson.org/wp-content/uploads/2013/06/06.-How-Does-ACH-Improve-Analysis_FINAL.pdf>.

Heuer, R. J. Jr. (2008), 'Computer-Aided Analysis of Competing Hypotheses', in Bruce, J. B. and George, R. Z. (eds), *Analysing Intelligence: Origins, Obstacles and Innovations*, Washington DC: Georgetown University Press.

Heuer, R. J. Jr. (2009), 'Evolution of Structured Analytical Techniques', Presentation to the National Academy of Science, Washington DC, National Research Council Committee on Behavioral and Social Science Research to Improve Intelligence Analysis for National Security, 8 December 2009.

Heuer, R. J. Jr. and Pherson, R. H. (2010), *Structured Analytical Methods for Intelligence Analysis*, London: CQ Press/Sage Publishing.

Heyting, A. (1956), *Intuitionism: An Introduction*, Amsterdam: North-Holland Publishing Company.

Higgins, E. T., Rholes, W. S. and Jones, C. R. (1977), 'Category Accessibility and Impression Formation', *Journal of Experimental Social Psychology*, 13, pp. 141–54.

Hilbert, M. (2012), 'Toward a Synthesis of Cognitive Biases: How Noisy Information Processing Can Bias Human Decision-Making', *Psychological Bulletin*, 138(2), pp. 211–37.

Hill, C. (2006), 'Modality, Modal Epistemology, and the Metaphysics of Consciousness', in Nichols, S. (ed.), *The Architecture of the Imagination: New Essays on Pretence, Possibility, and Fiction*, Oxford: Oxford University Press.

Hintikka, J. and Bachman, J. (1991), What If . . . ? Toward Excellence in Reasoning, London: Mayfield.

Hintzman, D. L., Block, R. A. and Summers, J. L. (1973), 'Contextual Associations and Memory for Serial Position', *Journal of Experimental Psychology*, 97, pp. 220–9.

Hitz, F. P. (2007), 'Human Source Intelligence', in Johnson, L. K. (ed.), *Handbook of Intelligence Studies*, London: Routledge, pp. 118–28.

Hoffding, S. and Vrist Ronn, K. (2012), 'The Epistemic Status of Intelligence: An Epistemological Contribution to Understanding Intelligence', *Intelligence and National Security*, 28(5), pp. 694–716.

Hofweber, T. (2012), 'Logic and Ontology', in Zalta, E. N. (ed.), *The Stanford Encyclopedia of Philosophy*, <http://plato.stanford.edu/archives/sum2012/entries/logic-ontology/>.

Hogarth, R. M. and Einhorn, H. J. (1992), 'Order Effects in Belief Updating: The Belief Adjustment Model', *Cognitive Psychology*, 24, 1–55.

Horsten, L. (2014), 'Philosophy of Mathematics', in Zalta, E. N. (ed.), *The Stanford Encyclopedia of Philosophy*, <http://plato.stanford.edu/archives/fall2014/entries/philosophy-mathematics/>.

Houghton, G. (1990), 'The Problem of Serial Order: A Neural Network Model of Sequence Learning and Recall', in Dale, R., Mellish, C. and Zock, M. (eds), *Current Research in Natural Language Generation*, London: Academic Press, pp. 287–319.

Hovland, C. I. and Mandell, W. (1957), 'Is There a "Law of Primacy in Persuasion"?', in Hovland, C. I. (ed.), *The Order of Presentation in Persuasion*, New Haven, CT: Yale University Press, pp. 115–29.

Huang, H. and Lee, T-H. (2010), 'To Combine Forecasts or to Combine Information?', *Econometric Reviews*, 25(6), pp. 534–70.

Huber, F. (2016), 'Formal Representations of Belief', in Zalta, E. N. (ed.), The Stanford Encyclopedia of Philosophy, <https://plato.stanford.edu/archives/spr2016/entries/formal-belief/>.

Huff, D. (1991), *How to Lie with Statistics*, London: Penguin Books Ltd.

Hulnick, A. S. (2010), 'The Dilemma of Open Source Intelligence: Is OSINT Really Intelligence?', in Johnson, L. K. (ed.), The Oxford Handbook of National Security Intelligence, Oxford: Oxford University Press.

Hume, D. ([1738–40] 2013), A Treatise of Human Nature: Being an Attempt to Introduce the Experimental Method of Reasoning into Moral Subjects, Scott's Valley, CA: CreateSpace Independent Publishing Platform.

Hunt, C. (2008), 'Black Swans', in Chesser, N. (ed.), *Anticipating Rare Events: Can Acts of Terror, Use of Weapons of Mass Destruction or*

Other High-Profile Acts Be Anticipated?, United States Department of Defense, <https://www.hsdl.org/?abstract&did=233523>.

Hunt, C. and Schum, D. A. (2008), 'Complexity-Based Reasoning', in Chesser, N. (ed.), *Anticipating Rare Events: Can Acts of Terror, Use of Weapons of Mass Destruction or Other High-Profile Acts Be Anticipated?*, United States Department of Defense, <https://www.hsdl.org/?abstract&did=233523>.

Hybel, A. R. (1986), *The Logic of Surprise in International Conflict*, Lexington, MA: Lexington Books.

Iemhoff, R. (2012), 'Intuitionism in the Philosophy of Mathematics', in Zalta, E. N. (ed.), *The Stanford Encyclopedia of Philosophy*, <http://plato.stanford.edu/archives/fall2012/entries/intuitionism/>.

Insko, C. A. (1964), 'Primacy versus Recency in Persuasion as a Function of the Timing of Arguments and Measures', *Journal of Abnormal and Social Psychology*, 69, pp. 381–91.

Jackson, G. (2008), 'The Accurate Anticipation of Rare Human-Driven Events: An ABA/SME Hybrid', in Chesser, N. (ed.), *Anticipating Rare Events: Can Acts of Terror, Use of Weapons of Mass Destruction or Other High-Profile Acts Be Anticipated?*, United States Department of Defense, <https://www.hsdl.org/?abstract&did=233523>.

Jackson, P. (2010), 'On Uncertainty and the Limits of Intelligence', in Johnson, L. K. (ed.), *The Oxford Handbook of National Security Intelligence*, Oxford: Oxford University Press.

Jahnke, J. C. (1963), 'Serial Position Effects in Immediate Recall', *Journal of Verbal Learning and Verbal Behavior*, 2(3), pp. 284–7.

Jahnke, J. C., Davis, S. T. and Bower, R. E. (1989), 'Position and Order Information in Recognition Memory', *Journal of Experimental Psychology: Learning, Memory and Cognition*, 15, pp. 859–67.

Janis, I. L. and Feierabend, R. L. (1957), 'Effects of Alternative Ways of Ordering Pro and Con Arguments in Persuasive Communications', in Hovland, C. I. (ed.), *The Order of Presentation in Persuasion*, New Haven, CT: Yale University Press, pp. 13–23.

Jenkins, H. M. and Ward, W. C. (1965), 'Judgement of Contingency between Responses and Outcomes', *Psychological Monographs: General and Applied*, 79(1), pp. 1–17.

Johnson, J. L. and Berrett, M. T. (2011), 'Cultural Topography: A New Research Tool for Intelligence Analysis', *Studies in Intelligence*, 55(2), pp. 1–17.

Johnson, L. K. (ed.) (2007), *Handbook of Intelligence Studies*, London: Routledge.

Johnson, L. K. (ed.) (2008), *The Oxford Handbook of Intelligence Studies*, Oxford: Oxford University Press.

Johnson, L. K. (2012), *National Security Intelligence*, Cambridge: Polity.

Johnston, R. (2003), 'Developing a Taxonomy of Intelligence Analysis Variables', *Studies in Intelligence*, 47(3), pp. 61–71.

Johnston, R. (2005), 'Analytic Culture in the US Intelligence Community: An Ethnographic Study', Center for the Study of Intelligence, Washington DC: Central Intelligence Agency.

Joint Military Intelligence College (2001), *Intelligence Warning Terminology*, Washington DC: United States Joint Military Intelligence College.

Jonas, E., Schulz-Hardt, S., Frey, D. and Thelen, N. (2001), 'Confirmation Bias in Sequential Information Search after Preliminary Decisions: An Expansion of Dissonance Theoretical Research on Selective Exposure to Information', *Journal of Personality and Social Psychology*, 80(4), pp. 557–71.

Jones, E. E. and Goethals, G. R. (1972), 'Order Effects in Impression Formation: Attribution Context and the Nature of the Entity', in Jones, E. E., Kanhouse, E. D. and Kelley, H. H. (eds), *Attribution: Perceiving the Causes of Behavior*, Morristown, NJ: General Learning Press.

Jones, E. E., Rock, L., Shaver, K. G., Goethals, G. R. and Ward, L. M. (1968), 'Pattern of Performance and Ability Attribution', *Journal of Personality and Social Psychology*, 10, pp. 317–40.

Jones, M. D. (1998), *The Thinker's Toolkit: 14 Powerful Techniques for Problem Solving*, New York: Three Rivers Press.

Jones, N. (2017), 'Critical Epistemology for the Analysis of Competing Hypotheses', Intelligence and National Security, 33(2), pp. 273–89.

Jordan, M. I. (1986), 'Serial Order: A Parallel Distributed Approach', ICS Report 8604, San Diego, CA: University of California.

Joyce, J. ([2008] 2016), 'Bayes' Theorem', in Zalta, N. E. (ed.), *The Stanford Encyclopedia of Philosophy*, <http://plato.stanford.edu/archives/fall2008/entries/bayes-theorem/>.

Jungermann, H., Pfister, H-R and Fischer, K. (1996), 'Credibility, Information Preferences and Information Interests', *Risk Analysis*, 16(2), pp. 251–61.

Kahneman, D. (1973), *Attention and Effort*, Englewood Cliffs, NJ: Prentice-Hall.

Kahneman, D. (1990), 'Experimental Tests of the Endowment Effect and the Coase Theorem', *Journal of Political Economy*, 98(6), pp. 1325–48.

Kahneman, D., Knetsch, J. L. and Thaler, R. H. (1979), 'Prospect Theory: An Analysis of Decision Under Risk', *Econometrica* 47(2), pp. 263–327.

Kahneman, D. and Lovallo, D. (1993), 'Timid Choices and Bold Forecasts: A Cognitive Perspective on Risk Taking', *Management Science*, 39, pp. 17–31.

Kahneman, D. and Morewedge, C. K. (2010), 'Associative Processes in Intuitive Judgement', *Trends in Cognitive Sciences*, 14(10), pp. 435–40.

Kahneman, D., Slovic, P. and Tversky, A. (1982), *Judgement Under Uncertainty: Heuristics and Biases*, 1st edn, Cambridge: Cambridge University Press.

Kane, M. J., Bleckley, M. K., Conway, A. R. and Engle, R. A. (2001), 'A Controlled-Attention View of Working-Memory Capacity', Journal of Experimental Psychology: General, 130, pp. 169–83.

Kaplan, M. F. (1971), 'Context Effects in Impression Formation: The Weighted Average versus the Meaning Change Formulation', *Journal of Personality and Social Psychology*, 19(1), 92–9.

Kareev, Y. and Halberstadt, N. (1993), 'Evaluating Negative Tests and Refutations in a Rule Discovery Task', *Quarterly Journal of Experimental Psychology*, 46(A), pp. 715–27.

Kareev, Y., Halberstadt, N. and Shafir, D. (1993), 'Improving Performance and Increasing the Use of Non-Positive Testing in a Rule-Discovery Task', *Quarterly Journal of Experimental Psychology*, 46(A), pp. 729–42.

Karmiloff-Smith, A. and Inhelder, B. (1974–5), 'If You Want to Get Ahead, Get a Theory', *Cognition*, 3, pp. 195–212.

Karvetski, C. W., Olson, K. C., Gantz, D. T. and Cross, G. A. (2013), 'Structuring and Analysing Competing Hypotheses with Bayesian Networks for Intelligence Analysis', *EURO Journal on Decision Processes*, 1(3–4), pp. 205–31.

Kent, S. (1949), Strategic Intelligence for American World Policy, Princeton, NJ: Princeton University Press.

Kent, S. S. (1994), 'Words of Estimative Probability', in Sleury, D. P. (ed.), *Sherman Kent and the Board of National Estimates: Collected Essays*, Washington DC: Center for the Study of Intelligence, Central Intelligence Agency.

Khalsa, S. K. (2004), *Forecasting Terrorism: Indicators and Proven Analytic Techniques*, Lanham, MD: Scarecrow Press Inc.

Khalsa, S. K. (2009), 'The Intelligence Community Debate Over Intuition versus Structured Technique: Implications for Improving Intelligence Warning and Analysis', *Journal of Conflict Studies*, 29, <https://journals.lib.unb.ca/index.php/jcs/article/view/15234/20838>.

Kidd, G. R. and Greenwald, A. G. (1988), 'Attention, Rehearsal, and Memory for Serial Order', *American Journal of Psychology*, 101, pp. 259–79.

Klahr, D. and Dunbar, K. (1988), 'Dual Space Search During Scientific Reasoning', *Cognitive Science*, 12, pp. 1–48.

Klayman, J. (1995), 'Varieties of Confirmation Bias', in Buesmeyer, J., Hastie, R. and Medin, D. L. (eds), *Psychology of Learning and Motivation: Volume 32, Decision Making from a Cognitive Perspective*, New York: Academic Press, pp. 365–418.

Klayman, J. and Brown, K. (1993), 'Debias the Environment Instead of the Judge: An Alternative Approach to Reducing Error in Diagnostic (and Other) Judgement', *Cognition*, 49, pp. 97–122.

Klayman, J. and Ha, Y.-W. (1987), 'Confirmation, Disconfirmation, and Information in Hypothesis Testing', *Psychological Review*, 94, 211–28.

Klayman, J. and Ha, Y.-W. (1989), 'Hypothesis-Testing in Rule Discovery: Strategy, Structure, and Content', *Journal of Experimental Psychology: Learning, Memory, and Cognition*, 15, pp. 596–604.

Klein, J. (2012), 'Francis Bacon', in Zalta, E. N. (ed.), *The Stanford Encyclopedia of Philosophy*, <http://plato.stanford.edu/archives/win2012/entries/francis-bacon/>.

Klement, K. (2016), 'Russell's Logical Atomism', in Zalta, E. N. (ed.), The Stanford Encyclopedia of Philosophy, <https://plato.stanford.edu/archives/spr2016/entries/logical-atomism/>.

Koch, B. S., Pei, B. K. W. and Reed, S. A. (1989), 'Auditor Belief Revisions in a Performance Auditing Setting: An Application of the Contrast-Inertia Model', unpublished manuscript, University of North Texas.

Koehler, D. K. (1991), 'Explanation, Imagination, and Confidence in Judgment', Psychological Bulletin, 110, pp. 449–519.

Koehler, D. K. (1994), 'Hypothesis Generation and Confidence in Judgment', Journal of Experimental Psychology, 20, 461–9.

Koslowski, B. and Maqueda, M. (1993), 'What Is Confirmation Bias and When Do People Actually Have It?', *Merrill-Palmer Quarterly*, 39(1), pp. 104–30.

Kripke, S. (1975), 'Outline of a Theory of Truth', *Journal of Philosophy*, 72, pp. 690–716.

Kripke, S. (1980), *Naming and Necessity*, Cambridge, MA: Harvard University Press.

Kripke, S. (2001), 'Identity and Necessity', in Loux, M. (ed.), *Metaphysics: Contemporary Readings*, London: Routledge.

Krizan, L. (1999), 'Intelligence Essentials for Everyone', Occasional Paper 6, Washington DC: Joint Military Intelligence College.

Kuhn, D., Amsel, E. and O'Loughlin, M. (1988), *The Development of Scientific Thinking Skills*, New York: Academic Press.

Kuhns, W. J. (2003), 'Intelligence Failures: Forecasting and the Lessons from Epistemology', in Betts, R. K. and Mahnken, T. G. (eds), *Paradoxes of Strategic Intelligence*, London: Routledge.

Kuipers, T. A. F. (1992), 'Naive and Refined Truth Approximation', *Synthese*, 93, pp. 299–341.

Kuipers, T. A. F. (2000), *From Instrumentalism to Constructive Realism*, Dordrecht: Reidel.

Lahneman, W. J. (2006), *The Future of Intelligence Analysis: Volume 1*, College Park, MD: Center for International and Security Studies.

Lahneman, W. J. and Arcos, R. (eds) (2014), *The Art of Intelligence: Simulations, Exercises, and Games*, Plymouth: Rowman & Littlefield.

Lana, R. E. (1961), 'Familiarity and the Order of Presentation of Persuasive Communications', *Journal of Abnormal and Social Psychology*, 62(3), pp. 573–7.

Langer, E. J. and Abelson, R. P. (1974), 'A Patient by Any Other Name . . .: Clinical Group Differences in Labelling Bias', *Journal of Consulting and Clinical Psychology*, 42, pp. 4–9.

Langer, E. J. and Roth, J. (1975), 'Heads I Win, Tails It's Chance: The Illusion of Control as a Function of the Sequence of Outcomes in a Purely Chance Task', *Journal of Personality and Social Psychology*, 32, pp. 951–5.

Laplace, P. S. ([1814] 1951), *A Philosophical Essay on Probabilities*, New York: Dover Publications Inc.

Laqueur, W. (1985), *World of Secrets: The Uses and Limitations of Intelligence*, New York: Basic Books.

Lashley, K. S. (1951), 'The Problem of Serial Order in Behavior', in Jefress, L. A. (ed.), *Cerebral Mechanisms in Behavior: The Hixon Symposium*, New York: Wiley, pp. 112–36.

Lee, C. L. and Estes, W. K. (1977), 'Order and Position in Primary Memory for Letter Strings', *Journal of Verbal Learning and Verbal Memory*, 16, pp. 395–418.

Lee, R. (2007), 'The Use of Ontologies to Support Intelligence Analysis', Ontology for the Intelligence Community (OIC-2007), Booz Allen Hamilton.

Lehrer, K. and Paxson, T. (1969), 'Knowledge: Undefeated Justified True Belief', *Journal of Philosophy*, 66(8), pp. 225–37.

Leslau, O. (2010), 'The Effect of Intelligence on the Decision-Making Process', *International Journal of Intelligence and Counterintelligence*, 23, pp. 426–48.

Levin, I. P. (1976), 'Processing of Deviant Information in Inference and Descriptive Tasks with Simultaneous and Serial Presentation', *Organizational Behavior and Human Performance*, 15, pp. 195–211.

Levin, I. P., Ims, J. R., Simpson, J. C. and Kim, K. J. (1977), 'The Processing of Deviant Information in Prediction and Evaluation', *Memory and Cognition*, 5, pp. 679–84.

Levin, I. P. and Schmidt, C. F. (1969), 'Sequential Effects in Impression Formation with Binary Intermittent Responding', *Journal of Experimental Psychology*, 79, pp. 283–7.

Levin, I. P. and Schmidt, C. F. (1970), 'Differential Influence of Information in an Impression-Formation Task with Binary Intermittent Responding', *Journal of Experimental Psychology*, 84(2), pp. 374–6.

Levine, M. (1966), 'Hypothesis Behaviour by Humans During Discrimination Learning', *Journal of Experimental Psychology*, 71, pp. 331–8.

Lewandowsky, S. (1994), 'Memory for Serial Order Revisited', *Psychological Review*, 101, pp. 539–43.

Lewandowsky, S. and Murdock, B. B. Jr. (1989), 'Memory for Serial Order', *Psychological Review*, 96, pp. 25–57.

Lichtenstein, M. and Srull, T. K. (1987), 'Processing Objectives as a Determinant of the Relationship between Recall and Judgment', *Journal of Experimental Social Psychology*, 23, pp. 93–l 18.

Lipton, P. ([1991] 2004), *Inference to the Best Explanation*, London: Routledge.

Locke, J. (1690), *An Essay Concerning Human Understanding*, Scott's Valley, CA: CreateSpace Independent Publishing Forum.

Long, K. (2008), 'Philosophical and Epistemological Concerns', in Chesser, N. (ed.), *Anticipating Rare Events: Can Acts of Terror, Use of Weapons of Mass Destruction or Other High-Profile Acts Be Anticipated?*, United States Department of Defense, <https://www.hsdl.org/?abstract&did=233523>.

Lopes, L. (1982), 'Averaging Rules and Adjustment Processes in Bayesian Inference', *Bulletin of the Psychonomic Society*, 23(6), pp. 509–12.

Lord, C., Ross, L. and Lepper, M. (1980), 'Biased Assimilation and Attitude Polarization: The Effect of Prior Theories on Subsequently Considered Evidence', *Journal of Personality and Social Psychology*, 37, pp. 2098–109.

Lord, C. G., Lepper, M. R. and Preston, E. (1984), 'Considering the Opposite: A Corrective Strategy for Social Judgement', *Journal of Personality and Social Psychology*, 47, pp. 1231–43.

Loux, M. J. (ed.) (1979), *The Possible and the Actual: Reading in the Metaphysics of Modality*, Ithaca, NY: Cornell University Press.

Loux, M. J. (2001), 'Realism and Anti-Realism', in Loux, M. J. (ed.), *Metaphysics: Contemporary Readings*, London: Routledge.

Lowenthal, M. M. (2002), Intelligence: From Secrets to Policy, 2nd edn, London: CQ Press/SAGE Publications Ltd.

Lowenthal, M. (2012), *Intelligence: From Secrets to Policy*, 5th edition, London: CQ Press/SAGE Publications Ltd.

Luchins, A. S. (1942), 'Mechanisation in Problem Solving: The Effect of Einstellung', *Psychological Monographs*, 54, pp. 1–95.

Luchins, A. S. (1957a), 'Primacy-Recency in Impression Formation', in Hovland, C. I. (ed.), *The Order of Presentation in Persuasion*, New Haven, CT: Yale University Press, pp. 33–61.

Luchins, A. S. (1957b), 'Experimental Attempts to Minimize the Impact of First Impressions', in Hovland, C. I. (ed.), *The Order of Presentation in Persuasion*. New Haven, CT: Yale University Press, pp. 62–75.

Luchins, A. S. (1958), 'Definitiveness of Impression and Primacy-Recency in Communications', *Journal of Social Psychology*, 48, pp. 275–90.

Luchins, A. S. and Luchins, E. H. (1962), 'Personality Impressions from Communications Reflecting Attitudes Toward Segregation', *Journal of Social Psychology*, 58, pp. 315–30.

Luchins, A. S. and Luchins, E. H. (1970), 'The Effects of Order of Presentation of Information and Explanatory Models', *Journal of Social Psychology*, 80, pp. 63–70.

Luchins, A. S. and Luchins, E. H. (1984), 'Conceptions of Personality and Order Effects in Forming Impressions', *Journal of General Psychology*, 110, pp. 165–96.

Luchins, A. S. and Luchins, E. H. (1986), 'Primacy and Recency Effects with Descriptions of Moral and Immoral Behavior', *Journal of General Psychology*, 113, pp. 159–77.

Lund, F. H. (1925), 'The Psychology of Belief IV: The Law of Primacy in Persuasion', *Journal of Abnormal Social Psychology*, 20, pp 183–91.

Lycan, W. G. (2002), 'Explanation and Epistemology', in Moser, P. K. (ed.), *The Oxford Handbook of Epistemology*, Oxford: Oxford University Press.

Lyden, M. (2007), 'The Efficacy of Accelerated Analysis in Strategic-Level Estimate Judgements', unpublished MSc thesis, Department of Intelligence Studies, Mercyhurst College.

Lyons, J. (1977), Semantics: Volume 1, Cambridge: Cambridge University Press.

McAndrew, F. T. (1981), 'Pattern of Performance and Attributions of Ability and Gender', *Personality and Social Psychology Bulletin*, 1, pp. 583–7.

McBeth, M. S. (2002), 'Approaches to Enhance Sense-Making for Intelligence Analysis', Final Report, US Naval War College, Newport, RI.

MacBride, F. (2014), 'Truthmakers', in Zalta, N. E. (ed.), *The Stanford Encyclopedia of Philosophy*, <http://plato.stanford.edu/archives/spr2014/entries/truthmakers/.

MacDowell, D. (2009), *Strategic Intelligence: A Handbook for Practitioners, Managers, and Users*, Lanham, MD: Scarecrow Press Inc.

McElree, B. and Dosher, B. A. (1989), 'Serial Position and Set Size in Short-Term Memory: The Time Course of Recognition', *Journal of Experimental Psychology: General*, 118, pp. 346–73.

McGuire, W. J. (1969), 'The Nature of Attitudes and Attitude Change', in Lindzey, G. and Aronson, E. (eds), *The Handbook of Social Psychology, Volume 3*, Reading, MA: Addison-Wesley.

McKenzie, C. R. M. (1994), 'The Accuracy of Intuitive Judgement Strategies: Covariation Assessment and Bayesian Inference', *Cognitive Psychology*, 26, pp. 209–39.

McKenzie, C. R. M. (1999), '(Non)Complementary Updating of Belief in Two Hypotheses', *Memory and Cognition*, 27, pp. 152–65.

McNichol, D. and Heathcote, A. (1986), 'Representation of Order Information: An Analysis of Grouping Effects in Short-Term Memory', *Journal of Experimental Psychology: General*, 115, pp. 76–95.

MacPherson, N. (2013), 'Review of the Quality Assurance of Analytical Models', HM Treasury Report, HM Treasury.

Madigan, S. A. (1971), 'Modality and Recall Order Interactions in Short-Term Memory for Serial Order', *Journal of Experimental Psychology*, 87, pp. 294–6.

Madigan, S. A. (1980), 'The Serial Position Curve in Immediate Serial Recall', *Bulletin of the Psychonomic Society*, 15, pp. 335–8.

Mahoney, M. J. (1980), 'Rationality and Authority: On the Confusion of Justification and Permission', *Social Studies of Science*, 9, pp. 349–75.

Marrin, S. (2009), 'Intelligence Analysis and Decision-Making: Methodological Challenges', in Gill, P., Marrin, S. and Phythian, M. (eds), *Intelligence Theory: Key Questions and Debates*, London: Routledge.

Marrin, S. (2012a), 'Is Intelligence an Art or a Science', *International Journal of Intelligence and Counterintelligence*, 25(3), pp. 529–45.

Marrin, S. (2012b), 'Evaluating the Quality of Intelligence Analysis: By What (Mis) Measure?', *Intelligence and National Security*, 27(6), pp. 869–912.

Martin, L. L. (1986), 'Set/Reset: Use/Disuse of Concepts of Impression Formation', *Journal of Personality and Social Psychology*, 51, pp. 493–504.

Maxwell, S. E. and Delaney, H. D. (2004), *Designing Experiments and Analysing Data: A Model Comparison Perspective*, vol. 1, London: Psychology Press.

Mayo, C. W. and Crockett, W. H. (1964), 'Cognitive Complexity and Primacy-Recency Effects in Impression Formation', *Journal of Social and Abnormal Psychology*, 68(3), pp. 335–8.

Mehle, T., Gettys, S., Manning, C., Baca, S. and Fisher, S. (1981), 'The Availability Explanation of Excessive Plausibility Assessments', Acta Psychologica, 49, pp. 127–40.

Mehle, T. (1982), 'Hypothesis Generation in an Automobile Malfunction Inference Task', Acta Psychologica, 52, pp. 87–106.

Mendelsohn, R. (2005), *The Philosophy of Gottlob Frege*, New York: Cambridge University Press.

Metzger, P. J. (2008), 'Automated Indications and Warnings from Live Surveillance Data', *Lincoln Laboratory Journal*, 18(1), pp. 66–78.

Mill, J. S. ([1843] 2002), A System of Logic, Honolulu, HI: University Press of the Pacific.

Miller, N. and Campbell, D. T. (1959), 'Recency and Primacy in Persuasion as a Function of the Timing of Speeches and Measurement', *Journal of Abnormal and Social Psychology*, 59, pp. 1–9.

Millward, R. B. and Spoehr, K. T. (1973), 'The Direct Method of Hypothesis Testing Strategies', *Cognitive Psychology*, 4, pp. 1–38.

Mole, C. (2012), 'Three Philosophical Lessons for the Analysis of Criminal and Military Intelligence', *Intelligence and National Security*, 27(4), pp. 441–58.

Moore, D. T. (2007), 'Critical Thinking and Intelligence Analysis', National Defense Intelligence College, Occasional Paper Number Fourteen, US National Defense Intelligence College.

Morris, W. E. (2013), 'David Hume', in Zalta, E. N. (ed.), *The Stanford Encyclopedia of Philosophy*, <http://plato.stanford.edu/archives/spr2013/entries/hume/>.

Moschovakis, J. (2010), 'Intuitionistic Logic', in Zalta, E. N. (ed.), *The Stanford Encyclopedia of Philosophy*, <http://plato.stanford.edu/archives/sum2010/entries/logic-intuitionistic/>.

Moser, P. K. (ed.) (2002), *The Oxford Handbook of Epistemology*, Oxford: Oxford University Press.

Moskowitz, G. B. and Roman, R. J. (1992), 'Spontaneous Trait Inferences and Self-Generated Primes: Implications for Conscious Social Judgement', *Journal of Personality and Social Psychology*, 62, pp. 728–38.

Murdock, B. B. Jr. (1968), 'Serial Order Effects in Short-Term Memory', *Journal of Experimental Psychology Monograph Supplement*, 76, pp. 1–15.

Murdock, B. B. Jr. (1983), 'A Distributed Model for Serial-Order Information', *Psychological Review*, 90, pp. 316–38.

Murdock, B. B. Jr. (1993), 'TODAM2: A Model for the Storage and Retrieval of Item, Associative, and Serial-Order Information', *Psychological Review*, 100, pp. 183–203.

Murdock, B. B. Jr. (1995), 'Developing TODAM: Three Models for Serial Order Information', *Memory and Cognition*, 23, pp. 631–45.

Musgrave, A. (1988), 'The Ultimate Argument for Scientific Realism', in Nola, R. (ed.), *Relativism and Realism in Science*, Dordrecht: Kluwer.

Mynatt, C. R., Doherty, M. E. and Dragan, W. (1993), 'Information Relevance, Working Memory and the Consideration of Alternatives', *Quarterly Journal of Experimental Psychology*, 46(A), pp. 759–78.

Mynatt, C. R., Doherty, M. E. and Tweney, R. D. (1977), 'Confirmation Bias in a Simulated Research Environment: An Experimental Study of Scientific Influence', *Quarterly Journal of Experimental Psychology*, 29(1), pp. 85–95.

Mynatt, C. R., Doherty, M. E. and Tweney, R. D. (1978), 'Consequences of Confirmation and Disconfirmation in a Simulated Research Environment', *Quarterly Journal of Experimental Psychology*, 30, pp. 395–406.

Nadkimi, S. and Shenoy, P. P. (1999), 'A Bayesian Network Approach to Making Inferences in Causal Maps', *European Journal of Operational Research*, 128, pp. 479–98.

Nadkimi, S. and Shenoy, P. P. (2004), 'A Causal Mapping Approach to Constructing Bayesian Networks Decision', *Support Systems*, 38(2), pp. 259–81.

Nagel, E. (1961), *The Structure of Science: Problems in the Logic of Scientific Explanation*, New York: Harcourt, Brace and World.

National Commission on Terrorist Attacks upon the United States (2004), *The 9/11 Commission Report: Final Report of the National Commission on Terrorist Attacks upon the United States*, Washington DC: National Commission on Terrorist Attacks upon the United States.

National Criminal Intelligence Service (2000), 'Intelligence Model', HM Government.

Neath, I. and Crowder, R. G. (1990), 'Schedules of Presentation and Temporal Distinctiveness in Human Memory', *Journal of Experimental Psychology: Learning, Memory and Cognition*, 16, pp. 316–27.

Newtson, D. and Rindner, R. J. (1979), 'Variation in Behaviour Perception and Ability Attribution', *Journal of Personality and Social Psychology*, 37(10), pp. 1847–58.

Nisbett, R. and Ross, L. (1980), *Human Inference: Strategies and Shortcomings of Human Judgement*, Englewood Cliffs, NJ: Prentice-Hall.

Nolan, D. (2011), 'Modal Fictionalism', in Zalta, E. N. (ed.), The Stanford Encyclopedia of Philosophy, <http://plato.stanford.edu/archives/win2011/entries/fictionalism-modal/>.

Nolte, W. M. (2010), 'Intelligence Analysis in an Uncertain Environment', in Johnson, L. K. (ed.), *The Oxford Handbook of National Security Intelligence*, Oxford: Oxford University Press, pp. 404–22.

Nozick, R. (1981), *Philosophical Explanations*, Cambridge, MA: Harvard University Press.

Nozick, R. (2001), *Invariances: The Structure of the Objective World*, Cambridge, MA: Harvard University Press.

Nugent, P. M. S. (2013), 'Primacy Effect', *PsychologyDictionary.org*, <https://psychologydictionary.org/primacy-effect/>.

Ockham, W. ([1323] 2011) Summa Logicae, South Bend, IN: St Augustine's Press.

Odom, W. E. (2008), 'Intelligence Analysis', *Intelligence and National Security*, 23(3), pp. 316–32.

Olsson, E. (2017), 'Coherentist Theories of Epistemic Justification', in Zalta, E. N. (ed.), *The Stanford Encyclopedia of Philosophy*, <https://plato.stanford.edu/archives/spr2017/entries/justep-coherence/>.

Omand, D. (2014), 'Understanding Bayesian Thinking: Prior and Posterior Probabilities and Analysis of Competing Hypotheses in Intelligence Analysis', in Lahneman, W. J. and Acros, R. (eds), *The Art of Intelligence: Simulations, Exercises, and Games*, Plymouth: Rowman & Littlefield.

Ormerod, T. C., Manktelow, K. I. and Jones, G. V. (1993), 'Reasoning with Three Types of Conditional: Biases and Mental Models', *Quarterly Journal of Experimental Psychology*, 46(4A), pp. 653–77.

Osgood, C. E., Suez, G. J. and Tannenbaum, P. H. (1957), *The Measurement of Meaning*, Urbana, IL: University of Illinois Press.

Parducci, A., Thaler, H. and Anderson, N. H. (1968), 'Stimulus Averaging and the Context for Judgment', *Perception and Psychophysics*, 3, pp. 145–50.

Park, J. H., Kumar, A. and Raghunathan, R. (2010), 'Confirmation Bias, Overconfidence, and Investment Performance: Evidence from Stock Message Boards', McCombs Research Paper Series No. IROM-07-10.

Payne, J. W., Bettman, J. R. and Johnson, E. J. (1990), 'The Adaptive Decision-Maker: Effort and Accuracy in Choice', in Hogarth, R. M. (ed.), *Insights in Decision-Making*, Chicago: University of Chicago Press, pp. 129–53.

Peirce, C. S. (1931–58), *Collected Papers of Charles Sanders Peirce*, ed. Hartshorne, C., Weiss, P. and Burkes, A., Cambridge, MA: Harvard University Press.

Pennington, N. and Hastie, R. (1993), 'Reasoning in Explanation-Based Decision Making', *Cognition*, 49, pp. 123–63.

Perrin, B. M., Barnett, B. J., Walrath, R. and Grossman, J. D. (2001), 'Information Order and Outcome Framing: An Assessment of Judgement Bias in a Naturalistic Decision-Making Context', *Human Factors*, 43(2), pp. 227–38.

Peters, R. G., Covello, V. T. and McCallum, D. B. (1997), 'The Determinants of Trust and Credibility in Environmental Risk Communication: An Empirical Study', *Risk Analysis*, 17(1), pp. 43–54.

Peterson, C. R. and Beach, L. R. (1967), 'Man as an Intuitive Statistician', *Psychological Bulletin*, 68, pp. 29–46.

Peterson, C. R. and DuCharme, W. M. (1967), 'Primacy Effect in Subjective Probability Revision', *Journal of Experimental Psychology*, 73(1), 61–5.

Pherson, R. H. and Pyrik, J. (2017), *Analyst's Guide to Indicators*, Tysons, VA: Pherson Associates LLC.

Pherson, R. H. and Saunders, K. (2012), 'Using Structured Analytic Techniques to Assess the Interrelationship between Warlordism and International Diffusion', Forum Foundation for Analytic Excellence.

Pherson, R. H., Schwartz, A. R. and Manak, E. (2006), 'Anticipating Rare Events: The Role of ACH and Other Structured Analytical Methods', Occasional Paper, Pherson Associates LLC.

Phillips Griffiths, A. (ed.) (1967), *Knowledge and Belief*, Oxford: Oxford University Press.

Phythian, M. (2012), 'Policing Uncertainty: Intelligence, Security and Risk', *Intelligence and National Security*, 27(2), pp. 187–205.

Pitz, G. F. and Reinhold, H. (1968), 'Payoff Effects in Sequential Decision-Making', *Journal of Experimental Psychology*, 77(2), 249–57.

Platt, J. R. (1964), 'Strong Induction', *Science: New Series*, 146(3642), pp. 347–53.

Pope, S. and Jøsang, A. (2005), 'Analysis of Competing Hypotheses using Subjective Logic', unpublished manuscript, University of Queensland.

Popper, K. ([1934] 2002), *The Logic of Scientific Discovery*, 2nd edn, London: Routledge.

Pratz, O. (1987), 'Computer Presentation of Pattern-of-Success: A Primacy Effect Verified', *Perceptual and Motor Skills*, 65, pp. 379–87.

Prioreschi, P. (2002), 'Al-Kindi, A Precursor of The Scientific Revolution', *Journal of the International Society for the History of Islamic Medicine*, 2, pp. 17–19.

Proops, I. (2013), 'Wittgenstein's Logical Atomism', in Zalta, E. N. (ed.), The Stanford Encyclopedia of Philosophy, <https://plato.stanford.edu/archives/sum2013/entries/wittgenstein-atomism/>.

Pruss, A. R. (2006), *The Principle of Sufficient Reason*, Cambridge: Cambridge University Press.

Psillos, S. (1999), *Scientific Realism: How Science Tracks Truth*, London: Routledge.

Putnam, H. (1956), 'Red, Green, and Logical Analysis', *Philosophical Review*, 65(2), pp. 206–17.

Putnam, H. (1981), *Reason, Truth and History*, Cambridge: Cambridge University Press.

Putnam, H. (1987), *The Many Faces of Realism: The Paul Carus Lectures*, Chicago: Open Court Publishing Company.

Pyszczynski, T. and Greenberg, J. (1987), 'Toward an Integration of Cognitive and Motivational Perspectives on Social Inference: A Biased Hypothesis-Testing Model', in Berkowitz, L. (ed.), *Advances in Experimental Psychology*, vol. 20, New York: Academic Press, pp. 297–340.

Quine, W. V. O. (1980), *Pursuit of Truth*, Cambridge, MA: Harvard University Press.

Ramsey, F. P. (1926), 'Truth and Probability', in Braithwaite, R. B. (ed.), *Foundations of Mathematics and other Essays*, London: Kegan, Paul, Trench, Trubner, & Co.

Ramsey, F. P. (1927), 'Facts and Propositions', *Proceedings of the Aristotelian Society*, 7, pp. 153–70.

Random, R. A. (1958), 'Intelligence as a Science', Studies in Intelligence, Washington DC: Central Intelligence Agency, <https://www.cia.gov/library/center-for-the-study-of-intelligence/kent-csi/vol2no2/html/v02i2a09p_0001.htm>.

Restall, G. (1996), 'Truth-Makers, Entailment and Necessity', Australasian Journal of Philosophy, 74, pp. 331–40.

Richards, J. (2010), *The Art and Science of Intelligence Analysis*, Oxford: Oxford University Press.

Richards, J. (2014), 'Competing Hypotheses in Contemporary Intelligence Analysis', in Lahneman, W. J. and Acros, R. (eds), *The Art of Intelligence: Simulations, Exercises, and Games*, Plymouth: Rowman & Littlefield.

Richey, T. (2003), 'General Morphological Analysis: A General Method for Non-Quantified Modelling', adapted from the paper 'Fritz Zwicky, Morphologie and Policy Analysis', presented at the 16th EURO Conference on Operational Analysis, Brussels, 1998.

Richey, T. (2009), 'Futures Studies using Morphological Analysis', Millennium Project: Futures Research Methodology Series, Version 3.0, Stockholm: Swedish Morphological Society.

Richey, T. (2011), 'Modelling Alternative Futures with General Morphological Analysis', *World Futures Review*, Spring 2011, pp. 83–94.

Riskey, D. R. (1979), 'Verbal Memory Processes in Impression Formation', *Journal of Experimental Psychology: Human Learning and Memory*, 5(3), pp. 271–81.

Robinson, E. S. and Brown, M. A. (1926), 'Effect of Serial Position Upon Memorization', *American Journal of Psychology*, 37, pp. 538–52.

Robinson, L. B. and Hastie, R. (1985), 'Revision of Beliefs when a Hypothesis is Eliminated from Consideration', *Journal of Experimental Psychology: Learning, Memory and Cognition*, 24, pp. 771–92.

Roby, T. B. (1967), 'Belief States and Sequential Evidence', *Journal of Experimental Psychology*, 75, pp. 236–45.

Rollington, A. (2013), *Strategic Intelligence for the 21st Century: The Mosaic Method*, Oxford: Oxford University Press.

Rosenbaum, M. E. and Levin, I. P. (1968), 'Impression Formation as a Function of Source Credibility and Order of Presentation of Contradictory Information', *Journal of Personality and Social Psychology*, 10, pp. 167–74.

Rosenberg, S. (1968), 'Mathematical Models of Social Behavior', in Lindzey, G. and Aronson, E. (eds), *The Handbook of Social Psychology, Volume 1*, Reading, MA: Addison-Wesley.

Rosenhan, D. L. (1973), 'On Being Sane in Insane Places', *Science*, 179, pp. 250–8.

Rosnow, R. L., Holz, R. F. and Levin, J. (1966), 'Differential Effects of Complementary and Competing Variables in Primacy-Recency', *Journal of Social Psychology*, 69, pp. 135–47.

Ross, L., Lepper, M. R. and Hubbard, M. (1975), 'Perseverance in Self-Perception and Social Perception: Biased Attributional Processes in the Debriefing Paradigm', *Journal of Personality and Social Psychology*, 32, pp. 880–92.

Ross, L. and Leper, M. R. (1980), 'Perseverance of Beliefs: Empirical and Normative Considerations', in Shweder, R. A. (ed.), *New Directions for Methodology of Behavioural Sciences: Fallible Judgements in Behavioural Research*, San Francisco: Jossey-Bass.

Rudner, M. (2004), 'Britain Betwixt and Between: UK SIGINT Alliance Strategy's Transatlantic and European Connections', *Intelligence and National Security*, 19(4), pp. 571–609.

Russell, B. (1905), 'On Denoting', *Mind*, 14(56), pp. 479–93.

Russell, B. (1908), *An Enquiry into Truth and Meaning*, London: George Allen and Unwin Ltd.

Russell, B. (1912), *The Problems of Philosophy*, London: Williams and Noorgate.

Russell, B. (1918), *Mysticism and Logic and Other Essays,* London: George Allen and Unwin Ltd.

Russell, B. (1948), *History of Western Philosophy and its Connection with Political and Social Circumstances from the Earliest Times to the Present Day*, London: George Allen and Unwin Ltd.

Russell, B. and Whitehead, A. N. (1910), *Principea Mathematica, Volume One*, Cambridge: Cambridge University Press.

Russell, B. and Whitehead, A. N. (1912), *Principea Mathematica, Volume Two*, Cambridge: Cambridge University Press.

Russell, B. and Whitehead, A. N. (1913), *Principea Mathematica, Volume Three*, Cambridge: Cambridge University Press.

Russell, R. L. (2010), 'Competitive Analysis: Techniques for Better Gauging Enemy Political Intentions and Military Capabilities', in Johnson, L. K. (ed.), *The Oxford Handbook for National Security Intelligence*, Oxford: Oxford University Press.

Rysiew, P. (2011), 'Epistemic Contextualism', in Zalta, E. N. (ed.), *The Stanford Encyclopedia of Philosophy*, <http://plato.stanford.edu/archives/win2011/entries/contextualism-epistemology/>.

Sainsbury, M. (1991), *Logical Forms: An Introduction to Philosophical Logic*, Oxford: Basil Blackwell Ltd.

Sanbonmatsu, D. M., Posavac, S. S., Kardes, F. R. and Mantel, S. P. (1998), 'Selective Hypothesis Testing', Psychonomic Bulletin and Review, 5, pp. 197–220.

Schoeffler, M. S. (1965), 'Theory for Psychophysical Learning', *Journal of the Acoustical Society of America*, 37, pp. 1124–33.

Schroeter, L. (2010), 'Two-Dimensional Semantics', in Zalta, E. N. (ed.), *The Stanford Encyclopedia of Philosophy,* <http://plato.stanford.edu/archives/win2010/entries/two-dimensional-semantics/>.

Schultz, D. P. (1963), 'Time, Awareness, and Order of Presentation in Opinion Change', *Journal of Applied Psychology*, 47(4), pp. 280–3.

Schweitzer, N. (1976), 'Bayesian Analysis for Intelligence: Some Focus on the Middle East', *Studies in Intelligence*, 20(2), pp. 247–63.

Schum, D. A. (1987a), *Evidence and Inference for the Intelligence Analyst: Volume 1*, Lanham, MD: University Press of America.

Schum, D. A. (1987b), *Evidence and Inference for the Intelligence Analyst: Volume 2*, Lanham, MD: University Press of America.

Schum, D. A. (1994), *Evidential Foundations of Probabilistic Reasoning*, New York: John Wiley & Sons, Inc.

Schum, D. A. (2001), 'Species of Abductive Reasoning in Fact Investigation in Law', *Cardozo Law Review*, 22(5–6), pp. 1645–81.

Schwartz, P. (1998), *The Art of the Long View: Planning for the Future in an Uncertain World*, Chichester: John Wiley & Sons.

Schwoebel, R. L. (1999), *Explosion Aboard the Iowa*, Annapolis, MD: Naval Institute Press.

Seamon, J.G. and Chumbley, J. I. (1977), 'Retrieval Process for Serial Order Information', *Memory and Cognition*, 5, pp. 709–15.

Searle, J. R. (ed.) (1971), *The Philosophy of Language*, Oxford: Oxford University Press.

Serfaty, D., Entin, E. E. and Tenney, R. R. (1989), 'Planning with Uncertain and Conflicting Information', in Johnson, S. E. (ed.), *Science of Command and Control: Coping with Complexity*, Fairfax, VA: AFCEA International Press. pp. 91–100.

Sessions, W. A. (ed.) (1990), *Francis Bacon's Legacy of Texts*, New York: AMS Press.

Shaklee, H. and Tucker, D. (1980), 'A Rule Analysis of Judgements of Covariation between Events', *Memory and Cognition*, 8, pp. 459–67.

Shanteau, J. C. (1970), 'An Additive Model for Sequential Decision Making', *Journal of Experimental Psychology*, 85, pp. 181–91.

Shanteau, J. C. (1972), 'Descriptive versus Normative Models of Sequential Inference Judgment', *Journal of Experimental Psychology*, 93, pp. 63–8.

Shapiro, S. (2013), 'Classical Logic', in Zalta, E. N. (ed.), *The Stanford Encyclopedia of Philosophy*, <http://plato.stanford.edu/archives/win2013/entries/logic-classical/>.

Shields, C. (2014), 'Aristotle', in Zalta, E. N. (ed.), *The Stanford Encyclopedia of Philosophy*, <http://plato.stanford.edu/archives/spr2014/entries/aristotle/>.

Shiffrin, R. and Cook, J. (1978), 'Short-Term Forgetting of Item and Order Information', *Journal of Verbal Learning and Verbal Behavior*, 17, pp. 189–218.

Shramko, Y. and Wansing, H. (2010), 'Truth Values', in Zalta, E. N. (ed.), *The Stanford Encyclopedia of Philosophy*, <http://plato.stanford.edu/archives/sum2010/entries/truth-values/>.

Simms, J. E. (2010), 'Decision Advantage and the Nature of Intelligence Analysis', in Johnson, L. K. (ed.), *The Oxford Handbook of National Security Intelligence*, Oxford: Oxford University Press, pp. 189–212.

Simon, H. A. (1955), 'A Behavioural Model of Rational Choice', *Quarterly Journal of Economics*, 69(1), pp. 99–118.

Singh, J. (2013), 'The Lockwood Analytical; Method for Prediction within a Probabilistic Framework', *Journal of Strategic Security*, 6(3), pp. 83–99.

Skov, R. B. and Sherman, S. J. (1986), 'Information Gathering Processes: Diagnosticity, Hypothesis Confirmatory Strategies and Perceived

Hypothesis Confirmation', *Journal of Experimental Social Psychology*, 22, pp. 93–121.

Skyrms, B. (2000), *Choice and Chance: An Introduction to Inductive Logic*, 4th edn, Stamford, CT: Wadsworth.

Sleury, D. P. (ed.) (1994), *Sherman Kent and the Board of National Estimates: Collected Essays*, Washington DC: Center for the Study of Intelligence, Central Intelligence Agency.

Smith, T. J. (2008), 'Predictive Warning: Teams, Networks, and Scientific Method', in George, R. Z. and Bruce, J. B. (eds), *Analysing Intelligence: Origins, Obstacles and Innovations*, Washington DC: Georgetown University Press.

Smyth, M. M. and Scholey, K. A. (1996), 'Serial Order in Spatial Immediate Memory', *Quarterly Journal of Experimental Psychology*, 49A, pp. 159–77.

Snyder, M. (1981), 'Seek and Ye Shall Find: Testing Hypotheses about Other People', in Higgins, E. T., Heiman, C. P. and Zanna, M. P. (eds), *Social Cognition: The Ontario Symposium on Personality and Social Psychology*, Hillsdale, NJ: Erlbaum, pp. 277–303.

Snyder, M. and Campbell, B. H. (1981), 'Testing Hypotheses about Other People: The Role of the Hypotheses', *Personality and Social Psychology Bulletin*, 6, pp. 421–6.

Snyder, M. and Cantor, M. (1979), 'Testing Hypotheses about Other People', *Journal of Experimental Social Psychology*, 15, pp. 330–42.

Snyder, M. and Swann, W. B. (1978), 'Hypothesis Testing Processes in Social Interaction', *Journal of Personality and Social Psychology*, 36, pp. 1202–12.

Stalnaker, R. (2003), *Ways a World Might Be: Metaphysical and Anti-Metaphysical Essays*, Oxford: Oxford University Press.

Stech, F. J. and Elseasser, C. (2004), 'Midway Revisited: Detecting Deception by Analysis of Competing Hypotheses', McLean, VA: MITRE Corporation.

Steele, R. D. (2007), 'Open Source Intelligence', in Johnson, L. K. (ed.), *Handbook of Intelligence Studies*, London: Routledge, pp. 129–47.

Sternberg, R. J. (ed.) (1994), *Thinking and Problem Solving: Handbook of Perception and Cognition*, 2nd edn, New Haven, CT: Yale University Press.

Steup, M. (2014), 'Epistemology', in Zalta, E. N. (ed.), *The Stanford Encyclopedia of Philosophy*, <http://plato.stanford.edu/archives/spr2014/entries/epistemology/>.

Stewart, R. H. (1965), 'Effect of Continuous Responding on the Order Effect in Personality Impression Formation', *Journal of Personality and Social Psychology*, 1(2), pp. 161–5.

Stewart, T. R. (2009), 'Uncertainty, Judgement, and Error in Prediction', in Sarewitz, D., Pielke, R. A. and Byerley, R. (eds), *Prediction, Science, Decision Making, and the Future of Nature*, Washington DC: Island Press.

Strack, F., Schwarz, N., Bless, H., Kübler, A. and Wänke, M. (1993), 'Awareness of the Influence as a Determinant of Assimilation versus Contrast', *European Journal of Social Psychology*, 23(1), pp. 53–62.

Strange, K. R., Schwei, M. and Geiselman, R. E. (1978), 'Effects of the Structure of Descriptions on Group Impression Formation', *Bulletin of the Psychonomic Society*, 12, pp. 224–6.

Strohmer, D. C. and Newman, L. J. (1983), 'Counsellor Hypothesis-Testing Strategies', *Journal of Counselling Psychology*, 30, pp. 557–65.

Sullivan, J. P. (2008), 'Analytical Approaches for Sensing Novel and Emerging Threats', Panel on Novel Risks, Future Threats: The Emerging Global Security Landscape, 49th Annual ISA Conference, San Francisco, CA.

Talbott, W. (2016), 'Bayesian Epistemology', in Zalta, E. N. (ed.), *The Stanford Encyclopedia of Philosophy*, <https://plato.stanford.edu/archives/win2016/entries/epistemology-bayesian/>.

Taplin, J. E. (1975), 'Evaluation of Hypotheses in Concept Identification', *Memory and Cognition*, 3, pp. 85–96.

Tarski, A. (1943), 'The Semantic Conception of Truth', *Philosophy and Phenomenological Research*, 5, 341–75.

Taylor, C. (1990), *Creating Strategic Visions*, Carlisle, PA: United States Army War College, Strategic Studies Institute.

Taylor, S. M. (2005), 'The Several Worlds of the Intelligence Analyst', *Proceedings of the First International Conference on Intelligence Analysis*, McLean, VA: MITRE Corp.

Tecuci, G., Schum, D., Bouci, M., Marcu, D. and Hamilton, B. (2010), 'Intelligence Analysis as Agent-Assisted Discovery of Evidence, Hypotheses and Argument', in Phillips-Wern, G., Lakhimi, C. J., Nakamatsu, L. C. and Howlett, R. J. (eds), *Advances in Intelligent Decision Technologies*, Berlin: Springer-Verlag.

Tesser, A. (1968), 'Differential Weighting and Directional Meaning as Explanations of Primacy in Impression Formation', *Psychonomic Science*, 2(8), pp. 191–8.

Tetlock, P. E. (1983), 'Accountability and the Perseverance of First Impressions', *Social Psychology Quarterly*, 46, pp. 285–92.

Tetlock, P. E. (1985), 'Accountability: A Social Check on the Fundamental Attribution Error', *Social Psychology Quarterly*, 48(3), pp. 227–36.

Tetlock, P. E. and Boettger, R. (1989), 'Accountability: A Social Magnifier of the Dilution Effect', *Journal of Personality and Social Psychology*, 57, pp. 388–98.

283

Tetlock, P. E., Skitka, L. and Boettger, R. (1989), 'Social and Cognitive Strategies of Coping with Accountability: Conformity, Complexity, and Bolstering', *Journal of Personality and Social Psychology*, 57, pp. 632–41.

Thompson, C. C. (1999), *A Glimpse of Hell: The Explosion on the USS Iowa and Its Cover-Up*, New York: W. W. Norton & Co.

Thompson, J. R., Hopf-Wichel, R. and Geiselman, R. E. (1984), 'The Cognitive Bases for Intelligence Analysis', Research Report 1362, US Army Institute for Behavioral and Social Sciences, Fairfax, VA.

Thornton, S. (2017), 'Karl Popper', in Zalta, E. N. (ed.), *The Stanford Encyclopedia of Philosophy*, <https://plato.stanford.edu/archives/sum2017/entries/popper/>.

Tiwari, B. D. (1978), 'Primacy-Recency Effects in Impression-Formation as a Function of Dependence-Independence Proneness', *Psychologia*, 21, pp. 143–9.

Tolcott, M. A., Marvin, F. F. and Lehner, P. E. (1989), 'Expert Decision-Making in Evolving Situations', *Institute of Electrical and Electronic Engineers (IEEE) Transactions on Systems, Man, and Cybernetics*, 19(3), pp. 606–15.

Tomassi, P. (1999), *Logic*, London: Routledge.

Treverton, G. F. (2009), 'Bridging the Divide between Scientific and Intelligence Analysis', Center for Asymmetric Threat Studies, Swedish National Defence College.

Treverton, G. F. (2011), 'Comparing Early Warning Across Domains', paper presented at a conference held in Stockholm hosted by the Center for Asymmetric Threat Studies, Swedish National Defence College.

Treverton, G. F. and Fishbein, W. (2004), 'Making Sense of Transnational Threats', Sherman Kent Center for Intelligence Analysis Occasional Papers, 3(1), Washington DC: Sherman Kent Center.

Treverton, G. F., Jones, S.G., Boraz, S., and Lipscy P. (2006), *Towards a Theory of Intelligence: Workshop Report*, Arlington, VA: RAND Corporation.

Trope, Y. and Bassok, M. (1982), 'Information Gathering Strategies in Hypothesis-Testing', *Journal of Experimental Social Psychology*, 19, pp. 560–76.

Tubbs, R. M., Messier, W. F. Jr. and Knechel, W. R. (1990), 'Recency Effects in the Auditor's Belief Revision Process', *The Accounting Review*, 65, pp. 452–60.

Turner, M. A. (2005), *Why Secret Intelligence Fails*, Dulles, VA: Potomac Books Inc.

Tversky, A. and Kahneman, D. (1974), 'Judgement Under Uncertainty: Heuristics and Biases', *Science*, 185, pp. 1124–31.

Tversky, A. and Koehler, D. J. (1994), 'Support Theory: A Non-Extensional Representation of Subjective Probability', *Psychological Review*, 101, pp. 547–67 .

Tversky, A., Sattath, S. and Slovic, P. (1988), 'Contingent Weighting in Judgement and Choice', *Psychological Review*, 95(3), pp. 371–84.

Tweney, R. D., Doherty, M. E., Worner, W. J., Pliske, D. B., Mynatt, C. R., Gross, K. A. and Arkkelin, D. L. (1980), 'Strategies of Rule Discovery in an Inference Task', *Quarterly Journal of Experimental Psychology*, 32, pp. 109–23.

United Nations Office on Drugs and Crime (2011), *Criminal Intelligence Manual for Analysts*, New York: United Nations.

United States Department of the Army (1998), *Intelligence Officer's Handbook FM 34-8-2*, Washington DC: Headquarters, Department of the Army.

United States Department of Defense (2014), *Department of Defense Dictionary of Military and Associated Terms*, Joint Publication 1-02, Arlington, VA: United States Department of Defense.

United States Government (2009), *A Tradecraft Primer: Structured Analytical Methods for Improving Intelligence Analysis*, Washington DC: Central Intelligence Agency.

Vaidman, L. (2008), 'Many-Worlds Interpretation of Quantum Mechanics', in Zalta E. N. (ed.), *The Stanford Encyclopedia of Philosophy*, <http://plato.stanford.edu/archives/fall2008/entries/qm-manyworlds/>.

Vaidya, A. (2011), 'The Epistemology of Modality', in Zalta, E. N. (ed.), *The Stanford Encyclopedia of Philosophy*, <http://plato.stanford/edu/archives/win2011/entries/modal-epistenology/>.

Van Atten, M. (2012), 'The Development of Intuitionistic Logic', in Zalta, E. N. (ed.), *The Stanford Encyclopedia of Philosophy*, <http://plato.stanford.edu/archives/fall2012/entries/intuitionistic-logic-development/>.

Van Frassen, B. (1980), *The Scientific Image*, Oxford: Clarendon Press.

Van Gelder, T. (2008), 'Can We Do Better Than ACH?', *AIPIO News*, 55, pp. 4–5.

Van Inwagen, P. (2001), *Ontology, Identity, and Modality*, Cambridge: Cambridge University Press.

Van Wallendael, L. R. (1989), 'The Quest for Limits on Non-Complementarity in Opinion Revision', *Organizational Behaviour and Human Decision Processes*, 43, pp. 385–405.

Van Wallendael, L. R. and Hastie, R. (1990), 'Tracing the Footsteps of Sherlock Holmes: Cognitive Representations of Hypothesis Testing', *Memory and Cognition*, 18, pp. 240–50.

Venn, J. (1876), *The Logic of Chance*, 2nd edn, London: Macmillan.

Vickers, J. (2014), 'The Problem of Induction', in Zalta, E. N. (ed.), *The Stanford Encyclopedia of Philosophy*, <http://plato.stanford.edu/archives/fall2014/entries/induction-problem/>.

Von Wright, G. H. (1951a), 'Deontic Logic', *Mind*, 60(237), pp. 1–15.

Von Wright, G. H. (1951b), *An Essay in Modal Logic*, Amsterdam: North-Holland Publication Company.

Von Wright, G. H. (1951c), *A Treatise on Probability and Induction*, London: Routledge and Kegan Paul Ltd.

Vrist Ronn, K. (2014), '(Mis-)Informed Decisions? On Epistemic Reasonability of Intelligence Claims', *International Journal of Intelligence and Counterintelligence*, 27(2), pp. 351–67.

Walker, L., Thibaut, J. and Andreoh, V. (1972), 'Order of Presentation at Trial', *Yale Law Journal*, 82, pp. 216–26.

Wallsten, T. S. (1976), 'A Note on Shanteau's Averaging versus Multiplying Combination Rules of Inference Judgment', *Acta Psychologica*, 40, pp. 325–30.

Wang, R. Y. and Zhu, H. (1995), 'An Information Quality Framework for Verifiable Intelligence Products', unpublished manuscript, Massachusetts Institute of Technology.

Warner, M. (2002), 'Wanted: A Definition of "Intelligence"', *Studies in Intelligence*, 46(3), pp. 15–22.

Warner, M. (2006), 'The Divine Skein: Sun Tzu on Intelligence', *Intelligence and National Security*, 21(4), pp. 483–92.

Wason, P. C. (1960), 'On the Failure to Eliminate Hypotheses in a Conceptual Task', *Quarterly Journal of Experimental Psychology*, 12(3), pp. 129–40.

Wason, P. C. (1968), 'On the Failure to Eliminate Hypotheses – A Second Look', in Wason, P. C. and Johnson-Laird, P. N. (eds), *Thinking and Reasoning*, London: Penguin, pp. 165–74.

Wasserman, S. and Faust, K. (1994), *Social Network Analysis: Methods and Applications*, Cambridge: Cambridge University Press.

Wastell, C. A. (2010), 'Cognitive Predispositions and Intelligence Analyst Reasoning', *International Journal of Intelligence and Counterintelligence*, 23, pp. 449–60.

Watson, B. W. (2008), 'Military Intelligence', *Encyclopaedia Britannica*, <https://www.britannica.com/science/intelligence-military#ref511593>.

Way, J. (2017), 'Reasons as Premises of Good Reasons', *Pacific Philosophical Quarterly*, <https://doi.org/10.1111/papq.12135>.

Weber, E. U., Böckenholt, U., Hilton, D. J. and Wallace, B. (1993), 'Determinants of Diagnostic Hypothesis Generation: Effects of Information, Base Rates, and Experience', *Journal of Experimental Psychology: Learning, Memory, and Cognition*, 19, pp. 1151–64.

Weiss, C. (2008), 'Communicating Uncertainty in Intelligence and Other Professions', *International Journal of Intelligence and Counterintelligence*, 21, pp. 57–85.

Weiss, D. J. and Anderson, N. H. (1969), 'Subjective Averaging of Length with Serial Presentation', *Journal of Experimental Psychology*, 82, pp. 52–63.

Weld, H. P. and Roff, M. A. (1938), 'A Study in the Formation of Opinion based Upon Legal Evidence', *American Journal of Psychology*, 51, pp. 609–21.

Whaley, B. (1969), *Strategic Deception and Surprise in War*, Cambridge, MA: The MIT Press.

Wheaton, K. J. (2001), *The Warning Solution: Intelligence Analysis in the Age of Information Overload*, AFCEA, Fairfax VA: International Press.

Wheaton, K. J. and Chido, D. E. (2006), 'Structured Analysis of Competing Hypotheses: Improving a Tested Intelligence Methodology', *Competitive Intelligence Magazine*, 9(6), pp. 12–15.

Whetherick, N. E. (1962), 'Eliminative and Enumerative Behaviour in a Conceptual Task', *Quarterly Journal of Experimental Psychology*, 14(4), pp. 249–59.

Whitesmith, M. (2018), 'The Efficacy of ACH in Mitigating Serial Position Effects and Confirmation Bias in an Intelligence Analysis Scenario', *Journal of Intelligence and National Security*, 34(2), pp. 225–42.

Whitney, P., Thompson, S., Wolf, K. and Brothers, A. (2008), 'Bayesian Assessments of Likelihood, Consequence and Risk for Comparing Scenarios', in Chesser, N. (ed.), *Anticipating Rare Events: Can Acts of Terror, Use of Weapons of Mass Destruction or Other High-Profile Acts Be Anticipated?*, United States Department of Defense, <https://www.hsdl.org/?abstract&did=233523>, pp. 99–104.

Whorf, B. L. (1956), *Language, Thought and Reality: Selected Writings*, Cambridge, MA: The MIT Press.

Windschitl, P. D. and Young, M. E. (2001), 'The Influence of Alternative Outcomes on Gut-Level Perceptions of Certainty', *Organizational Behavior and Human Decision Processes*, 85, pp. 109–34.

Wittgenstein, L. ([1921] 2002), *Tractatus Logico-Philosophicus*, London: Routledge Classics.

Wolf, F. M. (1986), *Meta-Analysis: Quantitative Methods for Research Synthesis*, Thousand Oaks, CA: Sage Publications.

Woodward, J. (2014), 'Scientific Explanation', in Zalta, E. N. (ed.), *The Stanford Encyclopedia of Philosophy*, <http://plato.stanford.edu/archives/win2014/entries/scientificexplanation/>.

Yachanin, S. A. and Tweney, R. D. (1982), 'The Effect of Thematic Content on Cognitive Strategies in the Four-Card Selection Task', *Bulletin of the Psychonomic Society*, 19, pp. 87–90.

Yates, J. F. and Curley, S. P. (1986), 'Contingency Judgment: Primacy Effects and Attention Decrement', *Acta Psychologica*, 62, pp. 293–302.

Young, J. O. (2013), 'The Coherence Theory of Truth', in Zalta, E. N. (ed.), *The Stanford Encyclopedia of Philosophy*, <http://plato.stanford.edu/archives/sum2013/entries/truth-coherence/>.

Zadny, J. and Gerard, H. B. (1974), 'Attributed Intentions and Informational Selectivity', *Journal of Experimental Social Psychology*, 10, pp. 34–52.

Zalta, E. N. (1988), 'Logical and Analytic Truths That Are Not Necessary', *Journal of Philosophy*, 85(2), pp. 57–74.

Zegart, A. (2009), *Spying Blind: The CIA, the FBI, and the Origins of 9/11*, Princeton, NJ: Princeton University Press.

Zlotnick, J. (1972), 'Bayes' Theorem for Intelligence Analysis', *Studies in Intelligence*, 16(2), pp. 43–52.

Zwicky, F. (1969), *Discovery, Invention, Research though the Morphological Analysis*, New York: Macmillan.

Index

abduction *see* logic (formal)
abductive logic *see* abduction
a posteriori *see* knowledge
a priori *see* knowledge
acoustic intelligence (ACINT) *see*
    measurements and signals
    intelligence (MASINT)
Analysis of Competing
    Hypotheses (ACH), 10–11,
    15, 61–96, 97–100, 107,
    109, 114–16, 119–21, 123,
    126–7, 155, 190–1, 198,
    200, 211–15, 224–5
analytical failure *see* intelligence
    failure
analytical judgements, *unused
    term*: analysis
anchoring bias, 13; *see also*
    anchoring effect; focalism;
    primacy
anchoring effect, 13; *see also*
    anchoring effect; focalism;
    primacy
appropriately caused true belief
    theory *see* knowledge
Aristotle *see* scientific method
art vs. science debate, 4–6, 7–9,
    12, 97–9, 227
Asch, S. E., 13, 145
authority, 83, 86; *see also* testimony

Bacon, F., 63, 64
Bayes, T. *see* probability
Bayesian logic *see* probability
Bayesian subjectivism *see*
    probability
belief acquisition, 7–8, 61–96
Belief-Adjustments Model (BAM),
    146, 150, 164–6, 168, 170,
    n.173, n.174, n.176–7
belief inertia effect theory *see*
    serial position effects (SPE)
bracketing *see* serial position
    effects (SPE)

Cabinet Office, 100, 103, 107,
    108, n.132, 213
Cheikes, B. A., 11, 99–100, 121,
    123, n.141, n.144, 146, 194,
    198, n.201, n.203, 214
cognitive bias, 2–3, 4–6, 10–12
    causes, 55, n.60
    mitigation, 4–6, 61, 94–6,
    97–9, 119–21, 126–8,
    198–200, 211–15, 221–7
coherence of truth theory, 68–73,
    n.103; *see also* consistency of
    information
communications intelligence
    (COMINT), 41; *see also*
    signals intelligence *(SIGINT)*

EU Authorised Representative: Easy Access System Europe Mustamäe tee 5

0, 10621 Tallinn, Estonia gpsr.requests@easproject.com

Printed and bound by CPI Group (UK) Ltd, Croydon, CR0 4YY

16/04/2025

01847011-0004